Dear Hulм,

In memory of o.
so much for being su.
early days,   Warmly Kaitlyn.

Sacred Space

Embracing the spiritual in person-centred therapy

Kaitlyn Steele

Published and printed by CreateSpace Independent Publishing Company.

ISBN – 13 978–1–4992–1529–8
ISBN – 10 1–4992–1529–0

The photograph on the front cover is by Kaitlyn Steele.

Dedication

For my anam cara

who has shared my journey of becoming

and helped awaken the wild possibilities within me.

I see you.

About the author

Kaitlyn Steele has been involved in the world of counselling and therapy for most of her adult life. She qualified originally as a clinical psychologist in the early 1970s and worked for a number of years in the NHS before eventually moving into working as a person–centred therapist, supervisor and tutor on a full time basis. She has taught for over twenty years on Further and Higher Education counselling courses in the UK. As the Director of Training at Network Counselling & Training in Bristol for more than sixteen years, she was responsible for developing an innovative four year university–validated professional counselling training programme with a strong emphasis on working with the spiritual dimension of experience.

For many years, she has had a strong interest in the integration of faith, spirituality and person–centred therapeutic practice and in her work as a therapist, has had considerable experience of working with people's spiritual issues and concerns as they have chosen to bring aspects of their spiritual lives to therapy.

Currently, Kaitlyn is the Programme Leader of the Network Training Diploma in Counselling course and has a private practice as a therapist, spiritual accompanier, freelance trainer and group facilitator. She is also the Director of Spaceforsoul, a newly emerging, inclusive spiritual community which aims to support and resource those people who are making their spiritual journeys outside the walls of organised religion.

She can be contacted at kaitlynsteele16@gmail.com

Acknowledgements

A book is never the product of just one mind and there are a great many people who have played a very important part in enabling me to bring this book to life. Firstly, I would like to thank my colleague and friend, Steve Griffiths, for it is in large part the fruit of our many long and stimulating conversations about the nature of the Divine, about the integration of faith, spirituality and therapeutic practice and about what it means to live out the person-centred philosophy that inspires us both. It was his engagement with the questions that really matter that so often inspired and challenged my own thinking and his belief in me as a writer that encouraged and sustained me, that helped me to trust that I have something worth saying and that enabled me to find my own voice.

Secondly, my thanks go to my supervisor of many years, Mike Fisher, who has given me the space to express not only the many struggles and frustrations I have experienced 'along the way', but also the passion and excitement that energised me. His attentiveness to the emerging writer in me also helped me to listen to and trust the sense of vocation I was experiencing and to have the courage to take a step into the unknown.

Thirdly, I want to thank my many past and present friends and colleagues at Network Counselling & Training in Bristol. I am very grateful to all of them for their support, encouragement and feedback and for the many thought–provoking and enlightening conversations I have had with them over the years. The ongoing dialogue we have been engaged in has undoubtedly shaped and enriched my own thinking and I have learnt a great deal from our joint wrestling with the questions that really matter.

I also want to acknowledge the many students and clients whose personal journeys I have had the privilege of sharing over the years. They have taught me so much about myself and have deepened my understanding of the therapeutic process and of the spiritual journey immeasurably. In addition, I want to acknowledge those writers whose work has stimulated, challenged and inspired me – writers such as David Elkins, John O'Donohue, Carl Rogers and Brian Thorne to name but a few.

Last but not least, I want to thank my sons, Simon and Richard and my daughter, Megan with whom I have shared the last thirty five years or so of my life and from whom I have learnt far more than they might realise about life, love and what it means in the words of Thoreau (1995), 'to live deep'. Their continuing love and support enriches my life immeasurably.

Foreword
by Emeritus Professor Brian Thorne

Kaitlyn Steele has produced a book of rare quality and one which is strikingly relevant at the present time. As she herself comments in the final chapter, we are living in a period when there is a developing interest in spirituality of all kinds. In some ways this is almost certainly related to the widespread disenchantment with organised religion and its perceived inadequacy in responding to the needs of those seeking for a deeper meaning and purpose in life. At the same time, the evolution of counselling and psychotherapy in recent years has brought about a situation where, increasingly, there is a willingness on the part of many people to undertake the task of self-exploration in the hope that they will discover within themselves a wisdom and a resourcefulness which in previous generations they might have sought in religious or political affiliations. This confluence of the spiritual and the psychological forms the background to Kaitlyn's book which is devoted to the study of how the spiritual dimension of human experience can find its rightful place within the theory and practice of person-centred therapy – a therapeutic orientation which through its non-prescriptive openness to experience is particularly well-suited to supporting those who find themselves on spiritual paths where there are few acknowledged sign-posts and not a few potential pitfalls.

The book is an impressive distillation of study and practice which extends over forty years. It is solidly based in personal, professional, and spiritual exploration and encompasses a vast clinical experience and many years as a tutor to those aspiring to be therapists. It also bears witness to the author's own struggles and her refusal to languish for long in inauthenticity. There is much pain in its pages but, at the same time, there is the exhilaration which comes from the determined pursuit of personal truth within the context of a growing conviction of the interconnectedness of all things. The result is a text which commands instant trust and respect. This is the testimony of a writer who speaks with the authority of someone who has wrestled hard and long with the deepest questions with which she has been faced as a practitioner, teacher and, more importantly, as a person in relationship who seeks always to be true to what she has come to recognise as her 'core self' – a term which she now employs to describe the underpinning concept of her therapeutic model.

Person-centred therapists will discover here a reliable description of the theory and practice of their orientation. They will also find in the numerous case-studies a powerful demonstration of the approach in action. For Kaitlyn, however, it is in the person-centred approach that she has experienced a gateway into the world of spiritual reality with all its unknowns and challenges. With meticulous care the reader is guided into this terrain with exemplary skill and no little passion. Kaitlyn's personal experience is buttressed by reference to numerous person-centred and spiritual writers and by her considerable knowledge of the research undertaken in this field. The result is a book which serves as an admirable text for those in training as well as an invaluable resource for seasoned practitioners who are perhaps less familiar with the role of the person-centred therapist as a spiritual companion. Readers will also be inspired by encountering an author who often writes in a style of rare beauty and expresses complex thoughts with exquisite clarity. The pages on 'soul love', for example, constitute one of the finest expositions of this compelling subject that I have ever read. To study this book is in itself to undertake a therapeutic and spiritual pilgrimage which may prove transformative.

Brian Thorne
Norwich, April, 2014

Contents

Introduction

This book has been many years in the writing and it is not the book I set out to write. Writing it has been a journey on many different levels. Perhaps most importantly, it has been part of my journey as a therapist as I have continued to develop and refine my theoretical understanding and my therapeutic practice, particularly over the last decade of my life. Each encounter with a client has played its part in the deepening of my knowing and understanding and the evolving of my way of being as a therapist. Each story that has unfolded as we have walked the path together has become woven into a rich and beautiful tapestry which tells its own story.

At another level, writing this book has been part of my journey as a teacher over the past twenty years. My own emerging thinking has been stimulated, challenged and refined by many meaningful encounters and dialogues with fellow tutors and practitioners and with my students. Their insights, ideas and perspectives have taught me far more than they might realise and have enriched my way of making sense of my own and others' experience immeasurably. The fruit of this process has been the development of a new therapeutic model – an adaptation and extension of humanistic person–centred theory which I have come to call the core self model.

Writing this book has also been part of my own personal journey of growth as I have sought to find my way back to the core self that is the heart and soul of who I am – or perhaps, more accurately, who I am becoming. The book has grown as I have grown and inevitably, it is in part a reflection of what I might call my own sacred story. I am now in the sixth decade of my life and of late, I have often found myself reflecting on what I have learnt along the way, whether as therapist, teacher, mother, daughter, lover, friend or spiritual seeker. This book is my attempt to draw together the fruits of that reflection in the hope that the process of doing so will open me up to the learning that is still to come. I share it with some trepidation because one of the most important things I am still learning is that I know so little and understand even less and that what I believe today may not be what I believe tomorrow. Some of it may speak to you; some of it may not. And so I share it in a spirit of openness to and respect for your truth, especially where it may differ from my own. My hope is that through engaging in open–minded and open–hearted dialogue with each other, we may together find our way to the truth that will set us free.

I was a clinical psychology student in the early 1970s when I first encountered the writings of Carl Rogers. It felt like coming home. For the first time, I was encountering ideas which engaged and excited me, which fitted with my own experience and ways of making sense of myself and life and about which I was and still am passionate. I felt powerfully drawn to the humanistic philosophy which lies at the heart of the person–centred approach with its essentially positive view of human nature, its affirmation of the dignity and worth of human beings and its fundamental belief in people's longing and capacity to grow and develop, to become more fully themselves.

Almost ten years later, I experienced a second home–coming. I returned to the Christian faith of my childhood (albeit a very different version of it) and embarked on a journey of integration – my own personal struggle, both as a woman of faith and a therapist, to 'choose a version of reality' that I can live in as McLeod (1993) puts it. In so doing, I have sought to draw together the person–centred philosophy and values that so challenge and inspire me and the developing faith and spirituality that give my life its meaning. Each has strengthened and enriched the other and both have changed and evolved as my encounter with life has deepened my understanding and challenged me to broaden my mind and my vision. Much has been left behind in the journey, but much has also been reclaimed, albeit in a different form.

My spiritual journey over the last twenty years has at times been a turbulent one, embracing both reassuring periods of stability and painful periods of transition in which my knowledge and understanding of the Divine and of the Christian spiritual tradition have been powerfully challenged and transformed by my experience, and not least by my experience as a therapist. For as long as I can remember, I have always been strongly drawn to the person and teachings of Jesus and by the way of being he evidenced in his encounters with others. I believe too that the path he invited us to follow can lead us to an awareness and experience of the Divine and of our inter–connectedness with all of life. At this point in my journey, if pressed to try and define my spirituality, I would say that I am most closely drawn to a progressive form[1] of Christian spirituality with its recognition of the value of personal and subjective spiritual experience, its inclusiveness, its acknowledgement that the teachings of Jesus offer but one of many pathways to the Divine and its emphasis on the primacy of love and compassion. I have, I believe, remained loyal to what Moore (2002) calls 'the soul of my religion' – the essential core of it as I understand it. I am also, however, deeply committed to engaging in genuine, open–minded dialogue both with scientific and psychological thinking and with the truths to be found in other faiths and spiritual and philosophical traditions. In later years, I have also become increasingly drawn to a more mystical and contemplative spirituality and to some of the insights of the Celtic spiritual tradition. And my person-centred philosophy now embraces the 'yearning for the spiritual' that Rogers (1980) spoke of towards the end of his life. The coming together of the two is a synthesis which continues to excite me.

This book is the fruit of that journey of integration and it remains 'a work in progress'. What I write today may not be what I would write tomorrow. It is an attempt to make sense of my experience and my work as a person–centred therapist in the light of my spirituality as both continue to evolve. It is also an attempt to draw together ideas and insights from the work of others who have made this journey too – philosophers, psychologists, religious and spiritual writers, person–centred writers and practitioners, all of whom have informed and immeasurably enriched my own thinking.

My aims in writing this book have been four–fold. Firstly, I believe strongly that any therapeutic model that seeks to do justice to the wonderful complexity and mystery of human nature must embrace the spiritual. At one level, this book is a plea for the field of counselling and psychotherapy to take more seriously the spiritual dimension of human existence and to equip its practitioners to work effectively with the spiritual problems and concerns clients may bring to therapy. It is a plea that others before me have made but one that has, I believe, not yet been fully heard.

Secondly, my aim has been to articulate more fully the integrative person–centred model which I have had the opportunity to develop over the last fifteen years in the context of my work as a therapist and as a teacher. What I am essentially offering is a version of reality that makes sense to me and often seems to resonate with others. It fits with my experience of myself, others and the world as I perceive it. It is a synthesis of what I have learned and come to believe so far, and this synthesis flows both from my own life experiences and from my encounters with the experience and thinking of others. At another level, then, the book constitutes an in–depth exploration of this evolving model, covering both its philosophical and theoretical assumptions and their implications for therapeutic practice.

Thirdly, I have wanted through the writing of this book to share something of my own experience of attempting to integrate spirituality and therapeutic practice. I have reflected on aspects of my own personal engagement as a spiritual person with the experience and thinking of other theorists and practitioners in the field. I have also articulated something of my own struggle to 'live the questions' that have emerged for me as I have tried to hold these different parts of myself in some kind of creative tension. As such, the book is inevitably a deeply personal statement rather than a purely academic exploration of philosophy and theory. I have drawn not only on the work of psychologists and therapists, but also on the work of writers who have explored the realms of faith and spirituality. At times, I have also drawn on my own personal experiences as well as those of others, because I believe that good philosophical and spiritual reflection must be willing to embrace the learning that flows from such experiences and to grapple with the questions they raise.

As well as reflecting on those aspects of Christian thinking which have particularly spoken to me as a person–centred therapist, I have also drawn on relevant ideas and insights from other religious faiths and spiritual traditions – in particular, on aspects of Jewish, Hindu, Islamic and Buddhist thinking. What has excited and inspired me in exploring these differing worldviews in much greater depth than I have done before is my growing conviction that essentially we are all pointing towards the same unknowable spiritual reality, that what we share in common far outweighs the differences between us. Consequently, there is, I believe, the potential for a mutually enriching dialogue between us if we can only overcome the fear of difference that holds us at arm's length. My own belief is that there is one Source, one Great Spirit, one Ultimate Reality, however we may conceive of it. I also believe, however, that there are many paths that lead to this one Source and that there is truth to be found in all of the world's major religions and wisdom traditions. From these beliefs flows a passionate commitment to open–minded and respectful inter–spiritual dialogue and at another level, this book is an outworking of that commitment.

Lastly, my hope is that this book will act as a useful resource for those therapists and other professionals wishing to explore what it might mean to encompass a focus on spirituality in their work. While it is written primarily from the perspective of person–centred philosophy, theory and therapeutic practice, my intention has been to offer the material in a way that makes it accessible not only to therapists from other orientations, but also to professionals working in related fields such as clinical psychology and spiritual direction or accompaniment.

Introducing the core self model

The model outlined in this book is an integrative model and as such is inevitably the product of many minds. It is fundamentally person–centred in that it draws heavily on the work of Rogers and other person–centred writers and shares with its humanistic counterpart many of the philosophical assumptions and theoretical hypotheses that shape person–centred theory and practice. It is also person–centred in that it rests firmly on the belief that 'the relationship is the therapy' (Mearns and Thorne 2000). In other words, it views the therapeutic relationship itself as the primary instrument of change.

On a number of levels, it is also, however, an integrative model. Firstly, it is integrative in that it seeks to draw together the person–centred and the spiritual in a meaningful synthesis. It is in effect a psychospiritual model. Initially, I struggled to find the right terminology to capture this as using the words 'spiritual' or 'transpersonal' seemed to imply a primary emphasis on the spiritual rather than the psychological which I did not want to convey. I then came across the term 'psychospiritual' which West (2004) uses to describe ways of working with clients that embrace the spiritual dimension of human existence. I believe that to speak of 'a person–centred psychospiritual model' of therapy reflects the nature of the model more accurately. It is psychospiritual in the sense that it sees people as spiritual beings, people who are body, mind, soul and spirit, who have spiritual experiences and a number of fundamental spiritual needs. It is psychospiritual in that it views the psychological and the spiritual dimensions of our being as closely intertwined. Finally, it is psychospiritual in that it recognises the importance of being willing to address the spiritual dimension of human experience in therapy.

Secondly, it is an integrative model in that it incorporates in an adapted form ideas, concepts and insights from other therapeutic approaches and related theories such as attachment theory, transactional analysis, cognitive–behavioural therapy, Jungian psychology and existential psychotherapy. What has excited me about my encounters with therapeutic approaches other than my own has been discovering how much we have in common. I have come to realise that it is the therapeutic jargon we use that so often obscures our understanding of each other's ways of seeing and makes it difficult for us to recognise that we are all pointing to the same reality.

Lastly, it is integrative in the sense that it seeks to draw together relevant insights from philosophy, theology, the psychology of religion and of psychosocial development and to integrate these with the theoretical knowledge and understanding that underlie person–centred therapeutic practice. Because my own spirituality is evolving within the wider context of progressive Christianity, I will inevitably draw to a greater extent on the writings of other Christians such as Nouwen, O'Donohue and Thorne to name but a few. I also seek, however, to incorporate aspects of the writings of others from a wider variety of spiritual and religious traditions. My own experience of engaging in this process of expanding my horizons spiritually has been both an enriching and challenging one. Not only has it enabled me to develop a much greater understanding of spiritual pathways that differ from my own, but it has also enhanced my knowledge and understanding of my own spiritual tradition immeasurably. It has opened up deeper layers of understanding and given me fresh insights and perspectives that I may not otherwise have reached. It has challenged me deeply and brought me face to face with my own ignorance and prejudice in relation to alternative spiritual perspectives. In so doing, it has enabled me to arrive at a place in my spiritual journey where I am able, for the most part, to honour and reverence others' spiritual questing, even when their path differs significantly from my own.

My use of language

The way in which we use language can obscure or reveal. It can clarify or mystify. It can enhance or inhibit understanding. It can include or exclude, empower or disempower. In this book and in articulating the core self model that shapes my practice, I have sought to use language as far as possible in a way that demystifies philosophy, theory and practice. I have also tried to express psychological and spiritual concepts and ideas in accessible language that is readily understood by others and particularly by those who may be encountering these ideas for the first time. Where I have drawn on more technical philosophical, psychological or therapeutic language, moreover, I have tried to clarify its meaning by translating it into everyday language with which we may be more familiar.

Another issue relating to the use of language concerns my use of the terms 'therapy' and 'therapist' in preference to the terms 'counselling' and 'counsellor' or 'psychotherapy' and 'psychotherapist'. There are two key reasons for this. The first is that I believe, as do many others, that in practice, the overlap between the processes of counselling and psychotherapy is so great that they could almost be regarded as indistinguishable. Moreover, I agree with West (2000) when he argues that it is much easier to distinguish between different therapeutic approaches than it is to identify how the practice of counselling differs from that of psychotherapy. This is, I know, a controversial position to take and the debate over this issue is still very much alive. When it comes down to what happens in the room, however, I am not sure that a client could tell the difference between a well–trained and experienced counsellor and a similarly well–trained and experienced psychotherapist. Using the words 'therapy' and 'therapist' perhaps enables me to circumvent the controversy. Secondly, the word 'therapy' is derived from the Greek word meaning 'attendant'. This fits better with my own person–centred philosophy of practice. The therapist is one who attends to the client, to his or her story and to the unfolding of his or her unique being. Just as a midwife attends to the process of birthing a baby, so the therapist attends to the process of birthing a soul (or psyche), a process that is reflected very clearly in the term 'psychotherapist'.

One final issue in relation to my use of spiritual language concerns the way in which I speak about the Divine. There are many ways of talking about the Ultimate Reality to which I believe all the world's major religions and spiritual traditions point. We may, for example, speak of God or Goddess, of Allah, of Yahweh, of Brahman, of the Great Spirit. Or we may speak in more abstract terms of the Absolute Reality, of the Source and Ground of Being, of the Tao, of the Divine. All of these are inadequate attempts to name and grasp hold of a sacred mystery that is essentially beyond our ability to know in full. Other than when I am recounting others' sacred stories (in which case, I use language that would be meaningful to them), I have chosen in this book to speak mainly of the transcendent, the Sacred or the Divine. This is partly because these are terms that are not gender–associated and partly because they hold meaning for me personally. They are also terms that are hopefully inclusive enough for most people to relate to.

Drawing on my therapeutic practice

I have drawn on my own therapeutic practice a number of times in this book. It is very difficult for therapists to write about their encounters and work with clients because of the highly sensitive and confidential nature of the stories we are told and of what happens in the room between us. I am also somewhat uncomfortable with asking clients if I can draw on their stories and journeys in my writing. In part, this is because clients sometimes agree to such requests out of deference or gratitude. In part, it is also because they may not always anticipate the possible consequences of having such deeply personal material made public, even when their anonymity has been protected. Consequently, none of the clients or stories that you will meet in this book are real. None of these clients actually exist. The clients I describe, the stories I tell and the journeys I portray are all composites drawn together from my work over the years with a wide range of people. I have worked very hard to ensure that none of my clients or their stories are recognisable in what I have written, while at the same drawing on situations and events that did occur in reality, on things that clients actually said or did and on processes that really did play themselves out in the room.

The structure of the book

This book is a book in two parts. In the first half of the book, I focus primarily on arguing that the therapeutic world needs to take much more seriously the spiritual dimension of human experience and on articulating the fundamental philosophical and theoretical assumptions of the core self model that informs my practice. In the second half, I explore the implications of these assumptions for the way in which I work with clients as an integrative person–centred therapist. I look at what it means to be a spiritually–oriented therapist, at the specific spiritual interventions therapists sometimes draw on in their work and at the ways in which we might work with the kinds of spiritual issues that may surface in the course of therapy.

In the first chapter, I add my plea to those of others such as Elkins (1998), West (2000) and Swinton (2001) that it is time to 'put the soul back' in psychotherapy. Drawing on recent research findings, I argue that spiritual experience is far more widespread than we might imagine and that, despite the decline in organised religion in this country, spirituality plays an important part in the lives of many more people than we might have expected. I also explore what it might mean for psychotherapy to return to its roots and for it to be seen as both a psychological and a spiritual process – one which, at its best, addresses not only body and mind, but also soul and spirit.

In the second chapter, my focus shifts to an exploration of the fundamental philosophical assumptions that shape my thinking and way of being as a spiritually–oriented person–centred therapist. I try to articulate as fully and clearly as I can the philosophical and spiritual framework that shapes my practice and is a fundamental part of the core self model that constitutes my own version of reality. I introduce a holistic image of the person that includes the spiritual dimension and recognises its interconnectedness with all other aspects of our being.

My third chapter constitutes an in–depth exploration of the central theoretical assumptions of the core self model, assumptions about the nature and development of the self and about how our problems in living arise and are maintained. In articulating these assumptions, I have traced the journey of the developing self, particularly through the first half of life, and have introduced the concepts of the belief system and the survival self. These concepts have strong links with the humanistic person–centred concepts of the self structure and the conditioned self but adapt and extend them in a variety of ways.

In the fourth chapter, I explore aspects of the journey through the second half of life and the process of 'becoming a person' of which Rogers (1967) wrote. It is a journey which I see as being both a psychological and a spiritual one. I explore what it might mean in the words of Thoreau (1995), 'to live deep' psychologically, relationally and spiritually. I also identify what I see as the three key growth processes or tasks involved in the process of becoming – the processes of awakening, of letting go and of emerging.

The fifth chapter is an exploration of the spiritual journey. I look at various ways of making sense of the journey from both psychological and spiritual perspectives, including a core self model perspective. I consider the concept of spirituality as a developmental process, drawing both on what has emerged from psychological studies of the spiritual journey and on what we have learnt from the wisdom of the world's major spiritual traditions. I also explore what these differing perspectives have in common and how they might complement and enrich each other.

In the sixth chapter, I reflect in depth on Rogers' core conditions hypothesis (Rogers 1957b) and what it has taught us about the therapeutic process. I share his deeply held belief that it is the quality of our relationships with our clients that enables them to heal and grow. I explore a way of being as a therapist that I believe has the potential to be profoundly creative and liberating of others, both at a psychological and spiritual level. I also explore the concept of soul love and consider what it means to offer others the kind of love that is capable of loving them into being.

The seventh chapter moves into a focus on the practicalities of working with the spiritual dimension as a therapist. I explore what it means in practice to be a spiritually–oriented therapist and how we might offer people the kind of sacred space which might enable them to open up the deepest and most vulnerable part of themselves to another human being. I look at the concepts of soul listening (Kirkpatrick 2005) and sacred inquiry (Stairs 2000) and consider the ethical issues and challenges relating to the use of particular forms of spiritual intervention in the context of therapy. I also offer some basic guidelines for best practice drawn from my own experience as a therapist over more than thirty five years.

Finally, in the last chapter, I explore the kinds of spiritual issues that often surface in the context of therapy and consider how we might work with them as spiritually–oriented therapists. I discuss the key principles involved in working with spiritual issues in therapy and focus in particular on working with issues relating to forgiveness, to spiritual crises and transitions, to dealing with the impact of what Clinebell (1984) described as 'pathogenic religion' and to engaging in what I would call 'soul work'. I also consider the implications of embracing a spiritually–oriented approach for both the training and supervision of therapists.

A journey of integration

Writing this book has been a journey of integration – an integration of my journey as a person–centred theorist and practitioner and my journey of faith.

It is an integration of what I have learnt from my own experience, from my clients, from my students, from my colleagues and from my closest friends and family. All of them have played an important part in shaping what has emerged as I have engaged in the process of birthing this book. I also want to acknowledge those writers who have particularly inspired and challenged me and whose thinking has played a prominent role in shaping my own emerging 'way of being', both as a spiritual being and as a person–centred therapist. Elkins, Nouwen, O'Donohue, Rogers and Thorne have been my closest 'companions' along the way and immersing myself in their writing has been an especially rich and rewarding experience as I have sought both to discover who I am and to learn to live out that truth in my encounters with others.

What I hope I have done in this book is to articulate clearly my own particular blending of some of the insights that have emerged from the world's major spiritual traditions with the awareness and understanding of human nature and experience that we have gained through psychology. Indeed, many of the insights of modern psychology and psychotherapy are essentially, I believe, a reworking of much older spiritual truths. My hope is that by sharing something of my journey of integration, it will inspire others to embark on their own.

In drawing the introduction to this book to a close, I find myself thinking about the learning that I have valued most as I have struggled to grasp hold of the mystery of being human. Firstly, I have learnt that my life finds its deepest meaning and fulfilment in living out the truth of who I am becoming; that becoming has no ending; that we spend the first half of our lives forgetting who we are and the second trying to remember; that the way forward is also the way back home.

Secondly, I have learnt that what I believe is far less important than how I love; that ultimately love is all that matters; that to live deep is to love deep; that it is love that heals, love that transforms, love that liberates, love that creates persons.

Thirdly, I have learnt that our separateness – from others, from the world we inhabit, from the Source and Ground of our being – is but an illusion; that when we hold the boundary between self and Other too tightly, we succeed only in building walls that maintain the illusion; that the truth that lies at the heart of our existence is our essential inter–connectedness with all of life; that our deepest human yearning is for connection.

Lastly, I have learnt that there is truth and beauty to be found in all true religions and spiritual traditions; that there are many sacred paths but only one destination; that the language of psychology and the language of spirituality are not as different as they might seem; that what lies at the heart of both the psychological and the spiritual journey is soul.

This has been a journey worth the making.

Kaitlyn Steele

Introduction notes

1. There are progressive forms of all the major world religions. In general, what they have in common is their commitment to pluralism (the belief that there are multiple paths to the Divine); their belief in the equality of all people (which includes gender equality); their inclusiveness and welcoming of diversity (including diversity of sexual orientation); their recognition of the importance of mystical experience (direct experience of the Divine) and of individual spiritual autonomy; their sacralisation of both nature and the self (their view of both nature and the self as embodiments of Divine presence); their emphasis on the importance of moving towards an authenticity of being and on enhancing our human capacity for love, kindness and compassion; their search for religious forms which are intellectually credible in the light of modern scientific and psychological knowledge and understanding; and their commitment to genuine, open–minded interfaith dialogue. For a comprehensive exploration of progressive spirituality, see Lynch (2007).

1: Embracing the spiritual

We are not human beings seeking to be spiritual, we are
spiritual beings striving to be human.
De Chardin 2008

For most of my life, my experience of myself has been that I am first and foremost a spiritual being, that I am spirit, soul, mind and body[1]. I have deliberately changed the way in which these four constructs are normally ordered in order to reflect my sense that the essence of my being is spiritual in nature, that the innermost part or core of who I am is soul. Looking back at my life, I can see, moreover, that at the heart of my life's journey, there has always been a spiritual quest – a searching and reaching for what Elkins (1998) calls 'the sacred stream' – though I may not always have recognised or acknowledged this at the time. Over the years, my spirituality has at times lain dormant and at others, been powerfully awakened. It has led me to explore a number of different spiritual pathways and it has found expression in a variety of different ways. But it has always been there, sometimes a subtle presence waiting quietly and patiently to be attended to, sometimes a powerful presence which bursts into my consciousness and cannot be ignored.

Furthermore, I believe that I am most fully alive, most fully myself and most fully in touch with my humanity when I am most attentive to and most 'in tune with' this deepest, innermost dimension of my being. At such times, I invariably experience a greater sense of well–being, of integration, of fulfilment, of engagement with all that life has to offer. These times have also been the most growthful periods of my life, the times of most significant and far–reaching change and development, both psychological and spiritual. I have found that attending to and nurturing this spiritual dimension of my being or in other words, caring for my soul, enhances and enriches my life immeasurably. I believe it may also develop my ability to reach out to others in meaningful ways. It deepens my capacity to listen acceptingly, to feel compassion, to give of myself freely, to love unconditionally.

I would argue that any philosophy, any image of the person, any psychological or therapeutic model of human nature and behaviour which ignores, denies, dismisses or views the spiritual aspect of our being as immature, neurotic, dysfunctional or unhealthy fails to encompass the full complexity of our humanity. It denies the validity of the lived experience of many and fails to capture the depth and richness of it. Consequently, it diminishes us. Any model that seeks to be truly holistic and to make sense of the totality of human experience must therefore embrace the spiritual. What I mean by this is that it must do more than simply recognising the importance of the spiritual dimension of human nature and adopting a more open–minded, accepting and balanced attitude towards religious and spiritual experience. It must also be prepared to integrate an awareness and understanding of the complexity of human spirituality into its philosophical and theoretical framework and to equip its practitioners to work effectively with the spiritual issues and concerns that may emerge in the process of therapy.

There are a number of reasons why I believe this to be so important:

The universality of religious and spiritual experience

Firstly, it is important because there is strong evidence that religious and spiritual experience is of fundamental significance in many people's lives and, it seems, is becoming more so. Religious experience and belief has been a part of human nature for a very long time. Its history can be traced as far back as the beginning of written records and possibly further. While we do not know when human beings first became religious, Rossano (2006) argues that substantial archaeological and anthropological research points to the existence of religious ideas and behaviour from the Upper Paleolithic era onwards – in other words, from as far back as 50 thousand years ago. Evidence of religious behaviour in Middle Paleolithic times – that is from as early as 300 thousand years ago – is much less conclusive but, he argues, strongly suggests the existence of a very early form of religion. This is sometimes termed 'proto religion'. What is more, the emergence of more complex, organised religions can be traced as far back as the Neolithic period – about 9500BC. In her book 'The History of God', Armstrong makes an in–depth study of comparative religion. She writes that her study of the history of religion has convinced her that '…human beings are spiritual animals. Indeed, there is a case for arguing that Homo sapiens is also Homo religiosus'(Armstrong 1999: 3).

There is strong evidence, moreover, that religion and spirituality[2] still play an important part in many people's lives. A commonly held assumption in modern Western cultures is that religious belief and practice are on the decline, that society is becoming increasingly secularised and that religion is fast becoming irrelevant in the postmodern world. This is not borne out, however, by current worldwide demographic statistics. There is no doubt that, as measured by regular church attendance, what might be termed 'institutional' or 'organised' religion is currently in decline in the UK (Brierley 2006; Swinton 2001; West 2000). Nevertheless, around 40 to 50% of people in Britain still profess a belief in God and see themselves as actively practising their religion (British Social Attitudes Survey 2013; Eurobarometer survey 2010).

Moreover, when we include in the statistics those who have a belief in 'a higher power' and those who see themselves as 'spiritual but not religious', that figure increases significantly. Vernon (1968) noted that people who speak of themselves in this way are often reluctant to describe the spiritual experiences they have in explicit religious language and that they generally make sense of such experiences in ways that do not fit within the framework of specific faith traditions. The percentage of people who profess a belief in God, a higher power or 'some sort of spirit or life force' and regard themselves as having a spirituality is as high as 70 – 79 per cent in Britain (MORI poll 2003; Eurobarometer survey 2010). Recent worldwide religious demographic statistics also show a very similar pattern (Ipsos Mori poll 2011; Britannica Book of the Year 2012). What this appears to show is that, despite the well–documented post–war decline in institutional religion, at least seven in ten British people (and nine in ten people worldwide) see themselves as having a belief in God or in some form of higher power, force or spirit and as being either religious or spiritual.

There is also strong evidence that there has been a significant upsurge of interest in spirituality within Western cultures during the latter part of the twentieth century and into the new millennium. This is evidenced, for example, by increasing levels of media interest, an upsurge in the publication of books and articles about spirituality, a proliferation of websites about religion and spirituality and the setting up of a number of organisations and research institutes which seek to promote and study spirituality in its many forms (Swinton 2001; Richards and Bergin 2005). It seems clear from these findings that, at least in the West, our human longing for the spiritual appears, if anything, to have grown stronger, particularly over the last two decades. How do we make sense of these research findings? Swinton (2001) argues that while organised religion may be in decline, this does not necessarily mean that people are becoming less spiritual. What is happening here, he believes, is that while spirituality was once lived out primarily within the context of institutional religions, it is increasingly being expressed in the context of other diverse and less traditional forms of spirituality.

Religious and spiritual experiences are also a feature of many people's lives and appear to be more common than we might suspect. Hay (1982; 2006) is a zoologist with a longstanding professional interest in the boundary between biological science and the religious and spiritual dimensions of human experience. From the 1980s onwards, he has conducted extensive research into religious experience in this country. This research has included a number of national, in–depth surveys of reports of religious or spiritual experience in the United Kingdom and studies both of the spirituality of young children and of people who have no formal religious affiliations. His research has enabled him to demonstrate that spiritual experiences remain extraordinarily widespread in Britain, in spite of the decline of institutional religion. For example, a national survey carried out in Britain in the year 2000 showed that over 75 per cent of people reported being personally aware of a spiritual dimension to their experience (Hay and Hunt 2000). A similar earlier survey (Hay and Heald 1987) had reported a figure of only 48 per cent – an increase of around 60 per cent. In addition, 55 per cent of people reported seeing the pattern of their life events as 'part of an unfolding transcendent meaning which is not of their making' (Hay 2002); 38 per cent reported having been aware of the presence of God; and 29 per cent identified an awareness of 'the presence of the sacred' in nature (Hay and Hunt 2000). All of these figures, moreover, had increased significantly since the earlier 1987 survey.

It is important to recognise too that the results of such opinion poll surveys may actually underestimate how common such experiences are. Drawing on his considerable research experience, Hay (2002) points out that people are often very reluctant to disclose their spiritual experiences and that when individual qualitative interviews rather than opinion polls are used, the percentage of people reporting such experiences increases. Research carried out by Davis et al (1991) indicates that the most common reasons that people choose not to report or even refer to such experiences are that they are too difficult to describe in words; that they are regarded as very special, intimate and deeply personal experiences which people are reluctant to share with others; and that people are afraid their experience will be ridiculed or devalued by others.

How valid are these deeply personal accounts of mystical spiritual experience?[3] Recent scientific research in the field of spiritual neuroscience[4] strongly suggests that such mystical experiences are correlated with observable neurological changes in the brain. There have, for example, been a number of studies which have used brain scanning or neural imaging techniques to investigate changes in brain activity during meditative and contemplative prayer. Newberg et al (2001) reported the detection of a number of changes in brain activity during the process of meditation. When their subjects (Tibetan Buddhist meditators) were in a deep meditative state, they reported experiencing the loss of a boundaried sense of self and an intense awareness of unity with their surroundings. This subjective experience was associated with an increase in brain activity in the frontal lobes, that part of the brain that is concerned amongst other things with focusing attention – in this case on the particular focus of the meditation. At the same time, reduced brain activity was recorded in the left superior parietal lobe of the cerebral cortex, the part of the brain which is responsible for recognising the physical limits of the body. These results were confirmed in a later study by Newberg et al (2003) with Franciscan nuns who were using a different kind of meditative practice – a verbal meditation technique known as 'centering prayer' which involves the internal repetition of a particular word or phrase. A third study conducted with Carmelite nuns who regularly engage in contemplative prayer also correlated their subjective mystical experience with increased activity in a number of areas and systems of the brain (Beauregard and Paquette 2006).

Spiritual neuroscientific research is very much in its infancy and is fraught with difficulty. These initial findings, however, provide a degree of external validation of the reality of the mystical experiences people report. They suggest that our spiritual awareness and experience is indeed mediated by our neurophysiology, something that Hay (2006) regards as unsurprising given the fact that we are embodied human beings. What they cannot tell us, however, is what causes these mystical experiences. Some commentators have concluded from such findings that spiritual experience is nothing but a neurophysiological process. However, the fact that such experience appears to be associated with particular brain states does not necessarily mean, as Taylor (2010) points out, that such brain states produce the experiences. It is just as likely that they are the result of such experiences rather than their cause.

The inter–connectedness of body, mind, soul and spirit

Secondly, developing our awareness and understanding of the spiritual dimension of life is important because the worldview, values and assumptions clients may hold as spiritual beings will inevitably impact, whether positively or negatively, on their physical, psychological and social development and well–being. Body, mind, soul and spirit are inextricably intertwined, an assumption I will return to later.

The relationship between spirituality, religion and health is a very complex one. Drawing heavily on a number of earlier reviews such as those of Batson et al (1993) and Koenig et al (2001), Richards and Bergin's (2005) overview of the research literature and empirical findings from the previous twenty years concludes that overall, they provide strong support for a wide range of physical health benefits associated with religious commitment and involvement. These include a longer life span; lower rates of incidence of a wide range of diseases including heart disease, cancer, immune system dysfunction and age–related disabilities; better recovery rates from surgery; greater ability to cope with disease, pain and death and other forms of stress; and a lower likelihood of engaging in unhealthy behaviour patterns such as cigarette smoking, drug and alcohol abuse or high risk sexual behaviour. These studies also demonstrate a number of significant mental health benefits such as a greater sense of well–being and a higher level of satisfaction with life; lower levels of psychological distress including anxiety, depression and neurotic or false guilt; lower rates of suicide; greater self–esteem, strength of mind and emotional stability; greater ability to cope and adjust in the face of life crises and problems; higher levels of psychosocial competence; lower divorce rates; higher levels of marital satisfaction; and lower levels of antisocial behaviour.

At the same time, Richards and Bergin (2005) also recognise as does West (2000) that the picture is not always such a positive one. People who lead active spiritual lives are not invariably more psychologically healthy and may at times present with significant mental health problems which have been partially caused or aggravated by the particular religious beliefs they hold. Religious clients often struggle with spiritual problems (such as intense preoccupation with sinfulness or religious masochism) which may impact adversely on other aspects of their lives. Sometimes, moreover, they bring to therapy the profoundly damaging impact of having been persecuted because of their spirituality or in some way spiritually abused.

As a therapist who has worked for a number of years in pastoral settings, I have been deeply saddened by the number of clients I have encountered whose particular religious beliefs or interpretations of scripture have been in some way damaging of their mental and physical health and well–being. I well remember a young Christian youth leader I worked with who believed that her understandable and natural emotional distress over the suicide of a friend was a sign of spiritual immaturity and who consequently could not allow herself to express the emotional pain that was tearing her apart; a woman in her forties who had been forced into having an abortion by her parents when she became accidentally pregnant as a teenager and who believed that twenty five years later God was still punishing her for what she saw as an unforgivable sin; a pastoral care worker who was suffering from burnout as a result of denying and suppressing her own needs in an attempt to 'crucify the self'; and a pastor who was so preoccupied with what he saw as his inherent sinfulness and inadequacy as a Christian that he could not believe he would ever be acceptable to God. These are just a few of the painful stories I have listened to over the years. There are many more.

In addition, it is undeniably true that a minority of religious individuals and groups do commit violent and destructive acts in the name of their religion. Religion does indeed have its dark side. Over the centuries, organised religion has been used both as a vehicle and as a justification for the violation, manipulation, oppression and exploitation of countless human beings. Wars have been started in the name of religion. Genocides have been committed in the name of religion. Women and gay people have been discriminated against in the name of religion. Religion, as Clinebell (1984) recognised, can be both salugenic (health–promoting) or pathogenic (health–destroying). It can either enhance or diminish our health and well–being. It can both heal and harm. It can both liberate and oppress. An awareness and understanding of the complex inter–relationship between body, mind, soul and spirit and a willingness to attend to and work with the spiritual dimension of human existence is therefore essential if we are to work holistically with every aspect of our clients' experiencing.

Spirituality in therapy

Thirdly, I would argue that it is important for therapists to develop the capacity to work with the spiritual dimension of human experience because clients often bring to therapy issues and concerns which they themselves regard as being of an existential or spiritual nature. Whether religious or not, they may choose to bring into the room an agenda which centres around the deep questions of life – ultimate concerns such as the existence and nature of the transcendent[5] and our relationship to it, the meaning of life or the fear of death. While they rarely constitute part of the presenting problem, such questions often lie on or close to the surface and will readily become part of the overt agenda of the therapeutic process. This is, moreover, not a new phenomenon. As far back as the early 1930s, Jung who was the founder of analytical psychology asserted that, 'Amongst all my patients in the second half of life… there has not been one whose problem in the last resort was not that of finding a religious outlook on life' (Jung 1961: 264). Some fifty years later, Clinebell (1984) echoed this when he argued that while obvious, explicit spiritual issues may constitute part of the presenting problem in only a minority of cases, all problems have a hidden spiritual dimension.

While not wanting to go quite as far as Jung and Clinebell, I do agree that many problems that clients present in therapy have a hidden, spiritual dimension of which, at least initially, the client may not be consciously aware. At such times, the client's spiritual concerns may lie dormant beneath the surface and may therefore be harder to access. Alternatively, the questions or fears they are wrestling with may not be recognised as spiritual or existential ones. For example, one of the clients I worked with many years ago as a student entered therapy because he had begun experiencing panic attacks shortly after his fiftieth birthday. It emerged during our work together that his father had died suddenly and unexpectedly from a heart attack in his early fifties. The client himself had not made the connection between his father's death and the onset of his current problems. Nor was he consciously aware of the underlying existential anxiety that was fuelling his panic attacks. He was not religious; nor would he have described himself as a spiritual person. The closest he came in therapy to addressing the spiritual dimension of his concerns was his description of himself as agnostic and his acknowledgement that he would like to be able to believe in God. One of my deepest regrets is that I did not use this opening to offer him the space to explore this aspect of his experience in therapy. I recognise now that I missed an opportunity to work with the hidden spiritual dimension to which I think he was alerting me and as a result, I believe our work together was less helpful to him than it might have been.

Thorne (1998) asserts, that in his experience, it has become much more common in recent years for clients to bring to therapy their existential needs and concerns and even to insist on their therapists accompanying them as they explore this aspect of their experience. Drawing on the experience of therapists in the United States, Sperry and Shafranske (2005) echo this observation and argue that spirituality and spiritual issues should be seen as a valid focus in the therapeutic process, whatever the therapist's own worldview. Why then is this experience one that not all therapists share? Therapists often ask why spirituality does not come up more often in the course of their work with clients. Worthington (1986) argues that because of the well–known antipathy of mental health professionals to religion and spirituality, clients may often be reluctant to talk about their spirituality in the course of their therapy. Similarly, West (2000) maintains that clients will avoid exploring aspects of their experience that their therapist is 'deaf to' and that they are often able to sense their therapist's dismissiveness without it being disclosed.

This certainly fits with my own experience. When working with a psychodynamic therapist some years ago, I quickly became aware that I did not feel safe enough to raise the spiritual issues I was struggling with at the time. When I finally took the risk of testing this out by alluding briefly to an aspect of my spiritual experience, it was completely ignored by the therapist. In view of reactions such as this, it is perhaps not surprising that a number of studies have shown that religious clients often prefer to work with therapists who share their faith (or at least their general religious outlook) and are therefore less likely to ignore or misunderstand their perspective or to try to undermine their beliefs (Richards and Bergin 2005).

Spirituality as a resource

Fourthly, spirituality can often be a powerful resource in enabling people to cope with the problems in living they are facing as well as in supporting and sustaining them in their everyday lives. It is clear from the research findings that many people (50 – 80 percent across varying groups such as combat veterans, hospital patients and widows) report that their religion is helpful to them in coping with stressful or traumatic life events or circumstances (Pargament 1997). Pargament calls this 'religious coping'. Furthermore, the same appears to be true of people struggling with serious psychological and mental health problems. The results of a large study conducted in the USA (Tepper et al 2001) suggest that the majority of people facing such difficulties (around 80 per cent) draw on some form of religious activity, practice or belief in helping them to cope. Indeed, Tepper at al conclude not only that 'religious activities and beliefs may be particularly compelling for persons who are experiencing more severe symptoms' but also that 'increased religious activity may be associated with reduced symptoms' (p. 660).

Pargament identifies a range of spiritual coping strategies that people draw on when they are facing difficult times in their lives. These include seeking for a sense of connectedness with the transcendent and drawing on this connection as a source of love and care; seeking support from the spiritual communities to which they belong; and engaging in what he calls 'collaborative spiritual coping' – in other words, seeing themselves as being involved in an active partnership with God in attempting to resolve their problems (Pargament 2007; Pargament et al 1988). He also identifies the benefits of 'spiritual meaning making' in enabling people to come to terms with tragic or traumatic life events and gives the example of a survivor of the attack on the World Trade Centre in September 1993. When visiting the remains of the building, she noticed a set of steel beams that formed the shape of a cross. For her, these steel beams became a symbol of hope which reminded her of the possibility that resurrection and rebirth may flow out of even the worst suffering. This ability to reappraise negative life events positively from a spiritual perspective can enable people not only to hold onto hope and find meaning in their suffering, but also to retain their relationship with the transcendent. In this way, experiences of trauma and tragedy can become 'bearers of spiritual meaning and a spiritual presence' (Pargament 2007: 101).

It is clear that there are many personal testaments to the benefits of such spiritual coping strategies but do they actually work in practice? Pargament (2007: 109) reviews the existing research findings and concludes that such spiritual methods of coping are indeed effective not only in helping people to sustain and even enhance their mental health and well–being in difficult times, but also in enabling them to maintain their spiritual growth and well–being. He maintains that spirituality is 'exceptionally resilient to life stressors', even in the most extreme circumstances. As evidence of this, he cites a study of Jewish Holocaust survivors which found that 61 per cent of them reported no change in their religious behaviour before and immediately after the Holocaust or at the time of the study nearly forty years later (Brenner 1980). For many people, then, it appears that spirituality can be a powerful resource in coping with the difficulties they face in life. Furthermore, as Griffith and Griffith (2002) argue, in attending to the spiritual dimension of people's lives in therapy, we have the possibility of drawing on such resources as part of the process of facilitating healing and growth.

Therapy as a psychospiritual process

Fifthly, paying attention to the spiritual dimension of human experience in therapy is vital because the two processes of psychological and spiritual development are inextricably interwoven. In a sense, they are, as I see it, two faces of the same coin. What I am arguing is that there is a profound relationship or connection between the psychological and spiritual dimensions of human experience, between the psychological and the spiritual journey, between the process of psychotherapy and the process of facilitating spiritual growth. They are deeply interwoven. Sperry and Shafranske (2005) maintain that there are five possible ways of viewing this relationship. The psychological and spiritual dimensions of human experience and development can be seen as essentially the same, with either the psychological or spiritual dimension being primary; as essentially different though overlapping, with either the psychological or spiritual dimension being primary; or as fundamentally different, with neither having primacy nor being reducible to the other. I believe, however, that there is a sixth position: that they are both similar and different; that they are closely overlapping and deeply interconnected; that each has the capacity to enhance the other and that both are equally important. Sperry and Shafranske (2005) argue that the psychological and spiritual dimensions of human experience are 'contiguous' – that is, that they touch at the edges. I see them, however, as touching at the core. This is a viewpoint I will expand later in this book.

It seems, therefore, that there are very good reasons for embracing the spiritual in therapeutic work whatever approach we may adhere to. Why then is it so often neglected?

The neglect of the spiritual in counselling and psychotherapy

Counselling and psychotherapy have a problem with spirituality.
West 2000

At the turn of the century, West (2000) began his exploration of the relationship between spirituality and therapeutic practice with the assertion that the therapeutic world has generally failed to take the spiritual dimension of human experience seriously enough. Sadly, I believe that, over a decade later, this is still the case. The professions of counselling and psychotherapy still need to take much more seriously the spiritual and religious dimension of human experience. It is undeniably true that historically, many of the major counselling and psychotherapy approaches have tended to ignore, dismiss or pathologise the spiritual dimension of human experience. For too long, many therapists have been as dismissive of spiritual and religious experience as Freud, the founder of psychoanalysis was in the 1920s when he described religion as an illusion and as 'the universal obsessional neurosis of humanity' (Freud 1961: 43).

For example, Ellis (1980), the founder of Rational–Emotive Therapy, also described religion as a form of neurosis and saw it as being characterised by childish dependency needs and irrational thinking. He even went as far as advocating actively challenging the religious orientation and beliefs of clients and seeking to enable them to live successfully without such beliefs. Swinton (2001) points out, furthermore, that it has not been uncommon in the past for mental health professionals to view religious experience, beliefs and practice as a sign of mental illness, as a form of regression, as evidence of psychosis or even as the result of brain damage or dysfunction.

Writing in the States, Richards and Bergin (2005) paint a very similar picture. They maintain that in the latter part of the 20th century, the mainstream mental health professions consistently neglected religious and spiritual concerns; that psychological theory and research paid scant attention to the spiritual dimension of human experience; and that religion and spirituality were also largely excluded from training programmes for mental health professionals. They refer to a national survey undertaken by Jensen and Bergin (1988) which showed that only 29 per cent of psychotherapists in the States considered religious matters to be an important part of their work with clients. Even now, there is evidence that many psychiatrists and therapists retain a deep suspicion of and prejudice against religion and spirituality and tend to focus primarily on their potential for causing damage and distress rather than on their potential for enhancing well–being. To what extent does this apply to humanistic psychology and therapy?

Humanistic psychology and therapy

Maslow, Rogers and the other founders of humanistic psychology were concerned with developing a psychology focused primarily on human psychological health, strengths and potential rather than on the pathological or the dysfunctional. Interestingly, far from pathologising spirituality and religion as Freud and others had done in the past, this new emerging psychology viewed spirituality as an important dimension of human experience and as an integral part of human nature.

Maslow, for example, proposed the existence of a higher level of human motivation which he called self–transcendence. In 'Towards a Psychology of Being' (Maslow 1968: 206), we find him arguing that human beings need 'a religion or religion surrogate' to live by in the same way that we need 'sunlight, calcium, or love.' Indeed, he went as far as saying that humanistic psychologists would probably see those who are not concerned with spiritual or religious questions as existentially 'sick' (Maslow 1976). His in–depth study of human nature and motivation led him to believe that once people's fundamental physiological and psychological needs are met, they become less motivated by such basic needs and more motivated by the values associated with self–transcendence and by the desire to reach beyond the individual self (Maslow 1969). At this motivational level, Maslow argued, people are less preoccupied with fulfilling their own potential and more concerned with enabling others to fulfil theirs. Their lives are often devoted to a particular faith, ideal or cause and they tend to be drawn to vocations that involve serving others. They generally recognise the existence of some form of being or force beyond the boundaries of and greater than the self and experience a strong desire for communion or connection with this transcendent reality.

Maslow's recognition of the vital importance of spirituality and his conviction that it could be studied and researched scientifically eventually led him and others to launch what he called 'the fourth force' in American psychology – that of transpersonal psychology, the study of the spiritual dimension of human experience. Since then, transpersonal psychologists such as Cortright ((1997); the Grofs (Groff 1975; Groff and Groff 1989), Walsh (Walsh and Vaughan 1993); Wilber (1977); and Vaughan (1995) have written extensively about the incorporation of spirituality into psychological theory and therapeutic practice, often drawing heavily on insights from Eastern spiritual traditions such as Hinduism and Buddhism. This in turn led to the development of a number of transpersonal therapeutic approaches such as psychosynthesis (Assagioli 1975) and transpersonal psychotherapy (Rowan 1993). These have sought to broaden their focus and their aims through encompassing the spiritual dimension of experience and including a concern with facilitating spiritual as well as psychological development.

Elkins (2005) points out that in the United States, contemporary humanistic psychology has remained convinced of the importance of human spirituality. Elkins et al (1999) conducted a survey of humanistic psychologists which showed that the majority of those surveyed considered spirituality to be important in their lives (77 per cent), saw themselves as either spiritual (55 per cent) or religious (32 per cent) and held a belief in some form of higher power or transcendent force (75 per cent). Surprisingly, furthermore, 43 per cent of these professed faith in a personal God. Elkins sees this as challenging the myth that all humanistic psychologists are nontheistic.

It is certainly true that many humanistic psychologists and therapists have adopted a more holistic model of human nature which embraces the spiritual dimension of human existence. They also tend to see it as at least potentially healthy. They are in the main more accepting of spirituality and spiritual experiences and may even welcome the exploration of such phenomena in therapy should clients wish to focus on that dimension of their lives. When writing about spirituality, furthermore, they have tended to adopt either a positive or neutral position. Over the last twenty five years, furthermore, a number of person–centred writers such as Grant (1995), Hermsen (1996) Leonardi (2006), MacMillan, (1999) Moore (2001), Purton (1996, 1998) Thorne (1991; 1998; 2002) and others (Leonardi 2010; Moore and Purton 2006) have explored person–centred therapy from a variety of spiritual perspectives including Buddhism, Christianity, Sufism and Taoism.

Despite this more open–minded stance, however, West (2000) contends that humanistic practitioners have generally not been equipped to work with spiritual issues and concerns in a more systematic, in–depth way. While some training programmes may include a focus on the spiritual and the transpersonal, such topics are often addressed at a somewhat superficial level which fails to do justice both to the complexity of these phenomena or to the central part they play in many people's lives. Until recently, this has, I think, been true at least to some extent of person–centred training courses.

In view of this, it is interesting to note that in 'A Way of Being', the last book written by Rogers, we find him acknowledging his conviction that it is important for therapists to take seriously the spiritual dimension of human existence (Rogers 1980). In a paper exploring the foundations of the person–centred approach, we find him expressing his growing belief that he had underestimated the importance of 'this mystical, spiritual dimension' of human existence (Rogers 1980: 130). We find him making reference to early research into altered states of consciousness which he saw as 'confirming the mystics' experience of union with the universal' (p. 128). We find him describing his and others' experience of what he called 'transcendental phenomena', both in the context of individual therapy and of intensive person–centred group work. When introducing his concept of therapeutic presence, we also find him using such terms as 'inner spirit' and 'transcendental core' to describe a particular aspect of his experiencing of himself (p. 129). Later in the book, furthermore, when describing the characteristics of 'the person of tomorrow', we find him talking of their 'yearning for the spiritual', of their desire to find a deeper meaning and purpose in life that enable them to reach beyond themselves (p. 352).

A new Zeitgeist?

Richards and Bergin (2005: 50) believe that the influence of the naturalistic and atheistic worldview which was prominent amongst many of the leading thinkers in the fields of psychiatry and psychology in the previous century is gradually weakening. They argue that there is an increasing openness to a worldview that acknowledges the existence of supernatural realities and embraces the spiritual dimension of human existence. They see this is a new 'theoretical Zeitgeist', a new spirit of the time which is emerging in both the natural and behavioural sciences. Along with it, there is also, they believe, an increasing acceptance and valuing of therapeutic approaches that seek to address this aspect of our humanity. Sperry and Shafranske (2005) make a similar point when they make reference to increasing evidence that what they call 'spiritually oriented psychotherapy' is 'coming of age' as a specialist area of psychotherapy.

There are, I believe, some encouraging signs that suggest that Richards and Bergin (2005) may be right to speak of the emergence of a new Zeitgeist. In Britain, membership of BACP Spirituality – formerly known as the Association for Pastoral and Spiritual Care and Counselling (APSCC) and a division of the British Association for Counselling and Psychotherapy (BACP) – has doubled over the past five years. Furthermore, BACP's current policy and position statement in relation to pastoral care and spirituality (Thresholds summer 2010: 22) states that BACP 'considers it important to respect the convictions of clients who have an allegiance to a faith community'; that BACP 'encourages high standards of training and awareness in spirituality' and that BACP encourages therapists 'to engage with the aspects of faith and culture' should their clients present these in therapy.

There is still, however, a long way to go. Harborne (2008) acknowledges that there is anecdotal evidence from clients that some therapists appear to hold suspicious or even hostile attitudes to the subject of religion or spirituality. A recent APSCC draft report entitled 'Counselling and Spiritual Direction' (2009) also acknowledges that many counsellors are still not comfortable with clients bringing their spirituality into the counselling room to the point that some will display a degree of selective inattention. At times, as reflects my own experience, they may ignore any reference to it at all. Very few counselling training courses currently address the subjects of faith, religion and spirituality at a meaningful level and there is as yet no reference to spirituality in the current BACP core curriculum for Diploma level counselling training courses or in the Benchmark Statement for Degree level training in counselling and psychotherapy produced by the Higher Education Quality Assurance Agency (QAA 2013). The battle, it appears, has not yet been fully won. At least to some degree, counselling and psychotherapy still have a problem with spirituality as West (2000) asserted at the start of the century.

A re–visioning of psychology and psychotherapy

As others have before me (Elkins 1998; Hillman 1975; Moore 1992), I too want to argue that we urgently need to return to an earlier vision of psychology and psychotherapy. My experience both as a person–centred therapist and as a client has convinced me that therapy at its deepest and most meaningful level is not only or primarily about the relief of psychological distress or about problem–solving. At its heart, it is a profoundly creative, existential and spiritual process which has to do with being and becoming; with connecting with that which is to be found at the core of our being; with attending to the voice of the soul and trusting its natural wisdom; and with listening to and heeding the subtle prompting of the spirit which impels us towards growth.

It is creative in the sense that it is concerned with what Rogers (1967) called the process of 'becoming a person', a profoundly creative process that he saw as lying at the heart of every therapeutic endeavour. It is existential in the sense that it is concerned with the unfolding or emergence of the client's being – a process that is clearly reflected in the derivation of the word 'existential' from the Latin verb 'existere' which means 'to emerge'. It is spiritual both in the sense that the journey of becoming is inspired by that part of our being that I would call 'spirit', and in the sense that it is concerned not just with becoming the self that we have the potential to be, but also with transcending or reaching beyond it.

When we grow psychologically, when we allow ourselves to enter fully into that process of becoming a person that lies at the heart of the therapeutic journey, then it is likely, though perhaps not inevitable, that we will also grow spiritually. As we reach inwards to our truest self, so we begin to reach outwards to that which lies beyond that self. The more we become, the more we are able to transcend what we become. It is, I think, also possible that spiritual growth may lead to psychological growth, that the more I seek to transcend my self, the more I am likely to become my self. Therapy, as Benner (1988) contends, is not only a psychological journey. It is at the same time a 'spiritual quest'.

Therapy at this deeper level is not simply about wrestling with the psychological problems and distress we may be experiencing. It is about soul–making. It is soul work and as such is imbued with mystery, both the mystery of the unfolding of an individual soul and the mystery of a 'soul–to–soul' encounter between two human beings who are both engaged in their own unique ways in the process of becoming a person. Moreover, it is clear from the origins of such terms as 'psychology' and 'psychotherapy' that they reflected this earlier understanding of psychotherapy as both a psychological and spiritual process. The word 'psychology' originates from the Greek words 'psyche' which means 'soul' and 'logos' which in this context means 'study'. Literally, then, the word means the study of the soul. The word 'psychopathology' is derived from the same word 'psyche' and the word 'pathos', the Greek word for suffering. Its literal meaning, therefore, is the suffering of the soul. Similarly, the word 'psychotherapist' comes from the Greek words 'psyche' and 'therapist', the latter originally meaning 'servant' or 'attendant'. And so, etymologically, a psychotherapist is a servant or attendant of the soul.

What happened then to change this earlier vision of the process of psychotherapy? The answer, as Elkins (2009) sees it, is the advent of the medical model and its application to the field of psychotherapy. This is a process that began with the work of Freud as far back as the 1890s. Modern definitions of such words as 'psychology' and 'psychotherapy' clearly show the impact of this process of medicalisation. Psychology is now defined as 'the study of the human mind' and psychopathology as 'the study of mental disorders' (Oxford English Dictionary 2006). Following suit, psychotherapy is currently defined as 'the treatment of mental disorder by psychological rather than medical means' (Oxford English Dictionary 2006).

While it is certainly true that both the medical and so–called 'mechanistic' models of psychopathology (such as cognitive–behavioural therapy) have made significant contributions to our knowledge and understanding, I would

27

argue that when such models are regarded as the cornerstone of counselling and psychotherapy and soul is excluded, something fundamental has been lost. Because such spiritual terms as 'soul' and 'spirit' cannot be operationally defined, they are abandoned as unscientific. Because the experience of soul and spirit cannot be scientifically observed and measured, it is dismissed as meaningless and irrelevant. In an effort to be seen as scientifically credible, much of psychotherapy has in effect 'sold its soul' to the medical model and in so doing, has lost touch with its roots. It is also, I fear, in danger of losing its humanity.

There have, however, been many dissenting voices over the decades. As early as the 1940s, Rogers himself firmly rejected the medical model (Rogers 1951). He began using the term 'client' instead of 'patient'. He was strongly opposed to the use of diagnostic labels and psychological testing designed to uncover underlying 'pathology'. He cautioned against psychotherapists seeing themselves as 'the expert' on their client's problems in living and as we have already seen, towards the end of his working life, he began to recognise the fundamental importance of paying attention to the spiritual dimension of people's lives (Rogers 1980). More recently, Mearns and Thorne (2000) have spoken of their concern about the growing institutionalisation of the profession, of their sadness at its 'consequent loss of humanity' and of their conviction that at its heart, person–centred therapy is essentially a spiritual and existential process.

In the mid–seventies, Hillman (1975) argued strongly for the 'revisioning' of psychology, challenging it 'to return to its roots' by making the soul the primary focus of its study. Indeed, Hillman defines psychotherapy as 'soul–making' and sees the psychotherapist as 'an attendant' to this process. Moore (1992) also contends that modern thinking has separated both religion and psychology and spiritual practice and therapy and that the way forward lies in healing this artificial split through a 'radical re–imagining' of psychology. He views the care of the soul as 'a sacred art' and believes that psychological symptoms should be honoured and listened to as 'the voices of the soul'. Elkins (1998; 2009) makes a similarly passionate plea for psychology and psychotherapy to return to their respective roots as disciplines that are concerned with the study and care of the soul. He believes, as I do, that psychotherapy is much more of an art than a science and argues that the creative process should be seen as its central metaphor. At its best, he says, therapy eventually becomes focused not on problem resolution, but on what of him– or herself the client is seeking to bring into being. In so doing, it enables the client to engage in what he calls 'the creative process of becoming' (Elkins 1998). Carl Rogers, would, I think, have agreed.

'Putting the soul back' in psychotherapy

In arguing that at its deepest level, therapy is essentially a creative, existential and spiritual process, I am not in any way dismissing the importance of psychological problem–solving and of relieving psychological distress. And in wanting to return to a focus on what I call 'soul work' in our work as therapists, I am not setting aside the need to address other aspects of our problems in living such as our ongoing struggle to leave behind ways of thinking and behaving which are no longer working for us. Such work undoubtedly has an important part to play in the therapeutic process.

What I am saying is that if we are not prepared in addition to accompany our clients on their journey towards soul, then we may well be selling them short. Steere (cited in Kirkpatrick 2005:33) believed that, 'to listen another's soul into a condition of disclosure and discovery may be almost the greatest service any human being ever performs for another.' My own experience, both as a therapist and a client, tells me that he is right. Hence this impassioned plea that we might 'put the soul back' in psychotherapy, that we might recognise once again that psychotherapy is in its own right a vital and powerful way not only of bringing about psychological growth and healing, but also of nurturing the soul and embracing a deeper spiritual life, that it is in Elkins' words, 'a powerful path to the sacred' (Elkins 1998).

Chapter 1 notes

1. I am using the word 'spirit' here to refer to the life force within us that animates and energises us existentially and motivates our ongoing growth as persons. In using the term 'soul', I am speaking of the essence or innermost core of our being. For a more in–depth exploration of both concepts, see Chapter 2.

2. I would define our spirituality as our unique and constantly evolving way of being, experiencing and making sense of existence. This way of being and experiencing emerges within us in response to our lived experience, to the presence of the spirit within us and to our awareness and experience of the transcendent, however we may conceive of it. I have sought here to offer a broad and inclusive definition which embraces both religious and non–religious forms of spirituality; which recognises the uniqueness of each individual's spirituality and celebrates and values that diversity; and which acknowledges that our spirituality is not fixed or static but is, at least potentially, a fluid, dynamic process. It also affirms, moreover, that at the heart of our spirituality is our search for the transcendent.

In contrast, I would define 'religion' in the following way:

At a personal, experiential level, religion is our human response to the experience of the transcendent. It rests on a core belief in some form of transcendent reality, whether personal or impersonal, with whom (or which) human beings are in some form of relationship and to whom (or which) they may decide to commit themselves. Often, but not always, this takes the form of a core belief in and attitude of awe and reverence towards some form of higher unseen being(s) or power(s).

At a communal level, a religion comprises a body or system of shared beliefs, values, moral codes and practices which is concerned with enabling individuals to enhance their experience of the transcendent, to make sense of and find meaning in their experience of the sacred and to survive and deal constructively with the ultimate struggles and problems inherent in human life.

This definition recognises that religion has both an individual and deeply personal and private dimension (what might be called the individual's 'personal religion' or spirituality) and a corporate dimension (what we are referring to when we use the term 'organised religion'). Maslow (1970b) called these 'little r' and 'big R' religion.

3. Mystical experience is an experience of conscious awareness of or union or communion with an ultimate spiritual reality. For a more in–depth exploration of spiritual experiences, see Chapter 6.

4. Spiritual neuroscience operates at the crossroads of psychology, religion, spirituality and neuroscience. Its primary objective is the exploration of the kinds of brain activity that underlie religious, spiritual and mystical experiences (or RSMEs) in an attempt to identify the specific ways in which they are mediated by the brain.

5. The word 'transcendent' is derived from the Latin verb 'transcendere' meaning 'to climb over' or 'to go across' (Oxford Latin Dictionary). Dictionary definitions of the transcendent generally define it as (1) that reality which lies beyond or exists apart from the physical or material universe and is therefore not subject to its limitations or (2) that which lies beyond or above the range or limits of normal or ordinary experience and perception. The transcendent is also referred to as the sacred, the divine, the numinous or the otherworldly. For a more in–depth exploration of this concept, see Chapter 2.

2: An image of the person

An essential part of the process of becoming a counsellor is to choose
a version of reality that makes sense, that can be lived in.
McLeod 1993

Introduction

Since I first encountered the writings of Carl Rogers, I have always been powerfully drawn to the humanistic philosophy which lies at the heart of the person–centred approach with its essentially positive view of human nature, its affirmation of the dignity and worth of human beings and its fundamental belief in people's longing and capacity to grow and develop, to become more fully themselves. It fitted with my own experience and ways of making sense of myself and of my journey through life in a way that other philosophies and worldviews did not. In later life, however, my image of the person has also been profoundly influenced by the spiritual dimension of my experience and by the wisdom to be gleaned from the world's major wisdom traditions. What follows in this chapter is my attempt to articulate as fully as I can the philosophical and spiritual framework that shapes my practice as a therapist and is a fundamental part of the core self model[1] that constitutes my own 'version of reality'. I have also tried to 'show my working' – in other words, to make something of my own process of philosophical and spiritual reflection explicit.

The spiritual self

The central assumption of the core self model is that spirituality is a universal human experience. It rests not only on the belief that all of us have a spiritual as well as a psychological dimension to our being, but also on the belief that the essence of our human nature is spiritual. All of us are spirit, soul, mind and body. We are first and foremost spiritual beings. I also believe that our spirituality is an inherent aspect of our humanity, an innate potential as Elkins (1998) sees it. It is a fundamental part of what makes us human and, I would argue, it is embracing this deeper dimension of our being that enables us to become fully ourselves and fully alive.

In making this core assumption that spirituality is a human universal, however, what I am not saying is that all of us recognise or acknowledge our spirituality or that we are always attentive to this innermost dimension of our being. As I know from my own experience, there are often times when it goes underground, when it lies dormant, hidden beneath the surface of our lives –

a subtle presence of which we may be mostly unaware. What I am arguing is that, although we may not all think of or experience ourselves as spiritual beings, although we may at times ignore or deny our experiences of the transcendent or may not recognise them as spiritual experiences, this spiritual dimension is always present, always open to us whether we acknowledge and attend to it or not. Swinton (2001: 21) also makes a similar claim when he maintains that the spiritual dimension is always present in everyone we meet, whether implicitly or explicitly.

The search for the transcendent

This spiritual dimension of our existence manifests itself in our lived experience in a number of ways. First and foremost, it evidences itself directly in the longing and searching for what is variously referred to as the transcendent, the Sacred or the Divine. I experience this personally as an intense ache that seems to flow from the innermost core of my being for a deeper reality than my individual conscious self and the physical world I inhabit. I would argue that when the early Christian theologian, Augustine of Hippo spoke in the 4th century of the restlessness of the heart until it finds rest in God (Augustine 1999), when the philosopher, Thoreau (1995) spoke of his longing 'to live deep and suck out all the marrow of life', when the religious historian, Eliade (1961) spoke of what he called our 'ontological thirst' – our thirst for being – they were all describing the same essential longing.

What are we speaking of though when we use such words as 'transcendent', 'sacred' or 'divine'? All of these words are, I think, attempting to capture something of the nature of the same mystery. Attempts to define the transcendent are fraught with difficulty because it is essentially beyond our capacity to capture in words. It is something Other. It is beyond our normal human experience. It is mysterious, unknowable, beyond our capacity to grasp with the conscious mind. The experience of it is sometimes powerful, overwhelming and awe–inducing, but at the same time, compelling. The transcendent draws us towards it.

It seems to me that we generally make sense of our experience of the transcendent in one of two key ways. Either we see it as some form of supernatural being or reality which exists and originates outside the self, or we see it as a deeper layer of human nature, as originating from within the core of our being. Our images of the transcendent, furthermore, will both shape and be shaped by our experience of it. Writing in the early 20th century, James (1985) argued for the separate existence of a mystical or supernatural dimension of reality which he described as 'the reality of the unseen' (p.53).

He saw this as an invisible spiritual reality which transcends (or exists apart from) the physical world but which at times breaks into it through what he called 'invasions of consciousness'. For James then, the Sacred is this 'unseen order'. Elsewhere, he referred to it as 'the more' (pp. 511, 515). Eliade (1961: 66) described the Sacred in a similar way. He also thought of it as 'something of a wholly different order, a reality that does not belong to our world.'

In attempting to define the word 'holy', the Christian theologian, Otto (1926) coined the word 'numinous' from the Latin word 'numen' meaning divine power or spirit. When most of us use the word 'holy', we link it with the concept of goodness. Indeed, one of the definitions of the word offered by the Oxford English dictionary is that of 'moral or spiritual excellence or perfection'. Otto maintained, however, that this common usage of the term does not reflect the deeper original meaning it had when it was used in ancient languages such as Semitic, Latin or Greek. He described the experience of the numinous as a 'mysterium tremendum et fascinans' – literally, an overwhelming and fascinating mystery – and he saw the experience of the numinous as the deepest level or the essential core of all true religion. Having explored such numinous experiences from a phenomenological perspective (that is, from the perspective of our subjective experience), he characterised them as involving a number of key elements: the element of 'awefulness' or feelings of mystical awe; the element of 'overpoweringness' or feelings of being overwhelmed; the element of 'energy or urgency' or feelings of being compelled by a strong and urgent force; the element of the 'wholly other' or the sense of encountering a mystery which is wholly other than the self; and the element of 'fascination' or the experience of being drawn to and enthralled by the numinous (Otto 1926: 13 – 41). Clearly, Otto saw the numinous as something outside the self.

For others who do not believe in the existence of such a supernatural reality, however, the 'unseen order' that James (1985) spoke of might be seen as nothing more than 'the farther reaches of human nature' (Maslow 1971). While the transcendent may be experienced in a similar way, such encounters are seen instead as a reaching beyond our conscious self (what James referred to as 'the lower self') to the deepest layer of our human nature or to what Jung (1969) called the realms of the personal and collective unconscious[2].

Paradoxically, I have experienced the Divine as both within and beyond myself. At times, it has felt as if my encounter has been with something 'wholly Other', something outside of and greater than myself, some beautiful and mysterious presence that surrounds and enfolds me. At other times, it has seemed as if the encounter has taken place deep within me at the very core of who I am, as if the Source of the flow of energy that suffuses my being somehow lies within. I do not know how to make sense of this paradox; it is simply my experience. But what I do know is that with each encounter with the Sacred, the longing for it deepens.

For many of us, this search for the transcendent is lived out through embracing one or other of the world's great religious or spiritual traditions such as Christianity, Islam, Judaism, Hinduism or Buddhism. Others, whilst retaining a strong interest in spirituality, have turned away from mainline institutional or organised religion altogether and are exploring, for example, Native American traditions, New Age philosophies, Twelve Step programmes, Jungian psychology or a wide variety of forms of spiritual practice such as meditation, yoga and tai chi. Elkins (1998) points out that spirituality manifests itself in countless outer forms. Underlying all of these, however, are the deep longing for and experience of the Sacred that are a fundamental part of our humanity, whether we are religious or not.

Some people might contend that they do not experience this 'yearning for the spiritual' that Rogers (1980) spoke of towards the end of his life. I would argue, however, that it evidences itself not only directly in our search for the Sacred or the Divine, but also indirectly and often much less healthily in a variety of ways – for example, in an excessive craving for money, entertainment, fame, excitement, power, sexual intimacy or material possessions. It evidences itself too in the use of mind–altering drugs such as opium, cannabis or LSD in order to intensify or alter our normal state of consciousness. Effectively, we are trying, I believe, to quench the 'ontological thirst' Eliade (1961) spoke of, but in ways that will never fully satisfy the longing and that are sometimes damaging.

This longing for the Sacred is evident too in what Elkins (1998) might call the 'symptoms' of 'loss of soul'. When our means of quenching our ontological thirst consistently fail, we often experience a loss of vitality and passion for living, feelings of restlessness, emptiness or meaninglessness, a persistent vague depression or anxiety, a deep sense of disillusionment or resignation – what Thoreau (1995) called 'quiet desperation'. Moore (1992) believes that such 'symptoms' should be honoured and attended to as 'voices of the soul'. They are, as he sees it, the soul's way of expressing its pain.

It is of course possible, as Swinton (2001) points out, to view spiritual experiences as purely naturalistic phenomena – that is, to see them as nothing but physiological or psychological processes – and to describe our human needs for meaning and purpose, for connectedness and for transcendence as psychological survival and growth needs rather than spiritual needs. Swinton (2001: 25) also talks, however, of his deep intuitive sense that spirituality involves dimensions 'that include, yet at the same time transcend psychological explanation.' This is a perspective I share.

Positive at the core

Another of the core beliefs that lies at the heart of my philosophy and practice is that the core of human nature is essentially positive and that all of us have intrinsic value, worth and dignity as human beings. This echoes the affirmation of human worth and potential to be found not only in humanistic philosophy and psychology and in person–centred theory and practice, but also in every major world religion and spiritual tradition.

What does it mean, however, to say that the core of human nature is essentially positive? I believe that the essence or core of our being – what Seeman (1983) would have called 'the organismic self' – is fundamentally positive and trustworthy. This is not to say that we are morally good or perfect beings or that our behaviour is always positive and constructive. There is undeniably a darker side to human nature. Now and then, all of us behave in ways which are in some way destructive of ourselves or others. All of us know what it is like to struggle with ourselves, to find ourselves doing things we know to be wrong or failing to do things we know to be right. However, when we are most deeply connected with our innermost self, when we are able to live life from the core of our being, we can, I believe, be trusted to grow, to develop, to move towards wholeness at all levels of our being. We can be trusted to become the people we have the potential to be, to become more fully ourselves. We can be trusted to behave rationally, constructively and justly as we seek to meet our needs. We can be trusted to form closer, more loving and harmonious relationships with others.

This is also one of the central assumptions of humanistic person–centred theory. Humanistic psychology – described by Maslow (1962) as 'the Third Force' in psychology – emerged in the 1950s as a reaction to both psychoanalytical and behaviourist thinking which were predominant in the field of psychology at that time. Humanistic thinkers such as Maslow and Rogers believed that both psychoanalysis and behaviourism have a view of human nature which is too negative and pessimistic. In contrast, they affirmed the inherent worth, dignity and uniqueness of human beings and emphasised our innate potential and capacity for self–development. On the basis of his clinical experience, Rogers (1967: 90 – 1) argued that the core of human nature is fundamentally positive in nature as opposed to fundamentally evil, antisocial or destructive. By the word 'positive' he meant 'socialized, forward–moving, rational and realistic'. Elsewhere he also used the words 'constructive' and 'trustworthy' to describe human nature (Rogers 1957a in

Kirschenbaum and Henderson 1990b: 403). He believed as I do that when people experience a safe and non–threatening environment in which they have the freedom to choose and to be themselves, they are thereby freed from defensiveness and can be trusted to move towards self–development, wholeness, complexity, self–regulation, self–responsibility and harmonious co–operation with others.

It is widely assumed that humanistic person–centred theory believes that people are 'essentially good'. As Wilkins (2003: 60 – 1) points out, however, this is not a term that Rogers actually used. Indeed, he stated clearly that he did not see people as perfect (Rogers 1957a). It is important to understand that Rogers (1967) was not arguing that human behaviour is always rational, socialised and constructive. Indeed, it disturbed him to be thought of as an optimist in regard to human nature and he acknowledged that out of fear and defensiveness, people are sometimes capable of behaving in ways that are very destructive, either of themselves or of others. He saw every individual as having the capacity for evil and recognised that each of us struggles at times with the desire to control or inflict pain on others (Rogers 1982). His experience as a therapist convinced him, however, that the inner core of the human personality – that is, our organismic nature – is essentially both self–preserving and social (Rogers 1967).

Many critics of person–centred philosophy such as May (1982) see this positive image of human nature as an unrealistically optimistic and naïve one which underestimates its darker side. I do not believe this to be the case. I am well aware of the destructiveness of some aspects of human behaviour but like Rogers, have sought to hold this awareness in tension with what I have learnt about the essence of our humanity from my deepest encounters with others, both as a therapist and teacher and in my personal life. Like Rogers, I too struggle at times to make sense of aspects of human behaviour which I find profoundly shocking and am left sharing his uncertainty that the answer I have to the problem of evil is an adequate one. And yet, I remain convinced that Rogers was right.

All of the major world religions, moreover, view human nature in a similarly positive light. For example, the Buddhist understanding of human worth rests both on its belief that every individual human life is a manifestation of a universal life force and that all people have the potential to choose the path of self–perfection. In other words, all human beings possess the 'Buddha nature' and have the capacity for growth, development and creativity. Similarly, Hindus believe that it is the presence of Brahman – the infinite divine spirit or Ultimate Reality – in every human being that gives value and significance to each individual. Our worth and dignity is therefore seen as being derived from our embodiment of Brahman. Furthermore, Hindus also believe that because the 'atman' – the unchanging innermost core of the person or true self – is indistinct from and in union with Brahman, it is in essence divine in nature.

Within Christianity (as is also the case within Islam and Judaism), human beings are seen as having worth as a result of having been created in the image of God (Genesis 1: 26 – 7) and are viewed as a unique and distinctive creation which God values highly (Genesis 1: 31). The early Christian doctrine of original righteousness and deification – that is, the belief that men and women are partakers of the divine nature and are made for union with God – reflected this positive perspective and was a central aspect of Christian thought for the first one and a half millennia. It is true that there are other prominent strands of Christian thinking which stand in stark contrast to this positive view of human nature such as the classical Christian doctrine of 'the Fall' and of Original Sin formulated by the 4th century North African Christian theologian Augustine (421). Thorne (1992) argues, however, that more recently, the Christian church has been rediscovering the older, more positive teaching about human nature. He sees this earlier doctrine as offering a view of humanity which is closely aligned with that of Rogers. Indeed, Thorne (1991) views Rogers as one of its most important 20th century secular advocates.

This is a perspective that is also echoed in the idea of the 'sacralization of the self' which Lynch (2007) believes to be an important element in the ideology of emerging progressive religion and spirituality. Rather than seeing the self as intrinsically flawed or sinful, progressive spirituality views the self as a manifestation of the Divine. In exploring this progressive thinking, Lynch talks of each person 'carrying a spark of the divine essence'. He views the self as sacred and believes that, far from being alienated from each other, humanity and the Divine are closely interwoven. Because the Divine is present within us 'in the very fabric of our beings', the essence of our human nature is recognised to be inherently positive.

If this is true, however, how do we make sense of the darker side of human behaviour? Rogers (1951) maintained that people act in destructive or regressive ways because they wrongly perceive their behaviour to be self–preserving or self–enhancing. He argued that if our perceptions of our experience are distorted, we may at times make choices which we believe to be self–enhancing but which in fact are damaging for ourselves and sometimes for others. If, for example, my early life experiences were to convince me that people are invariably untrustworthy, hostile and abusive, I might feel driven to protect myself either by withdrawing and isolating myself from others, or by behaving in aggressive and rejecting ways towards them in order to drive them away or to destroy them before they destroy me. While this behaviour might appear very destructive, it makes perfect sense when viewed as a strategy for self–preservation based on a significantly distorted view of the world. The behaviour of men like Joseph Stalin and Saddam Hussein becomes comprehensible, though not excusable, when we learn of the rejection, abandonment and physical and psychological abuse they experienced at the hands of those who were supposed to love and care for them in early life.

I do not believe that our potential for destructive behaviour is innate. I see it as flowing from the depths of our human brokenness and woundedness, from the damage that we have sustained at the hands of the societies in which we live and of those that are meant to love and care for us. That damage disconnects us from who we truly are. It also distorts our view of ourselves, others and the world in which we live and, in an effort to survive, causes us to behave in ways that inflict further damage, both on ourselves and others. This is the tragedy of human existence.

The potential for growth

Related to and underpinning my belief that the core of human nature is positive is another of the core assumptions that lie at the heart of the core self model. This is the belief that there is within all of us a potential, a capacity and indeed a need for growth and development at all levels of our being and that this potential for growth is always there throughout the lifespan.

Humanistic person–centred theory rests on the assumption that throughout their lifespan, human beings are always (at least potentially) in the process of growing, developing or of 'becoming' and that, if the conditions are right, personality development naturally moves in a positive direction towards greater maturity and wholeness. It was the neuropsychologist, Goldstein (1939) who first introduced the term 'self-actualisation'. He defined self–actualisation as the organism's tendency or drive to actualise (literally, to make actual or real) its capacities as far as is possible and saw it as the fundamental driving force which shapes the life of the organism. Writing some ten years later, Maslow (1943), a colleague of Goldstein's, also used the term 'self–actualisation' but, as he recognised himself, in a somewhat more limited and specific way. He described self–actualisation as the process of actualising our potential, of becoming everything that we are capable of being. He saw it as being motivated by our deep desire for self–fulfilment. He argued that if our basic physiological and psychological needs are being adequately met, we will experience a new kind of inner restlessness which then pushes us in the direction of realising our full potential.

Later still, we find Rogers (1951: 488) describing 'a directional force in organic life' which has come to be known as 'the actualising tendency'. Like Goldstein, Rogers believed this to be the sole motivating factor in human development. In other words, he regarded all other drives and needs, whether physiological or psychological, as aspects of this one fundamental drive. In the fourth proposition of his theory of personality and behaviour, he describes this one basic tendency to actualise, maintain, and enhance the self (Rogers 1951). The use of the word 'tendency' is important here. What it indicates is that the presence of the actualising tendency does not guarantee that growth and development will take place in any one individual. It only creates the potential for it. It is, as Rogers (1967) put it, 'a directional trend' rather than an inevitability. Environmental conditions also need to be right if this potential is to be fully realised.

What Rogers was saying is that inbuilt within all of us, there is some kind of constructive or 'forward–moving' force which is present and active within us at all times from birth onwards. It seeks to preserve, sustain and develop us at all levels of our being. It is an intrinsic and fundamental characteristic of our biological make–up as human beings. We are in a sense biologically programmed not only for survival, but also for continuous growth and maturation. It is not something we consciously choose. Nor do we need to be aware of it for it to be operating within us. At the most basic level, it motivates us to protect and care for ourselves, to defend ourselves when we are threatened, to seek to reduce the tensions we become aware of in ourselves and to meet our basic needs. At another level, it pushes us towards acting autonomously, assuming control of ourselves and our lives and taking responsibility for ourselves. It stimulates us to grow, to mature, to realise our potential, to develop our capacities, to fulfil and enhance ourselves, to become more fully who we are. It drives us to learn, to expand our knowledge and understanding, to be creative. When it is expressed in the context of our relationships with others, it impels us towards forming and sustaining mutually enhancing social relationships. It moves us in the direction of socialisation. It is as Rogers (1967) described it 'the mainstream of life.'

How can we make sense of this concept of the actualising tendency from a spiritual perspective? As I have sought to integrate this humanistic philosophy with religious understandings of human nature, what has struck me is that there is clearly a considerable degree of overlap between Rogers' description of the actualising tendency and the concept of the human spirit. The word 'spirit' comes from the Latin word 'spiritus' meaning 'breath of life'. Etymologically, it is related to the Hebrew 'ruach' and the Greek 'pneuma', both of which are translated as 'spirit'. In their primary sense, though, they mean breath, air or wind. Modern dictionary definitions of the word 'spirit' describe it as a vital principle or animating force within human beings and see it as synonymous with a number of other words and phrases such as 'life force' or 'divine spark'.

I want to offer a tentative way of conceptualising the human spirit, recognising both that it is impossible to arrive at any meaningful kind of operational definition of such a mysterious and intangible phenomenon and that others' experience and way of making sense of the human spirit may differ from my own. In doing so, I am drawing both on the experience and thinking of a number of others as they have described it in their own writings and on my own personal experience of this dimension of my being. The spirit, as I see it, is the life breath which suffuses every aspect of my being. It is a subtle and mysterious presence that animates, energises and sustains me existentially. It motivates me to grow, change and actualise my potential in the ongoing process of becoming, integrating and transcending my self. It inspires my search for connectedness, for meaning, for purpose and for the transcendent. As do Hindus, I see my human spirit as 'a spark' of the Divine. For me, it is the creative energy within me whose ultimate source is the creative energy that sustains the universe. It is also that within me that connects me to every other living thing.

I experience the presence of the spirit at times as a deep inner restlessness, a sense of being gently but persistently impelled by some kind of subtle force or influence which seems to flow from the very core of my being. The Bushmen of South Africa might describe it as a 'tapping in my spirit'. It is unsettling but not disturbing. It is quietly insistent but not discordant. At other times, I experience it more as an inner flow of some kind of spiritual (as opposed to physical) energy which spreads through – and more rarely floods – my being. It brings with it feelings of aliveness and joy, a sense of my self expanding and being lifted up and what I can only describe as a mysterious lightness of being.

Swinton (2001) also sees the spirit as some form of animating life force or principle. He draws a helpful analogy between the human spirit and the process of human respiration. As we draw oxygen into our bodies to sustain our physical existence, so the spirit that is instilled into us maintains our existence on an ontological level. In other words, it sustains us existentially at the level of our being. Similarly, Liebert (2000) describes the spirit as the 'life breath' of our human personality. She locates it at the core of our being, something that also fits with my experience though I might prefer to speak of it as flowing from that innermost part of myself. Drawing these definitions together, we all seem to be talking about a personal life force or energy that is seen as lying at the very heart of our being and in some way 'brings us to life'.

While it may be very difficult to define exactly what the human spirit is, it is perhaps easier to capture something of the ways in which its presence impacts on us. As I think about the ways in which I experience the spirit working in my life, I associate it with such words and phrases as ascending, rising, soaring, energising, expanding, actualising, realising potential, becoming, growing into, transforming, integrating, seeking, reaching beyond and transcending. Interestingly, Elkins (1998) draws on very similar words. He describes such processes as 'movements of the spirit' and argues that they all involve some form of upwards movement. Another important aspect of the work of the spirit as I see it is the process of integration – that is, the drawing together of the different threads of our human personality into a unified whole. Ellison (1983) and Swinton (2001) also describe the spirit as an integrative force or presence. Ellison (1983: 331 – 2) argues that it 'synthesizes the total personality and provides some sense of energizing direction and order'. I would argue that this process of integration takes place at the deepest level of our being.

What strikes me about these processes that I have described is that they could all be characterised as growth processes. As I see it, the spirit is then at the heart of our desire to become and to reach beyond the self that we have the potential to be. Van Kaam (1976) puts this very succinctly when he argues that the spirit is responsible for creating within us the desire to keep growing and changing as part of 'a process of emerging, becoming and transcending of self' (cited in Swinton 2001: 15). For me, the spirit is the life breath that brings me to life, that energises me, that sustains my being. It is the source of my desire to grow, to develop, to become more fully human, to entrust myself as fully as I can to the process of becoming that draws me towards the fullest expression of the self that I am. It is also, however, that which drives me to reach into and beyond my self towards what Tillich (1964) would call the source, depth and ground of my being.

As we have seen, the actualising tendency is similarly seen as motivating, sustaining and maintaining human existence, as creating within us the momentum towards growth and constructive change and as playing a vital part in enabling us to move towards integration and wholeness. Clearly, in his later thinking, furthermore, Rogers' conceptualisation of the actualising tendency moved even closer to the concept of the human spirit in its recognition of the importance of the spiritual and the transcendent. Are we all talking about the same phenomenon? I believe we are.

So why is this potential for growth and development not always fully realised? Why do most if not all of us fail to become all that we have the potential to be? It is because the actualising tendency can be inhibited, blocked or distorted as a result of damaging life experiences, as a result of destructive relationships with significant others in our lives, or as a result of wider negative environmental influences such as the dysfunctional social and cultural systems within which we live out our lives (Rogers 1967). As a result of our human suffering and consequent woundedness, our inner longing for growth may be suppressed or denied. The psychological and spiritual damage we have sustained may be too great to enable us to continue to face the challenges of growth and change.

Swinton (2001:16) argues that the human spirit is not a fixed or unchanging impersonal force or energy that is unaffected by our experiences in life but that it can be affected, both positively and negatively, by such experiences. He points to such common expressions as 'her spirits are raised; his spirits are at a very low ebb'; her spirit has been quenched'; 'he is feeling rather dispirited'; 'she has lost her spirit' and sees these as illustrating the ways in which the spirit can be impacted by our experience of life. In other words, our spirit may be crushed or quenched by our encounter with the darker side of life. It is vulnerable to the impact of deeply painful and damaging life experiences.

Can it ever be totally destroyed? Rogers (1967) believed as I do that while the actualising tendency can be inhibited or suppressed as a result of negative environmental influences, it can never be totally destroyed. Indeed, he maintained that the only way to destroy the actualising tendency is to destroy the organism itself. He also believed that the actualising tendency can always be re–activated no matter how damaged it has become given the right environmental conditions.

The core self

Another of the key underlying assumptions that lie at the heart of the core self model is a belief in the existence of the true self – what I have come to call the core self. It is, as I see it, our essential or real self. It is the deepest, innermost core of our being and the source of our uniqueness and individuality. To be this core self is, to draw on the words of Kierkegaard (1941), 'to be that self that one truly is.' At the same time, it is also what I might call the sacred centre within us. In other words, it is that aspect or dimension of our being that connects us with the transcendent. Clearly the core self is not a thing or a fixed entity, although people's subjective experience often leads them to speak of having 'a true self'. Instead it is best seen as a particular quality or state of being and experiencing.

My own personal experience is that when I am able to come into rhythm with this dimension of my being, there is a strong sense of being more fully and naturally who I am, of being 'at home' in my own skin, of everything within myself 'coming together' in some kind of process of synthesis which is, I think, what Seeman (1983) would call 'psychological integration'. At such times, I am more in touch with my creativity and intuition. I feel more deeply connected both with others and with the Divine. When I am able to listen to and trust the inner wisdom of this core self, moreover, I invariably discover as Rogers (1980) did that it is fundamentally trustworthy. What I mean by this is that when I am able to allow its promptings to shape my responses to what is happening, I often find myself reacting in ways that are more intuitive and spontaneous and that in some mysterious way seem to be just what is needed in that moment.

Humanistic person-centred philosophy and theory also assumes the existence of a true or authentic self (Merry 1999). As we have seen, Rogers (1967: 90 – 1) made reference in his earlier writings to what he called 'the innermost core of man's nature'. He spoke too of what he called 'our organismic nature' (p. 103) although it was in fact his colleague, Seeman (1983) who first called this innermost core of our being 'the organismic self'. He argued too that making the choice to be 'that self that one truly is' is our 'deepest responsibility' as human beings (Rogers 1967: 110). Furthermore, in his later writings, Rogers used language such as 'the transcendental core of me' and 'my inner intuitive self' to refer to his innermost self (Rogers 1980: 129). While he did not directly link these ways of describing his inner self with the concept of the organismic self, I believe that what was happening here was that his understanding of the concept was expanding to embrace the spiritual.

Other psychologists and therapists have used a variety of terms to speak of what is, I think, essentially the same phenomenon – terms such as 'the true personality' (Jung 1960), 'the higher or transpersonal Self' (Assagioli 2000) or 'the Deep Self' (Rowan 1993). Rowan associates the transpersonal self with intuition, with creativity, with peak or mystical experiences of the sacred and with what he calls our 'inner voice' – what Clark refers to as 'the inner teacher' (Clark 1977: 76). Clark also describes the transpersonal self as a 'center of pure awareness' which simultaneously observes and transcends the conscious self – that is, the sensations, feelings, thoughts and images that constitute our stream of consciousness.

How can we make sense of this concept of the core self from a spiritual perspective? What has struck me here is that there appears to be a considerable degree of overlap between this psychological concept and that of the human soul and I would argue that from a spiritual perspective, when Rogers spoke of the 'organismic nature' or of his 'transcendental core', he was essentially speaking about the soul. The word 'soul' is derived from the Old

English word 'sawol' which is related to the Hebrew term 'nefesh', the Greek 'psyche' and the Latin 'anima'. All the major world religions with the exception of Buddhism have a concept of soul. For example, in modern Judaism, the soul or 'nefesh' is often seen as being separate from the 'ruach' or spirit and from the body. In Islam, some theologians also distinguish between the 'nafs' or soul – the essence of our human nature – and the 'ruh' or spirit which is seen as having a separate existence and as reflecting the presence of the Divine Spirit within. In Christianity, the soul is widely regarded as the immortal and immaterial essence of a human being and is often seen as being separate from the body. The word 'soul' is generally regarded as being synonymous with the word 'spirit', although some Christians see human beings as consisting of body, soul and spirit as a number of biblical passages seem to suggest. For many Christians, the soul is also seen as the place of God's indwelling. For example, Kirkpatrick (2005: 34) describes the soul as 'the centre of our encounter and experience' with God.

Elkins (1998: 38) describes the soul as the 'divine nature' that lies at the centre of our being. He does not see the soul as a thing or an entity but like Moore (1992: 5) views it as 'a quality or a dimension of experiencing life and ourselves'. Amongst other things, Elkins associates soul with depth, with creativity and the imagination, with darkness, with mystery, with connectedness, with the transcendent and with our true self or our essential nature. He argues that unlike spirit, the movements of the soul are downwards. They have to do not with ascending to the heights of the self and beyond, but with descending into the depths, to that which is innermost. Rowan (1993) also relates the concept of the transpersonal self to that of the soul and describes this dimension of the self as having 'a touch of the divine' (p. 113).

Drawing all of this together, I believe that human beings are both spirit and soul. The two are, as I see it, separate but interconnected aspects of our spirituality. I associate the word 'soul' with such words as 'core', 'essence', 'innermost', 'depth, 'centre' and 'true self' and have come to see the core self or soul as my essential, authentic self. It is what makes me uniquely me. It is who I am at the core of my being. It is what comes to light on the rare occasions when my defences and masks are largely stripped away and I am able to risk being more fully myself. At the same time, it is also for me the sacred core of my being where the ultimate Source and Ground of my being has taken root and can be encountered. It is the spiritual centre deep within me which, as Corbett and Stein (2005) put it, 'receives' the spirit and from which the spirit flows into the rest of my being. Indeed, it is, I believe, the soul which enables me to become aware of the presence of the spirit within me. It is also that dimension of my being that enables me to connect with the transcendent. Spirit animates and propels us towards connection with our innermost self, with others, with nature and with the transcendent. Soul is the sacred centre within us where the connection with what lies beyond the self takes place.

A multidimensional view of human nature

The core self model is a holistic rather than a reductionist model and adopts a multidimensional view of human nature. It sees human beings as complex living unities of body, mind, soul and spirit in whom the various aspects of being and experiencing are closely interwoven. Each aspect or dimension of our being affects and is affected by the others and to regard them as separate or distinct does not reflect the reality of our human nature and experience. When we are wounded or ailing physically, it is not just our bodies that are injured. When we are hurting or suffering emotionally, it is not just our minds that are damaged by the pain we experience. When we are disconnected from our core self or when our spirit has been crushed, it is not just our spirituality that is affected. Emerging evidence from the fields of medicine, psychology, psychiatry, neurobiology (the study of the brain and nervous system) and psychoneuroimmunology (the study of the interaction between psychological processes and the nervous and immune systems of the human body) clearly indicates that it is no longer possible for us to view the relationships between body, mind, soul and spirit as dualistic ones.

I have attempted to capture this holistic image of the person in Figure 1 (p. 46). A two dimensional diagram can never adequately capture the nature and complexity of our human nature but perhaps it may be helpful in highlighting some of the points I am making. As the diagram illustrates, the core self or soul – the innermost essence of our being – is seen as lying at the heart of the person. The spirit or actualising tendency that suffuses and energises every aspect of our being – the physical, the emotional, the rational or intellectual, the volitional and the social or relational – is represented by the arrows radiating out from the core. I have chosen in this diagram to represent the whole self as a broken circle and to extend the arrows representing the spirit beyond the boundary of the self. I have done so in order to indicate that as well as every dimension of our self being closely interwoven, our whole self is intimately connected with everything else that exists – with each other, with nature, with the universe and with the transcendent, however we may conceive of it.

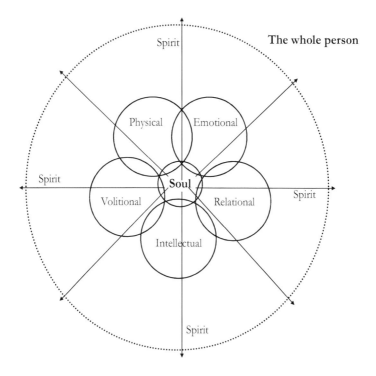

Figure 1

This is a view of human nature that is, at least in part, echoed in person–centred philosophy. Thorne (1992) expresses a similar holistic viewpoint when he talks of the person–centred conceptualisation of the human organism as 'a unity'. Merry (1999:17) also argued that humanistic person–centred philosophy views the person '...as a complex, organized whole' in which the various aspects of self are closely inter–related. He maintained that the concept of actualisation is in itself a holistic concept and that the actualising tendency is operating at all levels of our being simultaneously. As McMillan (2004: 2) puts it, the actualising tendency 'permeates' all aspects of our being and is engaged in both maintaining and enhancing the person 'as a whole'. From a spiritual perspective, this viewpoint is also echoed by writers such as Swinton (2001: 37) who describes the person as 'an indivisible whole' and as 'an inextricable continuum of body, mind and spirit'.

Human needs and the potential for growth

Another of the fundamental tenets of the core self model is the belief that we can only actualise our full potential as human beings if the conditions are right. In other words, our developmental journey is determined not only by our genetic blueprint and innate capacities and by the work of the actualising tendency, but also by the environment in which we live out our lives and by our life experience. What I mean by this is that if we are to become all that we have the capacity to be, we need to experience certain physical and psychological conditions throughout our lives. Our physical and social environment must, I would argue, provide us with the means of meeting our fundamental human needs, at least to a satisfactory degree, in order for us to realise our full potential, physically, psychologically and spiritually.

As Maslow (1943, 1971) did, I see human beings as having needs at a number of different levels – the physical, the psychological and the spiritual. In the 1940s, Maslow developed a theory of human motivation which was based on his concept of a 'hierarchy' of human needs. Maslow (1943: 375) assumed the existence of a number of key levels of motivation and saw our human needs as being organised into what he called 'a hierarchy of relative prepotency'. Maslow (1971) described what he saw as our lower levels of need (such as our needs for love, belongingness and self–esteem) as basic 'deficiency' or D needs because they arise as a consequence of deprivation and once adequately met, cease to be a source of motivation. They are essentially instinctual survival needs. He then distinguished these from what he saw as higher level needs such as the need for self–actualisation and self–transcendence. He saw these as our basic 'growth', 'being' or B–needs which stem from our desire to grow and develop as a person. In contrast to our D needs, once these needs have come to the surface, they continue to be felt and to motivate us and indeed are likely to grow stronger as they begin to be met.

What then are our deepest human needs? While acknowledging the importance of our lower level physiological and safety needs, I intend to focus here on our key psychological and spiritual needs as these play such an important role in determining the path of our psychosocial and spiritual development.

Our need for love and connectedness

I believe that our primary psychological survival need is the need both to be loved and to love. In order to grow and develop as human beings, we have a deep–seated need for love or rather for a particular kind of love that Rogers (1967) called 'unconditional positive regard'. We have a basic human need to know that we are loved, accepted and valued for who we are, irrespective of how we feel, think and behave. It is a need that is present from earliest infancy and that continues throughout our lives. It is, as Rogers depicted it, 'pervasive and persistent' (Rogers 1959: 223). It is also a very strong need and as such, a powerful motivator of our behaviour. Thorne (1991:29) describes the need as 'overwhelming'. O'Donohue (1997: 27, 30) argued that we need love 'as urgently as the body needs air' and that love is 'absolutely vital for a human life.'

At the same time, we also have a need to love. Our 'love needs', Maslow (1943) maintained, involve not only the receiving of love, but also the giving of it. The ability to love is, as I see it, an inherent capacity of the core self. In other words, it is in our deepest nature to be loving. We do not love solely in order to receive love; we love because at the core of our being, it is who we are. As O'Donohue (1997) put it, 'Love is the nature of the soul.' This is echoed in the more recent writings of Mearns and Cooper (2005). Drawing on the work of Stern (2004), they propose that in addition to the need to be loved, human beings also have an innate capacity and need to engage, interact and communicate with others, to share their subjective experience with others (what has come to be known as 'intersubjectivity') and to love as well as to be loved. This fundamental need to be loved and to love is what drives us into relationship. It underlies our need and longing for attachment (Bowlby 1979), for a sense of belonging (Baumeister and Leary 1995) and for closeness and intimacy (both emotional and physical) in our relationships with others.

Person–centred theory has always recognised that we are essentially relational beings. In the early 1950s, we find Rogers arguing that the actualising tendency appears to move people 'in the direction of socialization' – that is, that the tendency is in itself 'prosocial' (Rogers 1951: 488). Indeed, Rogers (1967: 103) saw the essential core of human nature as being 'deeply socialized'. More recently, other writers within the person–centred field such as Mearns and Cooper (2005: 6) have also proposed a more interdependent view of the self in which the self is not seen as an isolated being but as a 'being-in-relation'. Such a viewpoint clearly emphasises our essential interconnectedness and interdependence rather than our individuality and separateness.

Baumeister and Leary (1995) argue as a number of attachment theorists have done that the process of both infant and adult attachment formation serves an evolutionary function in that it is ultimately concerned with the survival of the species. They point to the physical survival value of social bonding and maintain that we are biologically programmed to be relational beings. I believe, however, that our need for intimate relationships is as important for our psychological survival, development and wholeness as it is for our physical survival. Firstly, our experience of loving intimacy and belongingness enables us to cope with our existential aloneness as individual human beings. The humanistic philosopher, Fromm (1956: 112) said that, 'Love is the only sane and satisfactory answer to the problem of human existence.' He argued that at an existential level, a sense of belonging and of being loved is vital to us because it enables us to cope with the basic problem of human existence – the awareness of our essential aloneness. It protects us from feelings of emptiness, isolation and loneliness that might otherwise paralyse us. Along with Elkins (1998: 230), however, I would argue that there is a deeper truth than that of our aloneness and that is our essential interconnectedness. Indeed loneliness, as Elkins views it, can be seen as the soul's longing for connection with others.

Secondly, it is, I believe, our experience of unconditional love that is the primary condition for both psychological and spiritual growth – an assumption I will return to later. As Clinebell (1984) pointed out, we grow and develop as people in the context of the relationships we have with each other. Our human personalities are at least partly shaped by our encounters with the significant people in our lives and the quality of those relationships will determine at least to some degree the extent to which we are able to realise our full potential, to become all that we have the capacity to be. As O'Donohue (1997) put it, 'Love is the condition in which we grow.' It awakens the soul. It reconnects us with the deepest, innermost part of ourselves. It enables us to embark on our own journey of becoming, of 'coming home' to our selves, of beginning to realise the unlived parts of who we are at the core of our being.

Our need for self–love

Another of our related fundamental survival needs is, I believe, that of the need for self–love. We need to be able to think of ourselves as people of worth and dignity, as having value, as deserving love and respect. We need to feel that we matter, that we have significance, that what we have to offer life is appreciated. We need to be able to see ourselves as fundamentally acceptable. We need to be able to love, respect and trust our core sense of self.

Healthy self–love is neither narcissistic nor egocentric. It is not the same as pride or arrogance and indeed both of these attitudes are in effect a defence against deeper feelings of low self–worth. It is not a belief in our own superiority over others or in our own perfection and it does not preclude a keen awareness of and willingness to be honest about our limitations, imperfections and 'growing edges'. True self–love is, moreover, not conditional. It is not dependent on a particular level of achievement or success or on a particular way of being. Nor is it dependent on the communication of others' respect or appreciation. It is rooted in a balanced and realistic self–perception and a depth of self–acceptance which enables us both to recognise and appreciate our own positive qualities, strengths and abilities and at the same time to face with equanimity the darker side of ourselves.

Maslow (1943: 381) did not speak of self–love, but he did see what he called our 'esteem needs' as some of our most basic 'D' or deficiency needs. Like Maslow, Rogers (1951; 1959) and other person–centred therapists have also recognised the importance of self–esteem – or what Rogers called 'positive self–regard' – and have seen it as being closely linked with the need for the positive regard of others. In one of his earlier papers, Rogers (1959) identified this need for positive self–regard, seeing it as a secondary learned need which develops as a result of the frustration of our need for the positive regard of others. Merry (1999) also acknowledged positive self–regard as a fundamental need of the developing self as does Thorne (1992). Thorne argues that without the ability 'to feel good' about ourselves to some degree, it is very difficult to function effectively. Where self–esteem is virtually non–existent, moreover, it is sometimes difficult to hold onto life. Suicidal feelings and behaviour are often closely linked with a profound absence of self–esteem.

The need for self–transcendence

In addition to these fundamental survival needs, I believe, as Maslow did, that we have a number of other basic psychological and spiritual needs which I call growth needs. I have already explored one of our primary growth needs – the need for self–actualisation. The second primary growth need is that of self–transcendence, our yearning to reach beyond our conscious selves, to be in relationship with the transcendent, to connect with whatever lies beyond ourselves however we conceive of it[3]. Because we are essentially spiritual beings, all of us, whether we are religious or not, have spiritual needs, our deepest human needs, which can only be adequately or fully satisfied in and through a meaningful relationship with the transcendent.

As we have already seen, it was Maslow, one of the founders of transpersonal psychology, who first introduced and explored the concept of self–transcendence. From a person–centred viewpoint, this is echoed in Rogers' later writings where he sought to describe how he saw 'the person of tomorrow'. Here, we find Rogers (1980: 352) identifying 'a yearning for the spiritual' as one of the characteristics of a fully functioning person. What he saw in such spiritual seekers was a belief in 'the more', a longing to find a deeper meaning and purpose in life, core values that motivate them to reach beyond themselves as individuals, and a desire to live life in a state of inner peace.

All of the major world religions also recognise this fundamental human longing as do the many forms of non–religious spirituality. We may see ourselves as seeking union with the Impersonal Divine as in the Advaita Vedanta school of Hinduism, in Taoism and Buddhism; we may be searching for communion with a personal God as in mainstream Islam, Judaism and Christianity; or we may see ourselves as striving to transcend our conscious selves by exploring the realms of the collective unconscious or the Higher Self. In essence, however, I believe the hunger that drives us is the same. At the deepest level of our being, we are always drawn to the search for the Sacred. There is within us an inner restlessness, an ache, an emptiness, a painful longing which can neither be wholly ignored nor fully satisfied other than through our connection with the Other, with that which lies beyond ourselves and the material world.

The need to know and understand

As did Maslow (1943), I would argue that we also have a fundamental need to know and understand ourselves and our world and to find meaning in our experience. Maslow referred to these as our cognitive needs. Human beings are born with a natural curiosity, a strong desire to learn, to know and understand, to explore and discover, to grasp the nature of reality. We are in effect constantly in pursuit of knowledge. We are also, I believe, storytellers. McAdams (1993: 27 – 28) argues that we are storytellers 'by nature', that we are born 'with a narrating mind' and that storytelling 'is a fundamental way of expressing ourselves and our world to others.' He also argues that we find meaning and purpose in our lives by telling ourselves a story about our lives – what McAdams calls 'a heroic narrative of the self that illustrates essential truths about ourselves' (p. 11). At particular times in our lives, we also have, I believe, a compelling need to tell our story to another, to someone we can trust to hear and receive the story with empathy and acceptance.

We are also meaning makers. At a psychological level, we need to be able to understand and make sense of our lived experience; at a spiritual level, we need to be able to find meaning and purpose in life. I believe we have a strong need to develop a sense of what Swinton (2001: 25) calls 'the ontological significance of life' – in other words, to determine what it is that gives significance both to human life and being in general and to our own individual lives in particular. For centuries, human beings have been wrestling with deep existential questions about human nature and identity, about our significance in the world, about the meaning of human existence. We have a fundamental need, it seems, to develop a viable philosophy of life. We also have a need to derive a sense of purpose from our lives, to determine the reason for our existence, to know what it is we are 'meant to be doing' with our lives. The concentration camp experiences of the Austrian psychiatrist and Holocaust survivor, Frankl, convinced him that what he called our 'will to meaning' is our most basic human motivation. Frankl (1997) believed that to live without meaning is to live in a painful existential vacuum, characterised by intense feelings of emptiness, inertia, apathy and boredom. In his later writings (Frankl 2000), he also argued that human beings have a need for ultimate meaning – what he called 'supra–meaning' – which he linked with our need for self–transcendence. This appears to be borne out by psychological research. Steger et al (2006) argue that such research is strongly supportive of the assumption of a link between a lack of meaning and psychological distress. Not having a strong sense of meaning in life appears to be associated with a number of forms of distress including the experience of depression and anxiety, suicidal ideation and substance addiction.

Alongside this need to develop a viable philosophy of life, we also have a need to develop and hold a set of ultimate values which give our lives direction and shape our life–styles and way of being in the world. The importance of the concept of values has been highlighted by humanistic psychologists such as Maslow and Rogers. McLeod (2009: 502) defines a value as 'an enduring belief that a specific end–state or mode of conduct is preferable.' He distinguishes between 'instrumental' values and 'terminal' or ultimate values. Instrumental values such as courage, ambition, competence and persistence are not ends in themselves, but the means or modes of conduct we need to adopt in order to achieve our ultimate goals. Ultimate values such as wisdom, truth, freedom and equality are, however, desirable end–states which have intrinsic value. Maslow (1968) made a similar distinction between what he called Deficiency or D values and Being or B values. He saw D values as 'lower values' which relate to our Deficiency needs – our basic physiological, safety, love and esteem needs – and may be thought of as 'survival values' or 'means–values'. He regarded B values as higher 'growth values' and believed that they are intrinsic in human nature, that they can be found in all or most human beings (albeit only weakly developed), but that they are most strongly developed in psychologically healthy and mature people whose D needs are being adequately met.

The need for beauty

Finally, I believe we have a need to experience beauty. Maslow referred to this as our 'aesthetic needs', our longing to experience symmetry, order and beauty in our lives. Beauty nourishes the soul. In some mysterious way, it brings us alive. It has the potential to reconnect us with our innermost self and with that which lies beyond the self. O'Donohue (2004) echoed this when he spoke of our human hunger and search for beauty. He saw beauty as nurturing the soul through enhancing our sense of aliveness and of 'homecoming'. Elkins (1998) believes that this need for beauty is, in part, what underlies our longing to connect with the natural world in a meaningful way. He argues that we have become increasingly estranged from nature and in so doing, have lost touch with one of our richest sources of nourishment for both body and soul and one of our most important 'paths to the sacred'. We have become increasingly inclined to objectify nature, to see it as something to be dominated, ordered and technologically manipulated rather than something to live close to and in harmony with. We often fail to recognise that we are part of nature, that we are in unity with it, that we are inextricably embedded within it rather than separate from it. This has resulted, Elkins believes, in our becoming increasingly cut off from nature, less able to contemplate and commune with it as we once did and therefore less likely to receive the gifts and nourishment it has to offer us.

In conclusion

Drawing all of this together, the image of the person that underpins this core self model is one that strongly affirms the essential worth and dignity of human beings; that sees the core of human nature as fundamentally positive and continually evolving; that recognises the uniqueness, complexity and mystery of our being and the inter–relatedness of all its aspects – spirit, soul, mind and body; that views people as relational beings with a deep need for belonging and for connectedness with our innermost selves, with others, with nature and with the transcendent; that acknowledges that human beings are always in the process of becoming; and that affirms the potential within even the most damaged of us for change and growth.

Chapter 2 notes

1. The core self model is an integrative person–centred model which is the fruit of my work over thirty years as a therapist and trainer. See the Introduction for a brief overview of the model and Chapter 3 for a discussion of its relationship with humanistic person–centred theory and practice.

2. In Jungian psychology, the collective unconscious is described as that part of the unconscious mind which is common to all human beings. It is universal rather than personal – that is, it is not particular to any individual – and does not owe its existence to individual or personal experience but to the common ancestral experience of all human beings. Jung (1973) believed it to be inherited and to contain

a vast reservoir of ancient human wisdom in the form of 'archetypes' (literally 'ancient patterns'). He saw archetypes as ancient, universal symbols or images which are manifested by all people in all cultures. For example, the mandala – a sacred geometric figure – is seen as an archetypal symbol of wholeness, a universal image of 'the totality of the self'. He believed that such images often appear in dreams and saw them as the common elements in myths, fairy tales and the literature of world religions. He argued that particularly at times of personal crisis, they emerge spontaneously from the collective unconscious in order to reveal deep inner truths or to direct the self towards self–actualisation or to what Jung called 'individuation'.

3. Heron (1998: 9 – 19, 89) points out that when talking about the transcendent or the transpersonal, some writers refer to that which is beyond the person 'as if personhood is something transcended and left behind' in this process of 'opening to the transcendent Thou'. He argues that when we talk of reaching beyond the individual self, that self does not completely disappear or dissolve. An experience of entering into a state of transcendent awareness, of encountering the Divine as 'transcendent spirit', does not involve the leaving behind of the self otherwise we would not be able to remember or recount the experience. Similarly, Lines (2006: 192) argues that 'transcending Self does not involve the abolition of personality but the heightening of humanity.'

3: The journey of the self – the survival self

In the beginning there was I, and I was good. In the beginning I was one person,
hearing only the voice of my own experience. But then came the other voices,
powerful voices telling me what was right and what was not right, what was
good for me and what was not, what I should be and what I should not be.
So many voices telling me so many different and often conflicting things.
I became lost in the confusion.

And then there were two, and three and four of I.
Steele (adapted from Rogers and Stevens 1973)

The emergence of the self

As infants, we are born with the capacity to encounter and receive
information about the world through our five senses and through our inner
feelings or visceral reactions. In person–centred terminology, this is
sometimes referred to as our capacity for 'organismic experiencing' (Merry
1999). The infant looks at his mother's face and sees her smiling at him. He
hears the sound of her voice, feels her touch on his skin as she holds him
close and smells the scent of her. He feels inwardly calm, content and
satisfied. These sensations and perceptions are essentially the raw, uncensored
and as yet unprocessed data of experience. We are not yet able to organise
them, make sense of them or give them meaning.

It is during this very early stage of life that our sense of self also begins to
emerge. As Merry (1999) puts it, some part of what we experience as reality
we begin to call 'I' or 'me' and we come to realise that this 'I' or 'self' is
separate and distinct from others and from the environment. Eventually as
our language skills and capacity for symbolisation develop, we also become
capable of naming and organising our experience. In person–centred
terminology, we develop the capacity to symbolise our experience consciously
in awareness (Rogers 1951).

The formation of the belief system

It is at this point in the process of self–development that what I call 'the belief
system' begins to be formed. As we acquire the ability to name and organise
our experience in some form of relationship with our self, we begin to
develop our own unique way of seeing and evaluating ourselves, others and
the world we inhabit. Rogers (1951) called this the 'self structure'. In the
context of attachment theory, Bowlby (1979) termed it 'the internal working

model'[1]. I prefer to use the term 'belief system'. I have adopted the term 'belief system' rather than 'self structure' partly because I believe such terminology more accurately reflects the nature of the phenomenon I am seeking to describe; partly because it is a term the majority of people can easily relate to; and partly because the core self model concept of the belief system is a broader one than that of the self structure and I want to highlight the differences between the two.

Tolan (2003) points out that developing such a belief system is important for our psychological survival. It gives us a framework for understanding our world, making sense of our experience and giving it meaning. McDowell (1985: 26) describes it helpfully as 'a set of lenses' through which we view reality. It also enables us to make predictions about how the environment that surrounds us and the people who care for us are likely to react if we behave in particular ways. As such, it helps us to 'fit in' to the family, society and culture into which we are born and to find a way of being in those contexts that will ensure as far as possible that our basic psychological needs are met.

Some of the beliefs and values that form part of our belief system emerge from the inner valuing process that enables us to evaluate our own experience. Others, however, do not flow from this inner valuing process and may even be at odds with it. How does this happen? During the very early stages of infancy, our actualising tendency or spirit (the force inherent within us that sustains us and motivates our growth and development) is functioning freely without inhibition. It motivates us to be open to all of our experiencing as this openness best serves the enhancement of our being. Research tells us that even as babies, we also have a clear, instinctive sense of what we need in the moment (Rogers 1973). We know what we like and value and what we do not and the origin of these value preferences lies solely within ourselves. As Rogers (1973) put it, 'the source or locus' of this ongoing valuing process is internal. We are able to listen to and trust our own inner signals. In person–centred terminology, this is known as the internal or organismic valuing process (Rogers 1951).

Gradually, however, we become aware that those who care for us do not always see our experience as we do, that they do not always like or value what we value, that they do not always approve of how we react to our environment. What feels good or natural to us often seems to be unacceptable or bad in the eyes of those who matter to us. And sometimes, when we behave in ways that they do not like, acceptance and love are temporarily withdrawn. We see the look of disapproval or disgust, hear the voice raised in anger and protest, and perhaps even feel the slap of a hand. We may be labelled 'bad', 'naughty', 'wicked' or 'stupid'. These are powerful 'messages' which communicate to us the beliefs, judgements, attitudes and values of the significant others in our lives. Such messages may be both verbal and non–verbal, both explicit and implicit. They may be communicated through words or through facial expressions, body language or particular actions or behaviour patterns. They may be communicated to us directly or indirectly – for example, through overhearing a conversation about us between two other people or through someone reporting to us what has been said about us by someone else. They may be either positive or negative and either accurate or distorted. For most of us, they are mixture of all of these.

When these messages come from those who our closest to us and are either particularly persistent or strongly expressed, we tend to 'take them on board'. In other words, we introject or unconsciously assimilate them even when they are foreign to us and do not fit with our own organismic experiencing. The word 'unconsciously' is used here because at the time we are not aware that we have assimilated them and experience them as if they were our own. This happens because our need for the love and acceptance of others – what Rogers (1951) called positive regard – and our fear of losing it are so strong that they over–ride our normal organismic functioning. We begin to be aware that being seen as lovable and being loved is conditional on feeling, thinking and behaving in a certain way, on pleasing those who care for us. Rogers (1959) called this the experience of 'conditions of worth'. In order to hold on to the love that is so important for our well–being, we learn, therefore, to distrust and dismiss our own inner signals and to adopt and try to live by the beliefs and values of those who are most significant to us. As Mearns and Thorne (1999) put it, we 'accept the straightjacket' of others' conditions of worth rather than risk rejection.

It is at this point that another self is being born. In person–centred terminology, this self been called 'the false or conditioned self' (Merry 1999). I prefer to call it 'the survival self' as I believe this reflects its primary purpose more accurately – that of enabling us to survive and cope with living in a less than perfect world. It is in a sense 'the mask' that we present to the world or in Jungian terms, the social self or 'persona' (Jung 1973) that we create in order to be acceptable to it. The survival self is not the same as the core self. As the survival self begins to emerge, the core self continues to exist and develop at the innermost level of our being. However, part of the actualising tendency inevitably becomes focused on actualising the survival self rather than the core self. Somewhat confusingly, Rogers (1959) referred to this process as 'self actualisation'. He argued that a 'sub–system' of the actualising tendency is formed as the belief system begins to emerge and that at times, the two will inevitably be at odds with each other. They will effectively be pulling in different directions and more often than not, the actualisation of the survival self will take precedence.

Is this not at least to some degree the inevitable consequence of the necessary process of socialisation? Rogers answer to this question would, I think, have been that it is not and this is a perspective I share. Rogers (1951) argued that if a child's caregivers were genuinely able to accept all of the child's feelings and values and to accept fully the child who experiences them while at the same time accepting and, where appropriate, expressing their own feelings that the child's behaviour is undesirable in the context in which it is being expressed, then a different outcome might become possible.

For example, on one occasion some years ago, I witnessed a father responding to his young son's attempt to hit his younger sister who would not let him have something he wanted. While he very firmly and clearly communicated to the little boy that he must not hit his sister, he waited until his son's anger had subsided and then made a point of verbally acknowledging that it was alright for him to want what his sister had and to feel frustrated and angry with her. He did not shame the child by labelling him 'bad' or 'naughty' and he did not hit him as a punishment. He also explained to him clearly and simply why his behaviour was unacceptable to him. At the end of this dialogue with his son, moreover, he gave him a smile and a hug and told him he loved him. I found this interchange both very moving (in part because it reminded me of my own father's way of being) and challenging. What particularly struck me about the father's handling of his child's behaviour was that while the child would undoubtedly have learnt that his father did not like his behaviour on this occasion, he would almost certainly have continued to feel loved and accepted by him and that he was still lovable despite his behaviour.

Rogers (1951: 502 – 3) argued that in such a relationship, the child's concept of himself as a lovable person is not undermined and his emerging self structure is not threatened by a potential loss of love. Consequently, the child does not need to deny or distort his own experience or to cut himself off from his own internal valuing process. He can fully accept his own feelings of anger and frustration and at the same time fully experience his perception that his aggressive behaviour is not liked by the person who loves him. He is then free to make a choice which will depend on how he weighs up the key elements in the situation – the strength of his own feelings of anger, the satisfaction he would get from expressing his anger physically and the satisfaction he would get from pleasing his father. Whether the outcome of such an exchange would always be positive is difficult to assess, but my own experience of being patiently and fairly disciplined in a very similar way by my father is that because of the depth and unconditionality of his love for me, even when he disliked or was angry about something I had done, I always knew myself to be accepted and valued. I also felt heard and that my perspective was important to him, even when he disagreed with it. Consequently, his disciplining did not undermine my sense of my own lovability and worth.

Where we have experienced relatively few conditions of worth and where we have received a sufficient degree of the love and acceptance we need in our early relationships with our parents and significant others, then the quality of our early relational environment will have been 'good enough'. The necessary conditions for growth are present which will enable us to grow and develop, to remain in touch with and trusting of our true or core selves, to form healthy belief systems and to relate to others and our environment in positive, constructive ways. The core self and the survival self remain reasonably closely aligned and there is unlikely to be any major conflict between the two. The actualising tendency can therefore continue to function in a relatively uninhibited way and to fulfil its task of enabling us to realise our full potential. In other words, we are likely to be relatively psychologically healthy. Such people do not become disconnected from their core self and are able to engage freely in the process of becoming.

We are, however, born into a less than perfect world. Often, we live out our early lives in the context of human systems which are at best imperfect and at worst profoundly 'toxic' and damaging to our spiritual and psychological well–being. We experience relationships with significant people in our lives which are at best partially flawed and at worst deeply destructive of us. For some of us, the psychological environment in which we find ourselves is so hostile that we can do little more than struggle to survive, tragically sometimes in ways which are in themselves harmful to ourselves or others. Hence, to some degree, all of us experience psychological conditions in our early lives which to some extent limit or block our psychological growth. Most, or perhaps even all of us, are at some point or other wounded by life.

Furthermore, experiences or relationships that we encounter later in life can also have a significant effect on our psychological development. My experience of being bullied at school as a teenager undoubtedly had a major impact on my self–image and self–esteem and one of the most destructive relationships I have encountered in my life did not develop until adulthood. It had a profound effect on the way in which I saw and felt about myself as a person and it took me many years to recover fully from the damage it inflicted. I believe though that the degree of impact these later experiences are likely to have will depend in part on the quality of the relationships we have experienced in early life. Where we have experienced difficult or damaging relationships in the first few years of life, the impact of later negative experiences is likely to be greater.

Thorne (1991: 31 – 33) argues that if the quality of our relational environment has been poor, we are likely to be relatively psychologically unhealthy. His experience as a therapist tells him that those of us who are victims of multiple conditions of worth in early life tend to show the following characteristics: a deeply negative self-concept; feelings of worthlessness over having failed to meet others' expectations and demands; an intense preoccupation with trying to make the grade; little sense of our own inherent value as unique persons; an external locus of evaluation and a deep sense of inadequacy. I would argue that our survival self is also likely to become significantly divorced from our core self. In other words, we become disconnected from our innermost self or soul. We lose touch with who we are at the core of our being in our search for the love and acceptance of others.

What happens then when we become disconnected from our innermost selves? Kierkegaard (1941) believed that the most common and most profound experience of despair is that which arises when we choose not to be ourselves. It is, as he saw it, a deep existential despair which he described as a 'sickness unto death'. Maslow (1962) used similar language when he argued that if we suppress or deny what he described as our 'essential core', we 'get sick' in a variety of subtle and not so subtle ways. The psychologist, Miller (1987) maintained that such a separation from the true self results in depression. The psychoanalyst, Horney (1950) sees it as leading to self–contempt.

One of my clients whom I shall call Mark came into counselling in his late thirties because he had been struggling with mild depression on and off for several years. Early on in our work together, he began to speak of feeling profoundly 'at odds' with himself but at that point, without knowing why. It transpired that very early in life, Mark had discovered in himself both a deep love of and talent for making music. He had known in his early teens that he wanted to become a musician but his father had strongly disapproved. As Mark had struggled throughout his early life to earn his father's acceptance and approval, he could not risk his rejection further by pursuing a career – or as he saw it, a vocation – to study music. So he chose to abandon his dream and embark instead on a career as an accountant (his father's chosen profession). Mark was, however, deeply unhappy in his job and still had not earned his father's approval. Uninhibited, his actualising tendency would undoubtedly have propelled him in the direction of developing his musical gifts. However, the subsystem that sought to actualise his survival self had pushed him in the opposite direction in order to gain the love and acceptance he so badly wanted from his father. As a result, he became significantly out of touch with his core self. For Mark, depression was the consequence.

I am not sure that I would have used words like 'depression' and 'despair' to describe my own growing awareness in mid–life of the extent to which I was disconnected from my innermost self. For me, it felt like being 'half alive'. When trying to capture my experience in my journal, I found myself using the images of living life 'in the trenches', of being trapped in a cul–de–sac from which I could see no escape. I vividly remember how disturbed I felt when I first came across Thoreau's (1995) assertion that most of us lead 'lives of quiet desperation' because somewhere deep inside myself, I knew that there was more than a grain of truth in it for me. I remember too a very powerful image that flashed into my mind one day when I was listening to a client, an image of a little girl almost buried alive in rubble. All I could see was one hand, still beckoning, still struggling frantically to be seen. I thought at the time that the image reflected something of my client's experience. And perhaps it did. But it also captured something of my own.

The nature of the belief system

There are a number of important things to note about the concept of the belief system. Firstly, the belief system is more than just a set of perceptions or beliefs. It is not only a cognitive framework; it also consists of a set of values attached to those perceptions and consequently has an affective component. For example, if when I experience or express anger as child, I consistently receive the message that such anger is unacceptable, I may come to dislike the angry part of myself, to see it as bad or unlovable. I begin to devalue this part of myself or even to believe that because I am a person who experiences anger, I have no worth. Secondly, the contents of the belief system consist not only of those perceptions and beliefs that we are consciously aware of but also those that are unconsciously held or that are on the edge of our awareness – in other words, in the process of emerging but not yet full present in awareness. The assumption here is that not all of the contents of our belief system exist in our conscious awareness, but that such unconscious material still has the power to impact on our emotions and behaviour.

In this sense, the concept of the belief system differs a little from the Rogerian concept of the self structure. The self structure as Rogers understood it contains only those perceptions of self that are 'admissible to awareness'. In other words, they exist in our conscious awareness, whether in the foreground or background of our perceptual field. Rogers (1951) did acknowledge that the perceptions and values we develop in early childhood are largely preverbal and are often not present in our conscious awareness. He also acknowledged the power of such unconscious material to influence behaviour. He recognised that even when they are not fully present in our consciousness, they are capable of functioning 'as guiding principles' (Rogers 1951: 498) and have the power to shape our interactions with our environment. Indeed, his decision to exclude such material from the concept of the self structure was essentially a pragmatic one. He did so because he believed it to be important to focus attention on what could be adequately operationally defined and researched within the research parameters of that time (Rogers 1959: 202 – 3). Interestingly, Mearns and Thorne (2000: 175) have since argued that the concept of the self structure should be broadened to include what they call 'edge of awareness material'.

Thirdly, the belief system is a highly complex, multi–faceted body of beliefs which is not always internally consistent. This is because our development as children is not just influenced by our parents or primary caregivers. It is also impacted by our relationships with other significant people in our lives – for example, by grandparents, siblings and other family members, by our peers, by our teachers and others in authority over us. There may also be a wider societal impact, for example via the media. Furthermore, the messages we receive from these different people may not be consistent or may conflict with each other. How one person perceives us may be very different from how another does. What makes us acceptable and valued in one context may not be acceptable in another. McMillan (2004) introduces the concept of an individual's overall 'regard matrix'. This matrix consists of all of the life experiences we have had which relate to our experience of the positive regard of others in our lifespace. Each person's regard matrix will be unique and complex. Some of the people in our lives will have communicated positive regard; others will not. Some people will have communicated their positive regard (or lack of it) consistently; others will not. Cooper (1999: 64) suggests that in order to maximise the positive regard we receive from different people in our lives, we may go on to develop 'a plurality of self-concepts: that is a different self to maximise positive self–regard in relation to each social grouping'. In other words, our survival self may come to have a number of different faces depending on which social environment we find ourselves in. We may behave very differently in one setting than we do in another.

It is interesting to note that Rogers himself spoke of observing 'violent fluctuations' in an individual's self structure at times (Rogers 1959). Furthermore, Mearns and Thorne (2000: 102) record their observation that clients often experience their self as having different 'parts'. They introduce the term 'configurations of self' to refer to these different dimensions of self, defining a configuration as a consistent pattern of feelings, thoughts and behaviours which we identify as reflecting a 'dimension of existence within the Self.' These configurations are not, however, experienced as separate entities within the self but as different but inter–connected parts of the self. We may even name these parts of ourselves that we are aware of, using particular descriptive or metaphorical terms such as the scared little boy, the critic or the free spirit. These may be very common descriptive terms or they may be highly idiosyncratic.

Mearns and Thorne (2000) see the formation of such configurations as a normal adaptive process, not a pathological one. They see it as enabling us to 'house' different or even conflicting aspects of the self. They recognise, however, that our configurations are often based on the particular beliefs about ourselves that we have introjected from others. For example, someone who frequently receives the message from others that she is stupid may develop a configuration based on this introjected belief – a part that she might, for example, call 'stupid me'. They may also be based on what Mearns and Thorne (2000) call 'dissonant self experiences' – that is, experiences of ourselves that conflict with our existing belief system. For example, clients who see themselves as placid and for whom anger is an unacceptable emotion may seek to contain their experience of anger within a configuration – 'the angry part of me' – as a way of maintaining the beliefs they have come to hold about themselves. This is an alternative to denial ('I wasn't angry') or to distorting or dismissing the experience in some way. Where a configuration is based around a negative internalised belief about self or dissonant self experience, clients are likely to find it difficult to acknowledge or explore that part of themselves and even more difficult to disclose it to others.

My experience tells me that configurations can also be based on the particular strategies we develop in order to ensure that our basic needs are met. One of the parts of myself that I became aware of later in life was 'the good little girl'. This part of me was always extremely well–behaved and would work very hard to obey the rules, even when internally, I disagreed with them. I see this part as having emerged from my people–pleasing strategy which was designed to enable me to secure the love and acceptance of others. Another part – the strong woman – was, I think, based on my self–protective strategy of being independent. This resulted in my not being able to articulate my needs to others, to acknowledge my vulnerability or to ask for help when I needed it. This part of me saw vulnerability as weakness and sought to protect me both from being let down and from being seen as unacceptably 'needy'.

Lastly, the belief system is neither fixed nor unchanging. Rogers (1959: 200) described it as 'a fluid and changing gestalt, a process' (where the word 'gestalt' refers to an integrated structure or pattern of elements). What I believe about myself, others and the world today may not be what I believed in the past or will believe tomorrow. Neither are our configurations of self static and unchanging. They evolve and develop (and sometimes disappear) as we continue to respond to our ever–changing social environment and the conditions of worth we encounter there; as our locus of evaluation becomes more internalized; and as we learn to 'reality test' the introjected elements of our belief system. For example, the client whose configuration, 'stupid me', is based on internalised messages about herself may become increasingly aware of elements of her experience that do not fit with this introject and may in time be able to reject it as invalid. As a result, her configuration, 'stupid me', may eventually cease to exist.

The key elements of the belief system

As I see it, the belief system is comprised of a number of different kinds of perceptions or beliefs: beliefs about ourselves, beliefs about others, beliefs about the world (including, where relevant, the transcendent as we understand it) and beliefs about how to 'make life work' – life strategies for meeting our fundamental human needs and for surviving emotional pain.

Beliefs about self

The traditional psychological term for this element of the belief system is the self–concept. It can perhaps usefully be thought of as having two separate but inter–related elements: our self–image which is the internal picture we have of ourselves and our self–esteem which is the evaluation we make of our worth. It has both a cognitive component – the way we think about ourselves – and an affective component – the way we feel about ourselves. Articulating it involves, therefore, both a process of self–description and a process of self–evaluation. Nelson–Jones (1988) identifies a number of key content areas within the self–image such as the physical, the emotional, the rational or intellectual, the social or relational and the sexual. I would want to add two other content areas – the volitional (that aspect of ourselves that is concerned with our capacity to make choices and decisions and to set and pursue goals) and the spiritual. Nelson–Jones (1988: 27 – 8) also distinguishes helpfully between central and peripheral perceptions of self. He regards central perceptions as those which are most important to us and which we regard as part of the essence of who we are and peripheral perceptions as those which are of relatively little importance to us.

At the root of many of our problems in living lie the negative core beliefs about ourselves that we have internalised. I would define a core belief as any belief that is concerned with or impacts on our sense of our acceptability, lovability and worth as a human being. Such beliefs are often, though not always, global beliefs – in other words, beliefs about ourselves as a whole person rather than beliefs about specific parts or aspects of ourselves. They tend to be absolute or black and white statements and they are generally rigidly held. Clients may, for example, talk about not being good enough, being 'second rate', or being inadequate. They may see themselves as a failure or a loser, as useless or worthless, as 'a waste of space'. They may think of themselves as mad or bad, as evil or sinful, as 'a weirdo' or 'a freak'. They may consider themselves to be unlikeable or unattractive, to be unimportant or insignificant, to be weak or pathetic. All of these are core beliefs that I have heard being voiced many times. They are generally the most damaging beliefs about self. It is important to recognise, however, that not all damaging core beliefs are global beliefs. We may also internalise a range of negative beliefs about specific parts or aspects of ourselves such as our appearance ('I'm ugly'), our intelligence ('I'm stupid'), our sexual attractiveness or responsiveness ('I'm frigid') or our emotional responsiveness ('I'm over-emotional'). While they may not be global beliefs, they are, I believe, always central as opposed to peripheral beliefs, to use Nelson–Jones' terminology.

In addition, as a result of the conditions of worth we have experienced, we also take on board messages about how we should be if we want to be acceptable to others – for example, 'Why can't you be more like your brother?'; 'Could try harder.'; 'Don't be such a cry baby.'; 'Why don't you grow up?'; 'If only you weren't so….'; 'You ought to be more…'. Underlying all of these core beliefs about self, there is, I believe, a central core belief – 'I am unacceptable' – which lies at the heart of any negative belief system. Writing from a Transactional Analysis perspective, Harris (1973) sees this as an 'existential decision' that we make about ourselves at a very early stage in life. As such, it is generally pre–verbal (and therefore, feelings–based) and unconscious.

Beliefs about others

In addition to developing a set of beliefs about ourselves as a result of our early life experiences, we also develop a set of beliefs about other people. These beliefs may have developed as a result of messages we have received from significant people in our lives or as a result of our own personal experiences of relating to other people. They may be beliefs about people in general or about particular kinds or groups of people – for example, men, women or authority figures.

Our core beliefs about others generally revolve around how acceptable and worthy of our love and trust we believe them to be. They are also concerned with how we believe other people are likely to relate to us. As a result of the way in which we have been treated by particular people in the past or as a result of what we have been told about others, we come to view people as more or less trustworthy and dependable, as more or less caring, as more or less sensitive and responsive to our needs. Core beliefs about others are again often global, absolute and rigidly held. Frequently, they are also over–generalisations. In other words, our perceptions of one or two key people in our lives are held to be true of everyone.

Negative core beliefs often revolve around issues of trust. Clients may talk about other people not being trustworthy, not being dependent or reliable and not being there for them when they are needed. They may see others as not liking them or caring about them, as rejecting or abandoning them or as being 'out to get' them. Sometimes they also project their own negative beliefs about themselves onto others – in other words, they assume others see them as they have learnt to see themselves. Again, underlying all of these core beliefs about others, there is generally, I believe, a central core belief that others are either acceptable or unacceptable, trustworthy or untrustworthy.

Harris (1973) identified a number of what he called 'basic life positions' that people come to hold as a result of their early life experiences. Essentially, these life positions consist of core beliefs about both self and others. He identified four key life positions: 'I'm OK – You're OK', 'I'm not OK – You're OK', 'I'm OK – You're not OK', and the most negative of the four, 'I'm not OK – You're not OK'. He believed that each of these life positions tends to be associated with particular emotional consequences and particular strategies for insuring that out need for acceptance and love is met. For example, he associated the 'I'm not OK – You're OK' life position with low self–esteem and depression and with a people–pleasing strategy for gaining acceptance.

Beliefs about the world

As a result of our life experiences, we also develop a set of beliefs about the world and about life in general as we perceive it. We come to view the world in which we live as more or less safe, as more or less hospitable, as more or less conducive to our living a life that is purposeful, meaningful and worthwhile. For many of us, this will include beliefs about the existence and nature of the transcendent, however we may conceive of it. If we have had one or more traumatic experiences, particularly early in life, we may develop the belief that the world is a dangerous or chaotic place, that to live is to suffer, that life is fragile or unfair or meaningless or that bad things are always 'just around the corner'. Such beliefs will inevitably shape both our emotions and our behaviour. We may, for example, struggle with persistent feelings of anxiety, fear or depression; we may become excessively cautious and self–protective and unable to take risks.

In a similar way, as a result of our life experiences, we may form beliefs about and images of the transcendent. For some of us, these beliefs will take the form of faith in a personal God or gods; for others, they may involve belief in some form of impersonal, unknowable Absolute Reality or in a Higher Self. Such beliefs and images will have been shaped partly by any spiritual experiences we may have had; by the messages we have received about the transcendent from significant people in our lives (for example, through what people tell us or through the ways in which we see people relating to the transcendent themselves); and by the wider culture within which we live. These beliefs will inevitably impact on the way in which we make sense of our spiritual experiences and on the way in which we relate to the transcendent.

Life strategies

In addition to developing a set of beliefs about ourselves, others and the world, we also develop a set of beliefs about 'how to make life work' – that is, we develop a number of life strategies for meeting our basic psychological and spiritual needs and for protecting ourselves from emotional pain. We are not usually consciously aware of these strategies, nor have we usually adopted them deliberately. They emerge in response to the conditions of worth we have experienced and are to a large degree shaped by the particular beliefs we hold about how we should be if we want to be acceptable to others. They may develop through a process of experimentation, through observing the ways in which other people try to 'make life work' for them or even perhaps by accident.

In the context in which they were originally formed (usually during early life), they 'worked for us' to a degree either in enabling us to meet our basic needs (at least partially) or to protect ourselves from potentially damaging or even overwhelming emotional pain. In other words, while they may be destructive for us now, they had a significant survival value for us in the past. Because they have worked well for us in the past, we tend to hold onto them, even if we have become aware that they are no longer needed, are not working for us now or are in some way inhibiting our personal growth. What keeps them in place is the fear of losing the acceptance they may have brought us (or may bring us in future) or the fear of having to face the emotional pain they protect us from. This is the case even when the damage they cause far outweighs any benefits they may bring. Some of the most commonly encountered life strategies are the following:

people pleasing (working hard to meet others' needs, wants or expectations or trying to be the person others want us to be as a means of achieving and maintaining their acceptance)

avoiding challenging, confronting, disagreeing or asserting ourselves with others (often accompanied by an underlying lack of trust in our own perceptions and beliefs)

'workaholism' (working harder than is necessary or healthy in order to achieve)

perfectionism (constantly trying to do better, achieve more or be a better person)

avoiding failure or making mistakes (setting goals which minimise the risk of failure thereby leading to under–achievement; avoiding situations in which we have to perform in public)

shyness and social withdrawal (avoiding social situations in which we may experience rejection by others)

avoiding intimacy (keeping others at a distance; working hard to maintain independence in order to avoid the possibility of rejection or abandonment)

hiding behind a mask (not letting others see our true self as a means of avoiding rejection)

rejecting others (behaving aggressively towards others; dismissing or 'putting others down' as a means of keeping them at a distance)

making ourselves unattractive to others (presenting ourselves to others or behaving towards them in a way that is designed to keep them at a distance)

suppressing emotions and denying emotional needs (both as a means of protecting ourselves from the pain of these needs being unmet and as a means of avoiding intimacy with others) constant activity and busyness (constantly 'doing' as a means of distracting ourselves from emotional pain, blocking off our emotional needs or avoiding intimacy)

developing addictive behaviour patterns (using food, alcohol, drugs and other addictive behaviours as a means of numbing or suppressing emotional pain).

As will be evident from the above list of possible life strategies, moreover, those strategies we use to protect ourselves can sometimes block or inhibit the meeting of our basic psychological needs. For example, if we have a strong need to protect ourselves from further rejection and abandonment and do so by keeping others at a distance, this will make it very difficult for us to meet our fundamental needs for love, acceptance and intimacy and so impede our psychological growth.

How does the concept of life strategies relate to Rogers' concept of conditions of worth? The concept of life strategies embraces but goes beyond that of conditions of worth. Many of our life strategies emerge from the beliefs we have internalised about how we should be in order to be acceptable to others – in Rogerian terms, from our conditions of worth. They are also concerned, however, with the ways in which we seek to protect ourselves from emotional pain.

The maintenance of the belief system

One of the key things I have learnt, both from my own personal experience and from my work as a therapist, is that no matter how self–defeating or destructive of ourselves and others our belief systems are, we often cling tenaciously to them, even when we are confronted by strong evidence that they are distorted, destructive of us or others and are no longer working for us. There are, I believe, a number of reasons for this. Firstly, it is important to recognise that much of the content of our belief systems develops during the early stages of our development and often in the context of significant emotional pain or trauma. As we have seen, furthermore, the core beliefs we develop in early childhood are generally pre–verbal and are not fully present in our conscious awareness. Consequently, they are likely to be encoded in emotional rather than cognitive ways – that is, they are 'felt' rather than 'believed' – and are, therefore, difficult both to access and to change.

Secondly, our belief systems were functional (that is, they 'worked for us') at that time in our lives, either in enabling us to some degree to meet our basic psychological or spiritual needs or in enabling us to protect ourselves from the pain of those needs being unmet. Furthermore, they may still be perceived as functional in the present as a means of continuing to meet those basic needs. They were and may still be part of our survival strategy and as such, are very hard to let go of. Moreover, many of our core beliefs were internalised from messages we received as children from significant, powerful others in our lives whose acceptance and valuing of us was and may still be very important to us. It is consequently very difficult for us to challenge those beliefs, particularly if we fear that we may lose the acceptance we have worked so hard to gain.

Thirdly, when we experience what Rogers called 'incongruence' – in other words, when there is a mismatch between what we actually experience and what we believe – we generally feel a degree of anxiety, tension or unease. Our belief system is effectively under threat and with it, our psychological survival. The more deeply embedded and distorted the belief system is, the greater the degree of anxiety that will be experienced. Changing our belief system means therefore that we must first work through the anxiety of facing incongruence. Rogers argued that when we become aware of this incongruence, the belief system effectively 'reacts as does a piece of protoplasm when a foreign body is intruded – it endeavours to prevent the entrance' (Rogers 1951: 505). We deny or distort the experience in order to reduce the threat. He believed that this process occurs at a level below conscious awareness and perception. In other words, that it involves an unconscious defence mechanism.

Rogers (1951) argued that there are four possible ways in which we can react to what we are experiencing. What he was concerned with here is the way in which we process or make sense of our experiences through the 'lens' of our belief system. Firstly, the experience may be ignored either because it is irrelevant to our belief system – in other words, it neither reinforces nor contradicts it – or because it does not meet any significant need that we may have at that point in time. For example, if I am absorbed in reading a good book, I may only be barely aware of the sounds I can hear outside my window. As attending to them does not serve any need that I have at that time and as they have no particular relevance for my belief system, I ignore them as immaterial background noise. Secondly, the experience may be accurately perceived, accepted into our conscious awareness and become part of our self structure. This usually happens when the experience is both relevant for and consistent with that self structure. For example, if I have learnt to see myself as incompetent and am then told that I have not done a good enough job on a piece of work, I am likely to absorb this feedback unquestioningly as confirming what I already believe about myself.

Thirdly, the experience may be denied because it is inconsistent or incompatible with our self structure. For example, if I believe I am not an anxious person, when I do experience anxiety I may deny or repress my awareness of the physical sensations that accompany it. This denial can either be semi–conscious or unconscious. In other words, I may be half aware that I am denying the experience or I may have totally repressed it from my awareness, a process Rogers (1951) called 'subception'. Lastly, our perception of the experience may be distorted, again usually because it is inconsistent with our self structure. Instead of denying or repressing the physiological sensations that my anxiety is generating, I may symbolise them in a distorted way – for example, by seeing them as evidence of an upset stomach.

Mearns and Thorne (1999) identified two basic mechanisms of defence – perceptual distortion and denial. The most common defence of the two is perceptual distortion. This involves the unconscious distortion of experiences which are not compatible with our existing belief system with the result that they are perceived incorrectly. For example, if I believe myself to be unattractive and then receive conflicting feedback from a friend or partner, I may tell myself that he or she is 'only saying that' in order to make me feel better. This is known as 'discounting the positive'. It is an example of what Beck (1976) called 'cognitive distortions' – that is, specific distorted thinking patterns which operate to maintain the existing belief system. Alternatively, when we resort to denial as a defence, experiences which are not congruent with our existing belief system are prevented from entering our awareness at all.

For example, if I see myself as being selfish and then receive positive feedback from others about my unselfishness, I may not be able to 'hear' or remember the positive feedback given to me. Any positive messages I may receive are effectively filtered out whereas negative messages are absorbed without reality testing. Mearns and Thorne believe this to be a less common defence mechanism but more difficult to deal with when it does occur. In addition to perceptual distortion and denial, there are, I believe, other forms of distorted or faulty thinking patterns which also operate as defences. These may include, for example, all–or–nothing thinking (that is, seeing experience in absolute and rigid terms), over–generalisation, jumping to conclusions without reality testing our assumptions, mind reading (trying to guess the content of others' thoughts without checking it out with them) and confusing fact and evaluation.

Fourthly, Rogers argued that the more conditions of worth we have been exposed to, the more likely we are to be unable to react to others and our environment on the basis of realistic perceptions. This is because we are prone to be more distrusting of our own organismic valuing process and to be more dependent on others' judgments and perceptions rather than on our own. In other words, our locus of evaluation is liable to be externalised rather than internalised. Consequently, it is probable that we will deny or distort a significant amount of our experiencing. We are also unlikely to have the confidence to acknowledge and face the mismatch between our perceptions and our experience, or to trust our own way of seeing and making sense of our experience rather than relying on the perceptions and beliefs we have internalised from others.

Finally, our distorted belief systems often have behavioural consequences which are destructive either of ourselves or of our relationships with others. Furthermore, these destructive patterns of behaviour themselves have consequences which can create a kind of 'negative feedback loop' and thereby serve to maintain the existing belief system. For example, if an individual sees himself as boring and uninteresting to others, he is likely to adopt behaviour patterns (for example, remaining extremely quiet and withdrawn around other people) which may result in others perceiving him as boring and uninteresting and avoiding spending time with him. The messages he receives from their avoidance of him then confirm his existing beliefs about himself ('Other people avoid me. Therefore, I am obviously as boring and uninteresting as I thought I was.')

Another form of negative feedback loop occurs as a result of what Freud (1920) originally called the 'repetition compulsion'. What I am referring to here is the marked tendency for people to be repeatedly drawn to situations and relationships which effectively trigger or replay unresolved traumas from earlier in their lives. For example, a woman who was abused by her father as a child is likely in later life to be unconsciously drawn to men who treat her in a similar way. This tendency has been explained in a number of ways – for example, as a tendency to return to what is familiar, however destructive it might be or as an attempt to triumph over the original trauma by replaying it in the hope that we will be able to deal with it in a healthier, more constructive way and thereby find healing. I see it as an unconscious process of seeking out evidence that confirms our existing core beliefs. Whatever the reason for it, the most likely consequence of such a compulsion to repeat the original trauma is that the experience will reinforce the negative messages we internalised as a child. History repeats itself and we wonder how we managed to find ourselves in the same position over and over again.

The impact of a negative belief system

The significance of our belief system lies in the fact that we carry the perceptions and beliefs we develop with us into our relationship with ourselves and into our interactions with others and with our environment. It plays an important part in shaping the way in which we both make sense of and respond to our experiencing. Indeed, many of our seemingly irrational feelings only make sense when we view them as the consequences of our belief system. Similarly, much of our apparently illogical behaviour only makes sense when we reach an understanding of how it 'works' for us. Satir (1972: 22) argued that, 'The crucial factor in what happens both inside people and between people is the picture of individual worth that each person carries around with him.' In other words, our belief system has a crucial impact on the way we feel and act both towards ourselves and others.

One of the key messages I frequently received about myself as a child was that I was not sociable or outgoing enough, that I was too quiet and introspective and that this was not an acceptable way to be. Having taken this message on board, I came to devalue the introverted part of myself, to see it as a weakness or an inadequacy and to lose confidence in my ability to relate to others. I also tried desperately hard for a while to change my introverted behaviour patterns in an effort to secure the approval and affirmation I needed. This was a strategy that inevitably had very limited success and left me feeling even more inadequate when I failed to achieve the changes I was trying to make. The beliefs I came to hold about myself therefore affected not only the way I saw and felt about myself but also my behaviour.

Through its impact on our emotions and behaviour, our belief system also has wider consequences. It may, for example, have physical consequences. Because we are embodied beings and body and mind are intimately inter–connected, it may affect our physical health and well–being. For example, if my strategy for gaining acceptance is that of driving myself to work harder in order to achieve more, I may push my body too hard through not getting enough sleep, exercise or relaxation. Furthermore, if I hold within me an unrealistically negative and distorted belief system and if I am unable to accept and value myself, then I am likely to find it difficult to acknowledge and allow myself to meet my own needs. My belief system can therefore determine the way in which I relate to and care for myself at all levels of my being, including the physical.

Our belief system may also have social and relational consequences. For example, those of us who have been badly hurt by others in early life may fail to develop a sufficient degree of 'basic trust' in others in the same way that we have failed to develop trust in ourselves (Erikson 1968)[2]. This is likely to impact adversely on our capacity to form and sustain secure attachments with others, both in infancy and throughout life (Bowlby 1979). We may develop a life strategy of denying or suppressing our needs for intimacy and of avoiding close relationships with others in order to protect ourselves from further hurt. We may pride ourselves on our independence and keep people at a distance rather than allow them to get close enough to be able to wound us again. If the fear is great enough, we may even allow ourselves to become socially isolated, preferring to endure the pain of loneliness rather than the pain of rejection or betrayal.

In addition, our belief system may have spiritual consequences. The way in which we think and feel about ourselves may also impact on aspects of our spirituality. For example, people who believe in the existence of a loving personal God but see themselves as bad or worthless may not be able to see themselves as loved and accepted by God. They may be constantly driven by the need to become a better person in order to gain God's acceptance and may live in fear that they will never be good enough. Even though the scriptures of their spiritual tradition may tell them that God loves them unconditionally, they may not be able to believe that of God or trust it for themselves.

Finally, we lose touch, at least to some degree, with the essential core of our being and are diverted from the path of becoming our true selves – also a spiritual consequence as I see it. I believe this to be the most damaging and far-reaching consequence of an adverse psychological environment. Not only does our survival self lead us to adopt ways of feeling, thinking and behaving that are inconsistent with our own organismic valuing process and core self, but we also lose touch with parts of ourselves that effectively 'go underground' because they are deemed by others – and consequently by ourselves – to be unacceptable or undesirable. This is essentially a defensive process that results in the formation of what I call the unlived self. Essentially, the survival self 'exiles' (Bly 1988) or relegates to the unconscious all those aspects of self which it wants to conceal both from others and itself. This process is similar to the formation of 'the shadow' in Jungian analytical psychology (Jung 1973). As does Page (1999), I believe that this process of suppressing or repressing parts of the self does not just take place in childhood but may extend into adulthood. In an effort to survive, we may become who we are not, and at the same time, fail to become who we are. The tragedy is, moreover, that we may not even realise what we have lost.

The core self model and its relationship with humanistic person–centred theory

In seeking to make sense of the variety of problems in living which people bring to therapy, the core self model that shapes my practice adopts many of the concepts and core assumptions that form part of the humanistic person-centred approach. It shares with its humanistic counterpart its emphasis on the importance of our early life environment and experiences – and in particular, our relational environment – in shaping the way we choose to be in the world. It draws to a significant degree on a number of humanistic person–centred concepts such as that of the organismic self, the self structure, the false or conditioned self, conditions of worth, introjection and the locus of evaluation.

However, it also adapts and develops some of these concepts further in a number of ways and introduces new ones such as the unlived self. In that sense, it is an adaptation and extension of humanistic person-centred theory. As part of an attempt to clarify meanings and make the theory more accessible, at times I use slightly different terminology to describe similar concepts – for example, 'belief system' rather than 'self structure', 'survival self' rather than 'conditioned self'. I have also broadened the Rogerian concept of the self structure which is central to person–centred theory in a number of ways. Firstly, I have included within the concept of the belief system the beliefs we develop about 'how to make life work' – that is, our life strategies for meeting our basic psychological and spiritual needs and for surviving the emotional pain and suffering that is the inevitable consequence of those needs being unmet.

Secondly, I have sought to embrace the spiritual dimension of our being more explicitly through recognising that for many of us, the perceptions and beliefs we develop about the world include perceptions and beliefs about the transcendent (however we may conceive of it) and about the meaning and purpose of human life. It recognises that such beliefs shape the way we relate not only to the transcendent, but also to ourselves, others and the world. It also focuses on the way in which our spirituality impacts and is impacted on by the development of the belief system and the survival self. As such, it is more explicitly spiritually–oriented than humanistic person–centred theory.

I have also adopted a more holistic viewpoint in seeking to make sense of people's problems in living, a viewpoint which stems from my belief in the inter–connectedness of body, mind, soul and spirit. The model sees people as complex living unities in whom the various aspects of being – physical, psychological, social and spiritual – are closely interrelated and as such is best thought of as a biopsychosociospiritual model. In paying attention more explicitly to the importance of the wider socio–cultural context of our being–in–the–world, it acknowledges that we exist and live out our lives not just in the smaller social systems of which we are a part such as family and friendship groups, but also in a range of wider contexts – our educational context, our work context, our cultural and political context and our philosophical or spiritual context. What we encounter in each of those wider contexts will also influence how we think, feel and behave and may therefore play a part in giving rise to the problems in living we experience.

In embracing the spiritual dimension of our being, furthermore, the model acknowledges the full complexity of our humanity. It sees psychological and spiritual problems in living as being multi–faceted and recognises that the causes of such problems are very rarely uni–causal or simple. Their causes generally involve a wide range of factors – physiological or genetic, psychological, social and spiritual – which interact together in a highly complex way both to give rise to and maintain specific problems. I would argue that if we are too narrowly focused on the psychological factors that underlie psychological distress, we may miss the wider picture and rely on over–simplistic theories which do not fully do justice to the complexity of human behaviour and experience.

In order to illustrate how this model may be applied in enabling us to make sense of the problems in living clients present in therapy, I intend to draw in some detail on my work with a client whom I shall call Emma. I will begin by recounting part of Emma's story.

Emma's story

Emma was a single woman in her thirties whose presenting problems were depression, lack of self–confidence, low self–esteem and difficulty in making and sustaining close relationships. She presented as a very controlled person, significantly 'out of touch' with her feelings and a little distant and aloof. She recognised that she was a perfectionist and 'a bit of a workaholic' and felt 'driven' to achieve ever higher standards in everything she undertook.

Emma was an only child. Her father left her mother when she was four years old and she had not seen him or heard from him since. She barely remembered him. Over the years, Emma had tried a number of times to ask her mother about him but she refused to talk about him or about why he left. Her mother also told her that if she ever tried to find her father, she would have nothing more to do with her. Emma's mother was retired and lived on her own nearby. Despite the fact that she had always had what she described as a 'very difficult' relationship with her mother, Emma contacted her and saw her very regularly. She described her as a strict disciplinarian who had very high expectations of her, both academically and in relation to standards of behaviour. Throughout her childhood, Emma was constantly pressurised to work harder and to do better academically. When she succeeded in obtaining high grades, her mother always urged her to aim higher. When she failed to do so, she earned her anger and disapproval. Whatever she did or achieved, Emma felt that she was never quite 'good enough' and that she never 'made the grade'. Her mother had rarely been affectionate to her or affirming of her and Emma felt that much of the time she had been a disappointment to her.

Emma acknowledged she had always found it difficult to make friends. She thought this was partly because she was too quiet, serious and introspective and that people generally found this off–putting. She described herself as 'a bit of a loner' and prided herself on being independent and self–sufficient. She occasionally socialised with two or three colleagues from work but would not have described any of them as close friends. She also recognised, however, that she had always lacked the confidence to approach or open up to people and did not feel at ease in social situations. She remembered having one close friend at school in her early teens but this friendship broke up after a couple of years when her friend became involved in another friendship group and subsequently rejected her. She still found it very painful to think about this experience many years later.

Emma lived on her own and did not have a partner at the time she entered therapy. She had never had a long–term relationship with a man. She had had two brief relationships in her late teens and early twenties, both of which ended in her being abandoned or betrayed by her boyfriend. She said she was too busy to commit herself to a serious relationship at this point in her life and that she was happy being single. She also admitted, however, that she did not feel comfortable around men and tended to avoid their company. She acknowledged that her mother had very negative views about men and had not had any subsequent partners since her divorce. Her mother's father had had frequent affairs when she was a child and as a result, her mother had always felt very angry and bitter towards men in general. She would often warn Emma that men were 'a waste of space and could not be trusted'. She would describe them to her daughter as selfish, obsessed with sex and completely incapable of being faithful and frequently stated that women 'are better off without men'.

Emma had a successful practice as a solicitor. She admitted, however, that she did not enjoy the job and did not find it particularly fulfilling. She chose to study law largely because she knew it would please her mother. In her teenage years, she had wanted to be a teacher like her father but her mother was always very disparaging of teaching as a profession and made it very clear that she did not approve of it as a career choice for her daughter. From time to time, she still dreamt about giving up her job and doing a teacher training course. She worked very long hours and most of the little spare time that she had was taken up with doing things for her mother or for the church she belonged to. She considered her own needs as relatively unimportant and always puts others' needs before her own. She saw it as both sinful and selfish to do otherwise.

Emma was a practising Christian and attended church regularly on a Sunday with her mother. Her mother had started going to a local church shortly after her father left home and both she and Emma had attended the same church regularly ever since. Emma described herself as having been brought up in a 'pretty strict' Christian environment. She saw herself as failing as a Christian. She was constantly preoccupied with what she saw as her inherent sinfulness and believed that she would never be good enough to be acceptable to God. She recognised that her faith was a largely intellectual one in that, while she had a strong belief in the existence of God, she did not feel that she had ever had a personal relationship with him or experienced his presence. Her predominant image of God was of a distant, stern and critical judge. She lived in fear of failing or letting him down and was unable to experience herself as being accepted and loved by him.

Emma's belief system

Emma voiced a number of negative core beliefs about herself in the early part of our work together. These beliefs were largely internalised from both the verbal and non–verbal messages she had received about herself from her mother; through her mother's high expectations of her and difficulty in giving her praise or affection; and through her father's physical and psychological abandonment of her. They were also confirmed by the rejection she had experienced at the hands of her school friend and boyfriends. Emma saw herself as fundamentally unlovable and 'not good enough' – not a good enough daughter, not a good enough solicitor, not good enough at relating to others and not a good enough person. She felt that however hard she tried, she could never get things quite right and would always 'miss the mark'. She saw herself as a failure and as a disappointment to others and to God and was preoccupied by what she saw as her inherent weakness and sinfulness.

Emma's core beliefs about others were mixed. As her mother did, she tended to see men as untrustworthy, disloyal and selfish and as 'only after one thing'.

These beliefs were in part internalised from the powerful messages she received about men from her mother and then confirmed by her boyfriends' rejection of her in her early twenties. Her beliefs about people in general, however, were more positive. Generally, she blamed herself for others' reactions towards her rather than seeing them in a negative light. She saw other people as better and more successful than her and believed that people avoided her because they did not like her and found her too quiet, serious and withdrawn.

In Harris's terms, therefore, Emma's basic life position was 'I'm not OK – You're OK (Harris 1973). He termed this the depressive life position which certainly fits with Emma's experience of struggling with periods of depression for most of her adult life. In addition, her beliefs about the world were also predominantly negative. She saw the world as being full of pain, suffering and injustice. Life is not fair and bad things happen to good people. Her image of God was one of a God of judgement who demands perfection and she believed that God too saw her as a failure. She could not believe that God could accept or love her because she was not a good enough person.

Arising out these beliefs, Emma had a number of key life strategies. She was a people pleaser who always put others' needs and expectations before her own. She was a perfectionist and a workaholic who kept herself constantly busy doing things for others in order to distract herself from the pain of unmet emotional needs which she could not acknowledge. She also denied and suppressed many of her feelings. She kept other people (and God) at a distance and avoided intimacy despite her unrecognised longing for it.

Making sense of Emma's problems in living

Emma's problems in living were, I believe, predominantly shaped by three key early life experiences – her father's abandonment of her as a child, her difficult relationship with her mother and the painful loss of her only close friendship in her mid-teens. They were then reinforced by her rejection and betrayal by her two boyfriends in early adulthood. These experiences resulted in the formation of a belief system characterised by predominantly negative beliefs about herself, others and the world and the development of a number of life strategies which were no longer working for her.

Her feelings of depression, lack of self–confidence, low self–esteem and difficulty in forming and sustaining close relationships can best be understood as the emotional and behavioural consequences of the core beliefs she had internalised in early life. Her belief system also had indirect consequences for her physical health and well–being through her constant over–working; for her social and relational well–being through her relative social isolation, lack of emotional support and avoidance of intimacy; and for her spiritual well–being through her unhealthy preoccupation with her sinfulness and her inability to experience herself as loved and accepted by God. All of these, I believe, further fuelled her feelings of depression. In addition, she had not yet fully grieved the loss of her relationship with her father.

There were a number of factors maintaining Emma's belief system. Firstly and perhaps most importantly, she was as an adult still receiving the negative messages from her mother which she had internalised as a child. Because they were consistent with her belief system, they were readily absorbed and served to reinforce her existing core beliefs. Moreover, she still did not feel accepted by her mother despite all her efforts to gain her approval and this awareness only served to reinforce her existing life strategies. Secondly, she appeared throughout her life to be drawn to relationships in which the early life trauma of her abandonment by her father was effectively replayed – for example, her teenage friendship and her short–lived relationships with men in her early twenties. The negative messages she received about herself and others from these experiences then further reinforced her existing core beliefs.

Thirdly, whenever she experienced incongruence and the anxiety it generates, her defence mechanisms would kick in to protect her current belief system. Emma was significantly out of touch with aspects of her own experiencing. In particular, she would persistently filter out or discount positive information and feedback and deny her own emotional needs. She also tended to over–generalise, jump to conclusions, engage in all–or–nothing thinking and mind read. Fourthly, there was a negative feedback loop operating in the context of her relationships with others. Emma believed that people did not like her or want to spend time with her. Consequently, she was often distant and withdrawn when she was with other people as she was in our early sessions together, causing them to see her as aloof and unapproachable. This tended to result in their avoiding her or not engaging with her at a meaningful level. Perhaps inevitably, she saw this avoidance as further evidence of her unacceptability. Lastly, Emma's locus of evaluation was highly externalised. She therefore found it very difficult to trust her own organismic valuing process and did not have the confidence in herself to begin to question and challenge the negative beliefs she had internalised as a child.

Finally, Emma had effectively lost touch with her core self. Expressing this in spiritual terms, we might say that she was no longer living soulfully. In the early stages of therapy, she would often speak of not really knowing what kind of person she was. She had spent so much of her life trying to be what others wanted her to be that she had almost forgotten who she was. She found it extremely difficult even to articulate her own needs and wants, let alone allow herself to meet them. She was also significantly out of touch with the flow of her own emotions. At one point in the later stages of our work together, she described herself as a nomad, wandering alone in the desert of her life, endlessly seeking the oasis that eluded her. What she needed was to come home to herself.

In conclusion

In this chapter, I have attempted to trace the journey of the developing self through the first half of life as I have experienced and come to understand it. But of course, this is not the end of the journey. Even when the survival self is firmly ensconced behind its defences, the actualising tendency is still at work, gently but persistently nudging us in the direction of growth, seeking to make actual what is as yet potential and drawing us back towards the self that waits to be reclaimed. It invites us to engage in this later journey of self – the inner journey, the journey of home–coming, the journey as Rogers (1967) described it, of 'becoming a person'. This journey is the subject of the next chapter.

Chapter 3 notes

1. Attachment theory is concerned with our fundamental human need for connectedness or attachment to other people. It explores the way in which we form and maintain attachments (that is, deep and lasting emotional bonds) to others across the lifespan and their importance for our physical and psychological health and well–being. Bowlby (1979) believed that our attachment patterns are largely shaped by the 'internal working model' of human relationships that we develop as a result of our early relational experiences. This working model involves not only beliefs about and expectations of others, but also about the self.

2. In his eight stage theory of psychosocial development, Erikson (1968) argued that the key psychosocial task in infancy is the development of 'a basic trust' in self, others and the world.

4: The journey of the self – the core self

The great law of life is: be yourself.
John O'Donohue (2007)

In entitling perhaps his best–known book 'On Becoming a Person', Rogers made it very clear that he saw the process of becoming that he sought to describe as lying at the heart of the therapeutic endeavour (Rogers 1967). His thinking echoes that of a number of key existential philosophers, psychologists and therapists. For example, Jung (1960) spoke of the importance of the struggle to bring about the birth of what he called our 'true personality'. He described this struggle as the process of 'individuation', of attaining 'selfhood' – of becoming a separate, fully integrated, whole person. Kierkegaard (1941: 29) argued that our deepest responsibility as human beings is to make the choice 'to be that self which one truly is'. Tillich (1952) maintained that what is asked of us as human beings is that we fulfil our destiny – in other words, that we become the people we are meant to be. More recently, Hillman (1996) has also spoken of the importance of giving ourselves to our 'destiny' and aligning our life with our 'calling' to become who we essentially are.

Looking back both on my own personal journey of growth and on my experience as a therapist, this certainly rings true for me too. When I have been in therapy myself, when I have been sharing the difficult or painful aspects of my experience with those to whom I am closest or when I have been wrestling on my own with what troubles me, I am often aware that at the heart of my struggle is a deep longing to become more fully myself, to discover and live out the truth of who I am. It is a longing that has grown over the years and that I have become more conscious of, especially in mid–life, to the point that it has begun to feel like an imperative, a need that will not be denied. I experience it as a yearning to reach within myself to what lies buried and forgotten, to recover what was lost, to release what has not yet come to be, to free 'the wild possibilities' within myself, to borrow O' Donohue's words (O'Donohue 1997). It is at heart a deep–rooted desire to 'come home' to my self, to live 'the truth, the whole truth and nothing but the truth' of who I am.

I have witnessed this struggle to become many times in therapy too. Sometimes, though clearly present, it remains implicit; sometimes it is explicitly voiced. I well remember one client whose opening words to me were that she had lost touch with her innermost self and wanted to know how to re–discover that part of her. Another voiced his deep disquiet that he had spent so many years of his life trying to be the person everyone else wanted him to be that he no longer knew who he was. A third brought with her into therapy two self–portraits that she had painted. One was a black and white portrait of a sad and seemingly lifeless young woman slumped in a chair. She was dressed entirely in gray. The other was a pale watercolour portrait of the same young woman but this time, the face had no features. This second portrait was entitled 'Who am I?'

What does it mean to 'become myself'?

I would argue that first and foremost, it means learning to live as fully as possible from the core of our being, from what Seeman (1983) called the 'organismic self', from the deepest, innermost part of ourselves that I would call the core self or soul. It is about living 'soulfully' and as such, is also about moving towards living out the truth of who we are – or perhaps more accurately, who we are becoming. Jung (1961) saw this journey of becoming as beginning in the second half of life. I see it, however, as a natural process that is, at one level or another, ongoing throughout much of our lives but one that becomes more heightened, more urgent in mid–life and beyond. This has certainly been true of my own experience.

How is this journey of becoming experienced? I have come to think of it as a form of spiritual midlife crisis. The word 'crisis' means amongst other things a crucial or decisive point, a turning point. It is also used to refer to a time of intense difficulty in our lives or a time when a difficult or important decision has to be made. Essentially, this midlife crisis is 'a turning point of the soul' as Monk Kidd (1990) puts it. It is also, I believe, a process of transition. Jung (1961) saw life as being divided into two halves: 'the morning of life' in which our central task is to develop a strong belief system that enables us to relate and adapt to our environment and 'the afternoon of life' in which we are drawn to turn inwards in order to develop the core self or soul. He likened the transition between these two halves of life to a difficult birth and argued that we often go into this birthing process 'wholly unprepared'.

As I have experienced it, both personally and as a therapist, this process of transition consists of three key psychological growth processes:

> the process of awakening
> the process of letting go
> the process of emerging

The process of awakening

It was in my early forties that I first became acutely aware of a growing inner tension and restlessness, a desire for change, a deep sense of yearning though I could not have identified then precisely what it was I was longing for. This was accompanied by a strong desire to re–connect with my own life story, to come to know it in all its richness and complexity. In so doing, I wanted to understand how it had shaped and was continuing to shape the person I was and so, I hoped, to come to know – and perhaps to be – myself more fully. I struggled at times with a deep sense of loss, of being disconnected from my self, or perhaps more accurately from parts of myself. Gradually, I began to recognise that what I was experiencing was a profound existential longing. I wanted to know who I was underneath all of the layers of conditioning that had shaped my survival self and to find my way back to the self that I had lost. This deep inner restlessness coincided with the onset of a prolonged desert experience; a period of intense spiritual dryness; a loss of meaning and of a sense of purpose and direction; a questioning of deep convictions once firmly held; a feeling of being profoundly disconnected from the Source and Ground of my being.

Monk Kidd (1990: 4) calls this the experience of 'midlife darkness'. Elkins (1998) sees it as a form of existential depression which is designed to reconnect us with our soul. What I was experiencing, I believe, was a particularly urgent 'tapping in my spirit'. It was, as Rogers would see it, the actualising tendency at work, quietly but insistently calling me to attend to what was unfolding within. It led over time to what I would now describe as a profound experience of awakening. It was an awakening on many different levels – an awakening to previously unacknowledged or disregarded parts of myself, to inner tensions and conflicts as yet unresolved, to brokenness and woundedness as yet unhealed, to deep needs as yet unmet, to gifts and capacities as yet undeveloped, to the inner voice of the soul as yet unheeded.

Rogers (1967) observed a similar existential longing in many of the clients he worked with as a therapist and in others he encountered in his journey through life. His portrayals of 'the fully functioning person' (1967: 183 – 196) and later of 'the person of tomorrow' (1980: 350 – 1) both describe a growing desire for authenticity, genuineness and 'a wholeness of life' in which all aspects of being are integrated in our experience. He described such people as 'process persons' who are always changing and growing, always engaged in the ongoing existential process of becoming (Rogers 1980). He observed that as his clients moved through the therapeutic process, they tended to move from being the self that is not towards being more fully the self that is. Gradually, they became less ruled by 'oughts' and 'shoulds', by others' demands and expectations. They moved towards greater self–direction, towards being more autonomous, towards choosing their own goals and taking greater responsibility for themselves. Increasingly, they became less inclined to suppress their individuality in order to fit in and conform.

Rogers himself recognised that for some people, such a state of 'ever–changingness' and fluidity would not be seen as a desirable goal or outcome. I believe that some might also find it a frightening prospect. Indeed, Van Belle (1980) voices the fear that in embracing this quality of changingness, there is a danger that we may become caught up in a process of excessive change and thereby lose any sense of having a secure or solid identity, that we might, in Thorne's words, 'be lost in an infinite process of becoming' (Thorne 1992: 89). That has not, however, been Thorne's experience. Neither has it been mine, nor that of the clients I have had the privilege of accompanying on this path. In reflecting on my own personal journey, particularly in mid–life, I can readily identify with the process of change that Rogers described. Moreover, it is a process that I have come to welcome and even actively seek out. There is no question that at times, it has been difficult, painful and scary and has left me feeling intensely vulnerable. I have, however, found it profoundly liberating, releasing, and often joyful and exhilarating and it has undoubtedly enriched my life immeasurably on many different levels. Paradoxically, furthermore, the more I have been able to embrace this process of becoming, to enter into it fully and without fear, the more solid and secure my sense of my own emerging identity has become.

The process of awakening then is a calling, a summoning, a beckoning. It is, as I see it, evidence of the actualising tendency at work. It is a movement of the spirit which creates within us a deep longing to be all that we have the potential to be, to break free of the straightjackets that have imprisoned our core self and to embrace a new freedom of being. It is often but not always triggered by those experiences in life which force us to confront the darker realities of pain, suffering and loss and the existential crises they give rise to. It is often accompanied by the experience of depression or darkness, by what we might call 'dark nights of the soul' to borrow the words of St John of the Cross (2003). Our task during the stage of awakening is a simple one. It is essentially one of listening, attending and responding to this inner prompting of the actualising tendency rather than ignoring, denying or suppressing it. Sometimes it manifests itself in quiet, subtle ways – perhaps in a persistent inner restlessness, a deep dissatisfaction with life as it is, a recognition that all is not what it should or might be, a growing sense that it is time for change.

Sometimes, the soul also speaks to us though our dreams or through powerful images that suddenly become important to us in ways that they had not been before. In some mysterious way, they seem to haunt us as if there is some important message they are trying to convey to us. Certainly, this has been true for many of my clients and for me personally. Part way through this stage of awakening that I am attempting to describe, I had a very unsettling and vivid dream of stopping my car at a lakeside to fill up my water bottle and finding a woman's body floating face up in the water at the edge of the lake. Her eyes were closed and I remember thinking that she must be dead. I felt intensely sad as I looked down at her but strangely, made no move to pull her out of the water. I decided to pour out the remaining water in my bottle before refilling it, but at the exact moment that the water broke the surface of the lake just above her face, her eyes opened wide and she looked intently at me. She seemed to be asking something of me. I was aware of a sudden feeling of exhilaration and reached down to help her out of the lake. As I did so, however, her body rose up unaided out of the water until we were standing face to face, gazing at each other.

This dream stayed with me for weeks afterwards and it still feels very vivid and real as I recount it now. While working with it over the following months, I uncovered layers of meaning and symbolism that I will not explore here but the dream undoubtedly spoke to me very powerfully at the time. As I see it now, what happened in the dream was, I believe, deeply symbolic of the process of awakening that I was experiencing at that time. The dream itself was also, however, a message, a summons which I instinctively knew that I could not afford to ignore, and the image of the woman submerged in the lake continues to play an important part in my journey to this day.

Finally, sometimes the soul 'shouts' to us through the symptoms of emotional distress that we begin to experience – the descent into a depression that we cannot make sense of, the surfacing of a nameless anxiety that threatens to overwhelm us, the eruption of an intense anger and frustration that seems to come out of the blue and sometimes leads us to lash out at life and others. These are, as Moore (1992) puts it, 'the voices of the soul'. They are the soul's way of expressing its pain. Psychopathology, Elkins (1998: 176) argues, 'is the cry of the soul' and psychological symptoms are 'messages of pain from the very core of our being.' He writes movingly of his own experience of existential depression and anxiety in midlife, seeing it as part of an archetypal or universal death–rebirth experience which eventually led to the stirring within him of new life. Depression, he argues, is often the soul's 'heavy artillery'. Perhaps if our survival self were less resistant to the voice of the soul, if we were to be more responsive to the gentler promptings of our spirit, such sledge–hammer tactics would not be necessary to get our attention. The soul, it seems, will not let us rest easy when we are only half living, when we are not being all that we have the potential to be, when there are unlived parts of ourselves that are hidden in the shadows. And if we do not heed the whisper, the pain will deepen and the voice will become louder and more strident – and more difficult to ignore.

It is when we are finally able to hear and respond to the cry of the soul that we move gradually into the next stage of the journey – that of letting go.

The process of letting go

The process of letting go involves the relinquishing of our old way of seeing ourselves and the world and of the self we have constructed in order to survive. At a psychological level, it can be thought of as a process of deconditioning, of breaking free from the conditions of worth that have shaped our way of being in the world. At an existential level, it can be thought of as the gradual dying or disintegration of the false or conditioned self – what I have called the survival self – in order to make way for the emergence of the true self.

In his stages of growth theory, Rogers outlined a number of key psychological changes that occur as we move into this phase of growth (Rogers 1967: 125 – 159). At a psychological level, embracing the process of letting go requires a profound shift in our relationship with our own inner experiencing. One of the consequences of the formation of the belief system and of the survival self is that we learn to filter out those aspects of our experiencing that conflict with what we have come to believe about ourselves and the world. As a result, we become 'out of touch' with the full flow of that experience. We are in effect holding parts of it at arm's length because we judge it to be in some way unacceptable or threatening to us. Consequently there is at times a remoteness about our connection with it. We may find it hard to access or capture in words some of what we feel, think or experience and may also struggle to identify and draw on its meaning for us. We also cease to trust what Seeman (1983) called our own 'inner signals'.

A key element of this process of letting go is that of becoming more in touch with the full range of our own inner experiencing. As we learn to listen to and trust our own inner signals, we become increasingly open to and accepting of all that we are experiencing and are able to access it more immediately. In other words, we become progressively more in touch with what is happening within us and more able to be aware of it as it is happening. Rogers (1967) describes this as moving towards a 'loosening of our experiencing' and towards 'living in an open, friendly, close relationship' with it. Gradually, we come to see it as a trustworthy resource rather than as something to be frightened of and to defend ourselves against. I would describe this as adopting an attitude of non–judgemental curiosity towards our experience. The more able we are to adopt such an attitude, moreover, the more able we are to turn to our experience both as a solid point of reference in the process of self–discovery, but also as a guide when we are making decisions about how to react to what is happening to us. Eventually, our experiencing comes to have what Rogers described as an 'increasing process quality'. In other words, we become able to accept and live in the flow of our experiencing and to draw on it readily in the process of making decisions about how to act (Rogers 1967).

On entering therapy, one of my clients whom I shall call John appeared to be significantly 'out of touch' with or cut off from key aspects of his experiencing. He was in effect holding much of it at bay. He found it hard to access or capture in words what he was feeling, thinking or experiencing and frequently struggled to identify and draw on its meaning for him. He seemed much more comfortable talking about externals rather than focusing on himself and his self–disclosure was very cautious and guarded. He clearly found it difficult to talk about himself other than in a very factual way. For much of the time in our early sessions, it felt as if he was holding me 'at arm's length'. He was perhaps most comfortable disclosing some of his thoughts but even then, would rarely use 'I' statements, preferring to speak of what 'one' thinks or feels. As he moved through therapy, however, I noticed a significant change in the way in which he was attending to his experience. Gradually, he became increasingly open to and accepting of a much wider range of what he was experiencing and there was clear evidence of his growing ability to access it more immediately. Indeed, in the later stages of therapy, he would sometimes stop mid–sentence and sit quietly with his eyes closed for a minute or two as he tried to access what it was that was surfacing within him. Alternatively, he might make a statement about what he was thinking or feeling but then acknowledge that 'that doesn't feel quite right. I'm struggling to find the right words…'

One key dimension of experience from which many of us become significantly detached is the emotional dimension and that process of disconnection has a profound impact on our ability to experience and express our feelings freely and uninhibitedly. We may be largely out of touch with and unable to recognise and name our own emotions. We may experience a fear or deep mistrust of feelings which consequently are either denied, suppressed or rigidly controlled. When we are able to access our feelings, moreover, we may experience and perceive them as being remote from or coming from outside the self. We may, for example, talk of a particular feeling 'coming over me'. We may also show little acceptance of our feelings; some might even be seen as bad, abnormal or even shameful.

Returning to my client John, he was at the start of therapy particularly cut off from the flow of his emotions. When asked what he was feeling, he would more often than not respond by telling me what he thought. Alternatively, he might say that he wasn't sure or didn't know. He was clearly mistrustful and even at times fearful of his feelings, particularly those he perceived to be negative or unacceptable such as sadness, fear and anger. He found it almost impossible to stay with his own emotional pain and I would often see him working very hard to contain the feelings that were surfacing inside him as we worked together. One of the first things that John told me about himself was that he 'didn't do feelings'. He was aware that he tended, as he put it, to live 'mostly in his head' as his father had done and indeed he saw this as a strength. One of his father's oft-repeated 'mantras' had been 'You can't trust your feelings' and John had fully taken this on board. His father had taught him to see his emotions as an unreliable guide when making choices or decisions and that emotional maturity lies in being able to control and contain the 'unruly feelings' that would almost certainly lead him into making bad choices. Being emotional for John was being weak and unmanly. The last time he remembered having cried was after the death of his mother from cancer when he was thirteen. His father had told him then 'to man up.' At one point early in our work together when he had been talking about his mother's death, he suddenly found tears welling up inside him and started to cry. He seemed deeply ashamed of this 'moment of weakness'.

As we become more accepting of ourselves, however, we slowly develop the ability to experience, own, describe and express our feelings, both past and present, more readily. We become more able to accept and own our feelings to the point where they are no longer denied, feared or struggled against and are often accompanied by what Rogers (1967) termed 'physiological loosening' – for example, moistness in the eyes or sighs. We are more easily and more deeply moved, whether to tears or laughter. There is also a much greater sense of an inner flow of feelings until eventually, we reach the point of being able to experience and express the full range of our feelings with both immediacy and richness of detail. There at this stage a deep acceptance of and trust in the flow of changing feelings within ourselves and these are increasingly used as an inner referent, even when they are negative feelings.

As therapy with John progressed, I witnessed a marked change in the way in which he engaged with his own emotions. He became much more able to experience, own, describe and express a broader range of his feelings, both past and present. From being fearful and dismissive of his feelings, he came gradually to accept, value and trust them and eventually to communicate them more freely to others. He described this as a process of 'thawing out' feelings that had previously been 'frozen' inside him. The grief that he had almost totally suppressed when his mother died began to surface and while initially he found this process frightening and overwhelming, eventually he learnt to allow it to be rather than trying to deny or control it.

In addition to developing our ability to attend to our own experience in a non–judgmental way, we also develop the ability to process that experience more fully and accurately. As a result of the conditioning we experience in early life, we often tend to perceive our experience and to articulate its personal meaning for us in largely 'black and white' or global terms. There is little 'differentiation in personal meanings' as Rogers (1967) put it. Our ways of making sense of our experience may be extremely rigid and are often perceived as indisputable facts. There may also be little or no awareness or recognition of any contradictions in our experiencing, other than at a very basic level. Furthermore, it is often 'structure–bound' to use Rogers' word. In other words, the way in which we make sense of what happens to us and in us is bound by the past and often bears little relation to what is actually happening in the present.

Drawing again on my work with John, in the early stages, his processing of his own experience was relatively inflexible. Amongst the other things John had admired about his father were his strongly held convictions and the fact that he was not easily swayed by others' viewpoints and perspectives. While he did recognise that his father's views could often be uncompromising and that he would rarely if ever admit that he might be in the wrong, he had to a large extent adopted his father's rigid way of seeing the world. Consequently, when he came into therapy, he tended to see the world in similarly inflexible, black and white terms. He would often make sweeping generalisations which he regarded as facts and tended to deny or distort aspects of his experience which were inconsistent with his black and white view of himself and the world. He was prone to reacting defensively when his beliefs and perceptions were challenged by others and like his father, would often insist that he was in the right even when there was strong evidence to the contrary.

Increasingly, however, in this stage of letting go, we begin to be able to process our experiencing in more complex ways. In Rogers' terms, our personal meanings become more sharply differentiated. We become more able to see our experience in less 'black and white' or global terms and to recognise and be concerned about the contradictions within it. We are more likely to question the way in which we have made sense of our experience in the past and more determined to capture the meaning of it more exactly. The contradictions and incongruities in our experiencing become much more vivid and we are also more willing to acknowledge and face them. Rogers called this process 'a loosening of the cognitive maps of experience' (Rogers 1967: 157). The constructs we use to make sense of our experience are much more loosely held and consequently much more readily modifiable as we encounter new experiences. We are more able to reality test our beliefs and assumptions, to recognise the influence of the past on the way in which we make sense of our experience and to resolve the inconsistencies in our experiencing through re–examining our existing beliefs.

As he engaged with the process of therapy, John also became more open to learning from his experience. He began to recognise the extent to which he had been influenced by his father's black and white view of the world and that his own rigid way of seeing things was not serving him well. He also became painfully aware of how many assumptions he was making in trying to make sense of his experience and of how strongly held these assumptions were. He became much less defensive when his experience challenged his expectations and he began to question the validity of some of his strongly held beliefs. As he put it himself, he began to see life 'in shades of grey'.

It is as we become more trusting of our own inner experiencing and valuing process and as our locus of evaluation gradually becomes more internal that our belief system inevitably begins to change. Gradually, as we find a new freedom to re–examine our assumptions and beliefs, we begin to divest ourselves of those that are inaccurate or distorted and therefore do not serve us well. We learn to see and think of ourselves, others and the world we inhabit in different ways, ways that are more in tune with our own inner experiencing. Moreover, it is at this point in the process of letting go that it becomes possible for us to begin to let go of the life strategies that we now recognise are not working for us, that are in some way constricting our growth and preventing us from actualising all that we have the capacity to become. At an existential level, this is the letting go of the survival self. We have to let go in order to become. We have to recognise that this self that has worked so hard to protect us and keep us safe for so long, that has enabled us to survive in the face of the pain and suffering that threatened at times to overwhelm us, is now restricting our growth. It is, albeit unintentionally, straight–jacketing us in its effort to ensure our survival.

For John, this process of letting go eventually led to a radical shift in some key elements of his belief system. He began to challenge some of the unhelpful messages he had received from his father in his early childhood and to recognise how they had shaped and were continuing to shape his way of being in the world. For example, he came to see his emotions as a valuable and trustworthy part of his experience and to become more accepting of his own vulnerability as a man. Crying was no longer unmanly, no longer a sign of weakness or inadequacy. He also faced his fear of abandonment by those closest to him and realised that his life strategy of avoiding intimacy, particularly in his relationships with women, was no longer working for him.

This process of deconstructing the belief system is a difficult, unsettling and therefore often a lengthy one. Letting go of past ways of seeing ourselves and the world and of surviving within it generally brings with it feelings of anxiety or even of fear. The most deeply rooted beliefs and strategies – and particularly those that emerged very early on in life or have been in place for many years – are the most difficult to uproot. I have likened this to the process of attempting to remove the stranglehold of bindweed from the stem and leaves of a plant to which it has bound itself. If bindweed gets too strong a hold, it becomes so entwined with the plant that it is extremely difficult to disentangle it and of course, if the root is not removed, it simply grows back. Furthermore, we may be fearful of damaging the plant in some way in the process of removing the bindweed that is straight–jacketing its growth. Or we may become so frustrated at the slow progress we are making in freeing the plant from its tenacious grip that we give up altogether.

So it is with the process of disentangling ourselves from beliefs and strategies that have, generally without our knowing it, shaped our way of being in the world, often for decades. What appear to be the smallest of victories are often hard won and hard to hold on to. I remember very clearly one of my clients who sat through her therapy session every week wearing dark sunglasses – evidence of her deep-seated fear of being seen by others. She was so convinced of her utter unacceptability as a person that she spent most of her time hiding, both psychologically and physically. To be seen was to be rejected. It took her many months to risk taking off the sunglasses as we talked, a seemingly small behavioural change but one which betokened a very significant emerging shift in her underlying belief system. When we are under stress or threat or feeling particularly vulnerable, moreover, it is all too easy to revert to our 'default' ways of thinking and reacting, often without any awareness at the time that we have done so.

It is clear from this that the process of letting go is far from an easy one, and for most of us, achieving it is likely to be a lifetime task. As I have experienced it, it is at times a joyful, exciting and liberating experience. At other times, it is a confusing, frustrating, disturbing and anxiety–provoking experience which has the potential to resurface past defensive strategies designed to hold in place the very survival self that we are trying to let go of. It may involve periods of intense struggle as the survival self and the actualising tendency seek to pull us in different directions. This is often experienced as an internal battle between different parts of ourselves – what

Mearns and Thorne (2000: 114) call our 'growthful' and 'not for growth' configurations of self.

I call one of my own configurations of self 'the Guardian'. She is the part of me that seeks to protect me from emotional pain and hurt. She is risk–averse and urges me to hold onto the life strategies that have served me well in the past. She is the voice of caution in my head when I seek to venture out of my 'comfort zone' or to take risks. The greater the risk I am contemplating, moreover, the more strident her voice becomes. She is so committed to ensuring my survival that she inadvertently and unintentionally restricts my growth. Though I understand her intention, I am learning not to listen to her voice, particularly when it conflicts with the inner promptings of my spirit.

Because of this internal struggle, the process of letting go is very much an 'up–and–down' experience. There are likely to be times of regression, of slipping back into old ways of thinking and being. We advance, only to retreat. We make changes, only to revert to old patterns when we fear where the process is leading us. There may be periods of 'stuckness' when movement is imperceptible and change feels out of reach. We become immobilised when we do not have the energy to struggle or when we are unsure that the benefits of making the changes will outweigh the costs. And in the process of letting go, we have to enter into the painful process of mourning the loss of the old self, the old life, the old ways of being to which we have been so strongly attached, even though somewhere deep within us, we know intuitively that they are stifling our growth. Speaking of his own personal experience in therapy, Elkins (1998: 187) describes having to face the death of his old self, of having to mourn it, conduct its funeral and bury it. He talks too of how hard this was, attached as he was to his old way of life and past way of being.

It is as we move further into this process of letting go, that another phase of the journey is set in motion – that of the emergence of the core self.

The process of emerging

The process of emerging is the process of reconnecting with the core self, of allowing this authentic or true self to emerge in all its richness and beauty from beneath the layers of conditioning that have constricted it. I believe this is what Rogers (1980: 129) was referring to when he spoke later in life of experiencing at times a greater 'closeness' to his 'inner intuitive self' or 'transcendental core'. In reality, the two tasks of letting and emerging overlap to a significant degree. As we begin to let go of the survival self, so we begin to re–connect with the core self and to rediscover, reclaim and re–integrate what I call 'the unlived self' – that is, those parts of the core self that we have denied or buried in an effort to survive.

My own personal experience of reconnecting with my core self is that when I am able to 'come into rhythm' with this deeper dimension of my being, there is a strong sense of being more fully and naturally who I am. I feel somehow 'more myself', more comfortable in my own skin, more grounded and there is something about this experience which feels like a 'home-coming'. There is also a sense of everything within myself coming together in some kind of process of synthesis which is I think what Seeman (1983) would call 'psychological integration'. This is a profoundly energising and enlivening experience. When I am able to listen to and trust the inner wisdom of this deeper self, moreover, I invariably discover as Rogers (1980) did that it is fundamentally trustworthy. What I mean by this is that when I am able to allow its promptings to shape my responses to what is happening, I often find myself behaving as he did in less predictable ways, in ways that are more natural, intuitive and spontaneous and that in some mysterious way turn out to be 'right'. Furthermore, when I ignore this inner voice – what some might call this 'gut instinct' – or fail to act on it, I am much more likely to react inappropriately or to miss the opportunity or opening with which I have been presented.

Part of this process of re–connecting with the core self may be what I will call a process of re–naming the self. For me personally, this process of 'home–coming' led in my early fifties to a strong desire to rename myself and at the age of fifty four, I changed my forename by deed poll to Kaitlyn. The decision to adopt this name was not a sudden or impulsive one. It arose out of a deep inner restlessness, a sense of being gently but persistently compelled by the mysterious force or energy which seems to flow from the very core of my being. It was a kind of 'still small voice' that seemed to emanate from some older, wiser part of myself. At one level, this was a simple decision to rid myself of a name which I had always strongly disliked and which had never seemed to 'fit' the person I experience myself to be. At another level, however, making this change was, I believe, a symbolic act. It was part of the process of connecting at a deeper level with my innermost self and at the same time of distancing myself from the self that had been. In some cultures, it is not uncommon for an adult to take on a new name in later life and often this name will be seen as having some kind of spiritual significance. I have come to think of Kaitlyn as my 'soul name', as a name that in some mysterious way reflects something of the essence of who I am, or perhaps more accurately, who I am becoming.

This desire to rename the self is, I suspect, not an unusual one, although it may not always be acted on symbolically in quite the same way. One of my clients changed her forename in a similar way in her early sixties following an intensive therapeutic journey of recovering from childhood sexual abuse. Another chose to start using his middle name rather than his forename as he believed that his middle name reflected more truthfully the person he now recognised himself to be. A third reverted to using her full forename rather than a shortened version of it and a number of others have chosen in the course of therapy to give their emerging core self a different name – one that they have, however, kept to themselves or perhaps only shared with one or two of those closest to them.

In her study of women's spiritual development, Christ (1986) refers to a phase in the journey which she calls 'a new naming' and I believe this reflects something of the process I am trying to describe. Drawing on Christ's work, Slee (2004: 38) argues that this process of renaming the self effectively 'articulates' the new sense of self and reality that is emerging. This process of renaming is, moreover, generally accompanied by a process of reclaiming lost or buried parts of the core self. Often, this is a process of recovering aspects of ourselves which have been repressed as a result of the negative messages we have received from others. For one of my clients, this involved reclaiming his 'musical self', a part of him that his parents had been unable to accept or value. For another, the process of therapy enabled her to recover her 'feminine self', an aspect of herself that she had suppressed for many years because her father had wanted a son rather than a daughter. For a third, it meant befriending her 'vulnerable self', a part of herself that went into hiding as a child because being vulnerable was seen in her family as being weak and weakness in any guise was unacceptable.

In addition, it sometimes involves a deeper process of embracing our destiny as Elkins (1998) portrays it. He writes movingly about reclaiming the creative writer and poet in himself as a result of experiencing his own existential crisis in midlife and describes this process as 'the stuff of ultimate concerns'.

The therapeutic journey

At its heart, the therapeutic journey is then, as I see it, a journey of becoming. It is a process of transition from an old to a new identity, from an old to a new way of being. It is a process of both disintegration and re–integration – the disintegration or dismantling of the old survival self and the reclaiming and re–integration of the unlived parts of the core self. It is a process of transformation in which the survival self gradually gives way to the emerging core self. As such, it is clearly a psychological journey. Fundamentally, however, the therapeutic journey is also a spiritual journey. It is inspired by spirit. We are drawn to it by spirit. It is a journey of descent into the depths of the soul. It is a process of recovery of what has been lost along the way. It is a process of rebirth, of resurrection – a coming to life again of soul. It is a homecoming – a coming home not only to soul, but also to the Source and Ground of our being, however we may conceive of and experience it. The process of re–connecting with our core self leads us into another phase of the journey – that of transcending or reaching beyond that self. We are most fully human and fully alive, I believe, when we are most deeply engaged in our search for the Sacred and it is this search for the Sacred that I will explore in the next chapter.

5: The journey beyond the self

The paths are many, but the goal is the same.
Hindu maxim

When we talk about 'the spiritual journey' what do we mean? This is a difficult question to answer because there are different ways of thinking about the spiritual journey, different ways of experiencing it and different ways of making sense of what we experience. Essentially, we are talking about the process of spiritual development, about the movement towards spiritual wholeness, however that might be envisaged. Implicit in the use of the word 'journey' is the recognition that our spirituality is not fixed or static, that it changes and develops in different ways as we move through life. In using the term 'spirituality' here, what I am referring to is our particular way of being, experiencing and making sense of our existence that emerges in response to our lived experience, to the presence of the spirit within us and to our awareness and experience of the transcendent. This way of being is, at least potentially, continually unfolding and evolving as we develop physically and psychologically, as we learn from and react to our life experiences and as we adapt to changes in the environment that surrounds us.

As I look back at my own spiritual journey over the years, what is immediately very apparent to me is that the shape of my childhood spirituality was very different to that of my spirituality now in midlife. While for much of my life, my spirituality has found its home somewhere within the Christian spiritual tradition, what I believe, how I image and relate to the Divine and how I experience and express my spirituality has changed and developed significantly over the years, particularly in the last two decades of my life. My childhood faith in a wise and kindly 'father God' whom I could trust to protect and look after me when life seemed unpredictable, chaotic or frightening has in later life gradually evolved into a progressive and mystical spirituality which is grounded in my experience of the profoundly loving presence of the Divine. The journey, moreover, has not been an easy or straightforward one. There have been peaks and troughs, mountain–top and desert experiences. There have been times when I lost my way and when I thought I had lost my faith. There have been times when I felt certain and secure in my convictions and times of being plagued by doubts and questions and uncertainties. There have been times of holding on and times of letting go, times of stability and times of crisis and transition. As I have worked with clients and students over the years, furthermore, it has become clear to me that this is true for most if not all of us.

Three stories:

Rachel is in her late teens. She has been feeling stressed and low over the past few months and has not been able to 'shake herself out of it'. She was brought up in a family of practising Christians. Both her parents have attended the local conservative evangelical Anglican church for as long as she can remember and both she and her brother were regularly sent to Sunday school from an early age. She was christened as an infant and confirmed when she was 16. Until very recently, she continued to attend her parents' church with them but, since leaving home to go to university, she has found herself beginning to question and doubt her childhood faith and beliefs and has drifted away from church. She knows that her parents are very distressed by what they see as her abandonment of Christianity and Rachel herself is feeling deeply unsettled and disturbed by her seeming inability to hold on to the faith that she feels has sustained her for many years. She no longer knows what she believes; she feels isolated and unsupported; and she is afraid of losing her faith altogether.

Ben is in his late forties. He has been struggling emotionally since his marriage broke up some months ago. His wife left him for another man, taking their two children with her. In the midst of his grief, he is trying to cope with a very demanding job and with adjusting to living on his own. He feels depressed and lonely and has become quite socially withdrawn. He has also started drinking too much. Ben has been a strident atheist for most of his life and has never seen himself as a spiritual person. Neither of his parents were religious and both were very dismissive and critical of those who are. Indeed, his father viewed the holding of religious beliefs as evidence of a weakness of character. The problem for Ben is one of making sense of a recent very powerful and moving encounter with something or someone 'beyond himself' and his feeling of being completely overwhelmed by this 'presence'. He is struggling to come to terms with his experience and to work out what it means for him. The atheist in him is trying to dismiss it as 'a moment of weakness', but another part of him desperately wants to believe that it was real.

Beth is in her early sixties. She is finding it very hard to come to terms with her mother's recent death from cancer. She had been very close to her mother and found it very distressing to watch her deteriorate gradually and then die a painful death. She is also struggling to make sense of her mother's suffering from a spiritual perspective. Her mother used to describe herself as 'spiritual but not religious' and her father was a practising Buddhist. Her parents had always encouraged her to find her own spiritual path and were very accepting of her exploration of a number of different religions. Beth believes she has had several spiritual experiences which have been very important to her and thinks of herself as a spiritual person. She cannot believe in a personal God but 'knows' there is 'something more' that she is searching for. So far, however, she has not felt 'at home' in the context of any of the organised religions she has explored and she is struggling to know where she 'fits'. She is still searching for a 'spiritual home' and sometimes worries that her inability to find her own path indicates that there is something wrong with her.

Rachel, Ben and Beth are all on a spiritual journey. Their respective spiritualities differ in many respects and they are all at different stages in their journeys. It is possible that any of them might bring their spiritual experience or concerns into the therapeutic relationship. It is my belief that if we are going to be able to meet people where they are spiritually and to support them as they work through the spiritual issues that concern them, we have to have developed some understanding both of the phenomenon of spirituality and of the process of spiritual development.

Friedman et al (2009) point out that there are many different kinds of maps of the spiritual journey. Every religious and spiritual tradition has its own understanding of the process of spiritual growth and development, its own concept of spiritual maturity, its own spiritual goals. Furthermore, there are often several different traditions within the same religion, each of which has a differing perspective. In addition, a number of models of spiritual development have emerged from the scientific study of the psychology of religion and have sought to understand the process of development from a psychological perspective. These include the work of Fowler (1995) and others on faith development. Finally, a number of transpersonal models have been developed by psychologists and therapists from a wide range of spiritual backgrounds in an attempt to make sense of their own and others' spiritual journeys (Daniels 2002). Some of the best known of these are Assagioli's psychosynthesis (Assagioli 1975), Jung's analytical psychology (Jung 1973) and Wilber's spectrum model (Wilber 1977).

It is far beyond the scope of this book to address the full range of these varying models of spiritual development in depth. My intention instead is to offer my own core self model perspective and in so doing, to draw on some of the key insights, themes and patterns that emerge from a study of other existing psychological, religious and transpersonal models.

The uniqueness of our spirituality

From a core self model perspective, the first assumption I make in thinking about the spiritual journey is that everyone's spirituality is unique. I believe that the starting point for any model of spiritual development has to be the importance of recognising both the infinite variety of spiritualities that exist and the distinctiveness of each individual's spirituality. Swinton (2001) argues that knowing an individual's spiritual tradition can only ever provide us with a general frame of reference in enabling us to understand their spirituality. I would add, moreover, that at times, such knowledge can be unhelpful if it leads us to make assumptions about a particular individual's spirituality which may bear little resemblance to reality.

Each one of us is a unique, individual human being. Our temperaments, our personalities, our ways of being in the world are different. Furthermore, we are born into different cultures, different environments, different circumstances. Our life experiences differ as do the ways in which we make sense of them. Our environment impacts on us and we interact with it in different ways. As a result, the form our spirituality takes and the way in which we experience and express it is also unique. This is true even when we share the same spiritual or religious tradition. There is, for example, no such thing as a definitive Buddhist spirituality. There are indeed as many Buddhist spiritualities as there are Buddhists.

Even where we do belong to the same religious or spiritual tradition, there may be differences in the specific beliefs and values we hold, the doctrines or teachings we adhere to, the symbols that are meaningful to us and the ways in which they speak to us. Our responses to particular sacred writings may also differ. We may view them in different ways. We may be drawn to different stories or passages and may interpret and make sense of them differently. Our spiritual experiences and the way we respond to them may differ too, as may the way in which we image and relate to the transcendent. We may value and be committed to different spiritual rituals, practices and disciplines and may relate to our own particular faith communities in a variety of ways.

We may also view the spiritual journey differently. For many, entering into the spiritual journey is essentially about embracing the path of religious faith. At its heart, this is not so much a matter of belief, but an opening up of the self to the Ultimate Reality, however it may be named or conceived of. For Christians, the ultimate goal of the spiritual quest is sanctification (the process of being made holy) and union with God. For Hindus, it is moksha or liberation from samsara (the cycle of death and rebirth) and the uniting of the soul with Brahman. For Jews, it is holiness. For Muslims, it is total surrender to Allah; for Taoists, it is being at one with the Tao. For others who do not believe in the existence of a transcendent being or reality, however, the spiritual journey may be viewed very differently. For Buddhists, for example, it is nirvana or the realisation of enlightenment. For humanists, it may be reconnecting with one's true or Higher Self or achieving unitive or cosmic consciousness (an awareness of union with all that exists in the cosmos).

The uniqueness of our spirituality is reflected in the many different traditions and denominations that have emerged within the major world religions. Momen (2009) points out that over a period of time, all of the major world religions have evolved a variety of religious expressions or pathways in order to meet the spiritual needs of different types of people. For example, within Christianity, there are not only the Eastern Orthodox, Anglican, Catholic and Protestant traditions, but also many thousands of smaller denominations. Furthermore, many religions also have their own mystical traditions[2] such as Kabbalah, the Jewish mystical tradition and Sufism, the Muslim mystical tradition. Individual differences in spirituality are also reflected in attempts that have been made within a number of the major religious traditions to identify and describe particular spiritual 'types' or 'personalities'. The assumption here is that while there are multiple ways of experiencing and expressing spirituality, each of us has a strong tendency to favour one particular type or form of spirituality over other types.

For example, Smith (2009) and Fisher (2011) point out that the Hindu tradition has paid a great deal of attention to the identification of basic spiritual personality types and the specific spiritual disciplines that are most likely to be effective for each type. It identifies four key pathways or 'margas'. These are known as the four 'yogas' – jnana yoga, the path of rational inquiry which particularly suits those who are predominantly philosophical and reflective in nature; karma yoga, the path of right action and selfless work and service for those people who are naturally active; bhakti yoga, the path of love and devotion for those who are strongly emotional in nature; and raja yoga, the path of disciplined mental concentration for those who are inclined towards meditation.

Within the Christian tradition, there have also been attempts to identify the different spiritual pathways people may choose to take. One of these is Holmes' (1982) theory of 'preferred spirituality types'. Holmes identified four key spiritual types:

> Type 1: a thinking or 'head' spirituality in which there is a primary focus on naming and making sense of the experience of the Divine, on theological reflection, on doctrine and on seeking guidance from scriptures and preaching

Type 2: an affective or 'heart' spirituality in which there is a primary focus on feelings, on the sharing of experience and on seeking guidance via the heart rather than the mind

Type 3: a mystic spirituality which is contemplative, introspective and intuitive, focused on the inner world, on being rather than doing and on seeking union with the Divine

Type 4: a kingdom spirituality which is a visionary, crusading, idealistic spirituality that equates prayer and theology with social action and has a primary focus on transforming society

The overlap here with the four yogas of Hinduism is very clear. There is in Holmes' work a recognition that each spiritual type is of equal value and that none of us will fit entirely into any one of these four categories. As in Hinduism, there is strong encouragement to experiment with and develop other ways of living out our spirituality alongside our preferred pathway. Indeed, this is seen as part of the process of spiritual development.

In addition to these religious typologies, there have also been a number of attempts to draw both on psychological knowledge and understanding and on traditional spiritual wisdom in reaching an understanding of the uniqueness of our spirituality. Within the Christian tradition, for example, attempts have been made to apply the Myers–Briggs Type Indicator (a psychometric questionnaire designed to measure psychological preferences) to the study of individual differences in spirituality (Goldsmith and Wharton 2004). The MBTI model identifies four different continuums along which spirituality may differ: the introversion–extraversion continuum, the sensing–intuitive continuum, the thinking–feeling continuum and the perceiving–judging continuum. Sixteen spiritual types then emerge from the way in which these different preferences come together in a particular individual.

Similarly, emerging originally from within the Sufi tradition in Islam, the Enneagram model of spiritual types identifies nine key personality types and nine corresponding paths of transformation or ways of moving beyond personality to the essential self. The Enneagram teaches that in response to our experiences in early life, we learn to meet our basic psychological needs and to protect ourselves from both internal and external threats by developing particular coping strategies. People of the same type are believed to have the same basic motivations, to view the world in similar ways and to draw on the same coping strategies such as perfectionism, pleasing others or acting as peacemaker. The Enneagram also recognises, however, that there are variations within each type, shaped by such factors as inherent personality traits, familial influences (such as our parents' types) and cultural values. Each type has both strengths and weaknesses and the aim of the Enneagram is to enable us to identify and let go of 'the dark side' of our particular gifts and in so doing, to break through to a new freedom in our spiritual lives (Rohr and Ebert 1990).

The potential benefit of such typologies is that they may help us to become more accepting and valuing of both our own and others' spiritualities. They may also help us to identify those particular spiritual practices and disciplines that are most likely to enable us to achieve our spiritual goals. The dangers of all such typologies, however, is that they fail to do justice to the uniqueness of our individual spiritualities, that they over–simplify something that is inherently very complex, and that we allow them to label us in ways which may be self–limiting. They may in effect force us into particular 'pigeonholes' in which we may then become trapped.

My own experience of learning about my spiritual type has been a predominantly positive one even though not every aspect of my spirituality fits neatly into 'the box' of my spiritual type. I have found myself identifying most strongly with elements of Holmes' heart and mystic spiritualities and in relation to the MBTI spiritual typology, recognise in myself much of what would be predicted by my spiritual type. This has been both a validating and a disinhibiting experience. It has helped me to accept and value my own spirituality at a deeper level and to trust my own inner sense of what is right for me. Therefore, it has also enabled me to recognise and embrace those spiritual paths and practices that I find most helpful, while letting go of others that I struggle to engage with. At the same time, it has deepened my acceptance and valuing of spiritualities that are very different from my own and encouraged me to experiment with other paths to the Sacred that might not come so naturally to me.

The implication of acknowledging the uniqueness of our spirituality is that of recognising that we cannot hope to come to a meaningful understanding of another's spirituality or spiritual journey unless we are prepared to adopt a phenomenological approach. The purpose of such an approach is to throw light on the specific rather than to identify patterns or norms. It is concerned with people's subjective experience, with their way of perceiving and making sense of their experience. It is a respectful, open–minded entering into the subjective world of the other in order to see it, as far as is possible, through his or her eyes rather than our own.

Spirituality as a developmental process

Another lens through which the phenomenon of spirituality can be viewed is that of a developmental framework. There are three key assumptions I make from a core self model perspective. The first of these is that just as our spirituality is unique, so too our spiritually journey is unique. No two spiritual journeys are alike, even when people live out their spirituality within the same spiritual tradition. Though we may be able to identify similar themes and patterns in people's individual spiritual journeys, if we are prepared to look beneath the surface, we will begin to see the differences – some clearly visible and readily articulated, others more subtle and harder to capture but no less significant.

This has implications for the way in which engage with the various maps and models of the spiritual journey that we encounter. Spirituality is such a complex, rich and multi–coloured phenomenon and so many factors may play a part in shaping its unfolding in our lives that no single map or model is likely to be able to encompass the full range of our human spiritual experience. To paraphrase the writing of the philosopher, Korzybski (1933), the map is not the territory and there are, I believe, dangers in making assumptions about the course that an individual's spiritual journey is likely to take. Furthermore, the maps we draw emerge from our experience; they should not shape or determine it. In paying too much attention to a map that someone else has drawn or trying to follow too closely the path that others have taken, we may fail to listen to the inner promptings of our own spirit and attempt to follow a path that will not lead us where we need to go. Or if our own spiritual journey does not conform to the patterns laid down in the maps of the journey that we encounter, we may come to see our own spirituality as somehow inferior or misguided.

The second assumption I make about our spiritual development is that our spirituality is not fixed or static, but is, at least potentially, unfolding and evolving throughout our lifespan. From a core self model perspective, I see this process of evolving as being the work of the spirit (or to use person–centred terminology, the actualising tendency) which motivates and sustains our spiritual growth. This mysterious life force not only animates, energises and sustains us existentially, but is also, I believe, the primary motivator and agent of our spiritual development as it is of our psychological development. It not only inspires our search for the Sacred, our reaching beyond ourselves to the transcendent, our longing for a deeper connection with the Source and Ground of our being, but also prompts and sets in motion the unfolding of our unique spirituality.

I believe this process to be at work throughout the lifespan but my experience tells me that it becomes more urgent and compelling – and harder to ignore – in the second half of life. This is, I think, reflected in Jung's assertion that the problems people experience in the second half of life almost always relate to the need to find 'a religious outlook' on life and in his belief that the process of individuation generally begins in the 'afternoon of life' (Jung 1961). Moody and Carroll (1997) echo this when they argue that while our spiritual potential can come to the surface at any point in our lives, it tends to become more compelling in the middle and later years. They point to contemporary research into people's level of religious commitment that supports this assertion and remind us that the middle adult years have always been recognised as the critical time for spiritual development by the world's major religious traditions.

For example, the Hindu view of the spiritual journey recognises four separate but related stages of life or 'asramas' (Smith 2009). The first is that of the 'brahmacarya' or the asrama of studenthood which is focused on studying the Hindu sacred texts and learning about the Hindu tradition. The second stage is that of 'grihastha', the stage of the householder in which life is primarily devoted to marriage, family, career and social or civic duties and responsibilities. The third stage, entered into in mid–life, is that of 'vanaprastha' or the stage of the forest dweller. At this mid–point in life, there is a 'gear shift' in the spiritual journey. This is a stage of withdrawal from the obligations and responsibilities of active life – whether familial, social, economic or religious – into contemplation and learning 'to let go and let be' as Teasdale (1999) puts it. Many will stay at this stage throughout the rest of their lives. Some, however, will move in later life into the final stage, that of the 'sannyasi' or renunciate who, letting go of all ties to the world, lives a purely contemplative life and wanders freely from place to place seeking to point us to Brahman, to remind us of who we are and why we are here.

Archetypal growth processes

The third assumption I make about our evolving spirituality is that while each person's experience of undertaking the spiritual journey is unique, it is possible to identify recurring patterns, processes or movements which seem to be characteristic of the way in which our spirituality evolves, whatever spiritual tradition we may belong to. As I have reflected back on my own spiritual journey and on the journeys of others as they have emerged in the context of my work as a therapist or a spiritual companion, what has struck me is that while there are undoubtedly observable differences between individual spiritual journeys, there are also observable similarities.

In portraying their spiritual journey, people often describe themselves as having gone through a number of phases or stages in their spiritual development. This is reflected in a wide range of religious and psychological maps of the spiritual journey which almost invariably make the assumption that our spirituality commonly unfolds in a series of identifiable steps or stages. In general, religious and transpersonal models of spiritual development seem to agree on this point. The majority of religious models of the spiritual journey talk in terms of such developmental stages. For example, the Zen Buddhist tradition draws on a ten stage model of the path of spiritual development which is reflected symbolically in the well-known Ox–Herding Pictures, an allegory of the search for enlightenment. Within the Christian spiritual tradition, a number of stage models of spiritual development have emerged such as the traditional 6th century three stage model of Pseudo–Dionysius (cited in Perrin 2007), the 16th century ten step model of St John of the Cross (2003) which uses the image of a 'ladder of ascent' and the more recent 20th century five stage integrative model of Underhill (Underhill 1995). Within Hinduism, there are a number of stage models such as the stages of life model I have already referred to and the more sophisticated eight step Yoga Sutras model of Patanjali (cited in Friedman et al 2009). Furthermore, in the mystical traditions of both Islam and Judaism, the spiritual journey is also viewed as a three stage process.

Similar patterns and themes are also evident in transpersonal models of spiritual development. This is perhaps unsurprising in that transpersonal psychology has always been interested in the integration of the wisdom of the world's major spiritual traditions with the knowledge and understanding derived from the study of psychology (Cortright 1997). Friedman et al (2009) point out that in contrast to the more objective and scientific approach that is taken in relation to the study of the psychology of religion, transpersonal psychology has instead been willing to adopt a more subjective and phenomenological approach to the study of the experiential aspects of spirituality. This has led to the emergence of a number of transpersonal models of spiritual development such as those of Assagioli (1975) and Wilber (1977, 1980, 2004).

For example, Assagioli (1975) made the assumption that full personal growth involves both psychological and spiritual development. He believed that all of us have a deeper 'centre of identity' – the equivalent of the concept of the soul – which he referred to in a variety of ways such as the Spiritual Self, the Higher Self, the Real Self and the Transpersonal Self. He saw this spiritual centre as our 'essential Being' and emphasised that it is different from the Conscious Self or 'I' which is the centre of our consciousness. He described this spiritual self as 'latent' in the sense that it does not generally reveal itself directly to our consciousness. Consequently, we often remain unaware of it, sometimes to the extent that we may deny its existence. He believed, however, that the Higher Self can be consciously realised when we are in a particular altered state of consciousness which he called 'cosmic consciousness'. This makes possible the transformation of the whole personality; its centre becomes the Higher Self. Furthermore, this inner shift in the personality is also accompanied by an encounter with the realm of the Divine which may be known and experienced in a variety of different ways. Assagioli called this process 'spiritual or transpersonal psychosynthesis' and saw it as the principal goal of spiritual development. Assagioli's model of the process of psychosynthesis is essentially a three stage one: the first stage of personal psychosynthesis which involves the achievement of a degree of what he calls 'psychological integration'; the second stage of the discovery or 'realization' of the Higher Self; and the third stage of transpersonal psychosynthesis in which the individual enters into an ongoing relationship and dialogue with the Higher Self and with the Divine.

What strikes me in exploring these differing religious and transpersonal maps of the spiritual journey is how much they have in common rather than how they differ and it is the awareness of this commonality that has led a number of writers to develop what might be called integrated models of the spiritual journey. These seek to draw on those processes and themes that cross religious boundaries in order to develop a map with which people from any spiritual tradition can identify. For example, as a result of extensive research into human spiritual development, Moody and Carroll (1997) have developed what they regard as an integrative model of the spiritual quest. They describe the spiritual journey as a process of 'soul realization' – the awakening of a 'higher part of ourselves' that they call the soul. They too believe that our spirituality unfolds in a series of steps or stages which tend to follow one another in sequence though they argue that this sequence is not 'written in stone'. Not everyone will pass through each of the five stages and some will not even begin the journey. Movement through the five stages is seen as a process of shifting the centre of our being towards the inner life of the soul; encouraging a disengagement from the ordinary problems of everyday life; increasing our commitment to what they call 'virtuous behaviour' such as love, kindness and generosity; raising our normal state of consciousness to a higher transpersonal level; and creating in us the desire to devote ourselves to service to others. Progression through the stages is not, however, automatic as it requires struggle, effort and a deep level of commitment.

Rather than viewing the process of spiritual development in terms of a series of sequential steps or stages, however, I prefer to see it as involving a number of fundamental archetypal[1] or universal growth processes which to a degree parallel those that characterise the process of psychological development. As I have come to see it, the spiritual journey is both a soul journey (a journey of becoming) and a journey of spirit (a journey of transcending). These growth processes are therefore designed both to enable us to reconnect with our core self or soul – the first key component of the spiritual journey – and to enable us to reach beyond or transcend the conscious self – the second key component of the journey. While these processes may occur sequentially, in my experience the sequence is not necessarily invariable and the processes often overlap with each other. I find Harris's image of 'the dance of the spirit' very helpful in capturing the complex interweaving of these processes (Harris 1989). In articulating her own particular model of spiritual development, she outlined a sequence of seven key developmental 'steps' which she likened to the steps of a dance. Unlike developmental stages, however, she did not see these steps as hierarchical or uni–directional but as flowing and dynamic. She viewed them as a series of steps which 'like the dance can go backward or forward, can incorporate one another, can involve turn and re–turn, can move down as well as up, out as well as in…' (Harris 1988: 14 – 15). As I see it, the music of the dance is the flow of the actualising tendency or spirit within us and all that we have to do is to give ourselves to the dance, to allow ourselves to feel and move to its rhythm. There is something in this of surrender, of letting go, of entrusting ourselves to the dance as it unfolds. While at one level this is simple, at another level it is extraordinarily difficult.

Awakening

The first of these archetypal growth processes is that of awakening. In addition to awakening us to our disconnection from our soul, this process also involves the development of our capacity for spiritual awareness. It is an expansion of our conscious awareness to embrace both our core self – our deeper spiritual self – and the transcendent, the Ultimate Reality which is both within and beyond us. Harris (1989) described it as a coming alive to body, inner self and spirit. In varying spiritual traditions, this might be referred to as a conversion experience, as a change of heart or as the process of 'metanoia', the literal meaning of which is 'going beyond the mind'. From the perspective of their five stage model of spiritual development, Moody and Carroll (1997) describe awakening as a process of learning to hear 'the inner voice of the soul' and they see it as the first stage of the soul's journey. The soul, as they see it, is both the core of our being and the sacred centre through which we connect with the transcendent.

In our everyday life, they argue, our minds are not in direct contact with this 'deeper point of consciousness'. The soul, however, is continually reaching out to our conscious minds – for example, through sacred writings, through myth, through art and music, through dreams or through engaging in spiritual practices. When this happens, what we are experiencing is 'a spiritual Call.' Some will experience it as a profound inner restlessness, a deep sense of dissatisfaction with life as it is. Some will be seized with an intense yearning to be more of the person they really are. Some will sense a growing longing for the Sacred, however they may envision it, or a desire for a deepening of the spiritual life. Others will experience it as hearing the call of God or the Divine. Moody and Carroll (1997) point out that the Call can happen at any stage of adult life and is best thought of as a process rather than a one–off event. The Call, they argue, is in itself 'a journey of stages'. It can occur in many different circumstances and can take many different forms. More often than not, though, it is undramatic and therefore not always easily recognised.

Looking back over my own spiritual journey, I can identify a number of periods in my life which I would describe as times of spiritual awakening. Sometimes these have occurred in the midst of difficult and painful life experiences. At other times, they seem to have come 'out of the blue' and it has been hard to identify any specific trigger. What strikes me, however, about the most powerful of these experiences is that each time, they have coincided with my developing a deep friendship, one that I would characterise as a 'soul–to–soul' or 'anam cara' relationship (O'Donohue 1997). For me at least, such experiences of awakening often seem to occur in the context of relationship. Elkins (1998) speaks of people awakening each other's souls, an experience with which I can readily identify.

The process of awakening can also be triggered by what Moody and Carroll (1997) describe as a 'breakthrough experience' – that is, some form of spiritual or mystical experience which gives us a glimpse of the transcendent. Momen (2009) observes that such experiences can occur at varying times in the spiritual life of an individual and are often triggered by specific circumstances or activities – for example, in the midst of engaging in some form of prayer or meditation; during the performance of sacred rituals; during acts of worship or the chanting of verses from sacred texts or mantras (sounds, syllables, words or group of words that are believed to take people into a place of spiritual transformation); while entering into silence; through reading from sacred texts or engaging with works of art, music, dance or drama; through being in nature; or even during childbirth or sexual intercourse. He identifies four key types of spiritual experience: regenerative, charismatic, mystical and paranormal experiences. Regenerative experiences are the kinds of experiences to which most people are referring when they speak of a religious experience. Essentially, they are experiences of coming into contact with a reality that is felt to be greater than or beyond the boundaries of the self. The experience is often so powerful that it is transformative. Momen points out that these experiences may take a number of different forms. Conversion experiences such as the biblical account of the conversion of the apostle Paul on the road to Damascus lead people to align with a religious movement to which they have not previously been committed (Acts 9: 1 – 9). Such experiences can be both mild and gradual or sudden and dramatic. Often, they have a profound impact on the person's life. Momen (2009: 94) gives the following example of a conversion experience:

> In the blessed pages of the Holy Qur'an I found solution to all my problems, satisfaction to all my needs, explication for all my doubts. Allah attracted me to His Light with irresistible strength, and I gladly yielded to Him. Everything seemed clear now, everything made sense to me, and I began to understand myself, the Universe and Allah… My whole world was shattered in one instant; all concepts had to be revised.

Confirming experiences do not involve a conversion but result in a regeneration or revival of faith within the context of a religious tradition to which people already belong. In the context of evangelical Christianity, experiences of being 'born again' (a spiritual rebirth experience) are examples of such confirming experiences. Finally, commissioning experiences take the form of a 'call' or divine commission to carry out a particular action or take up a new way of life. Another type of religious experience is the charismatic experience. This involves the sense of having been given some form of sacred gift such as a deep sense of being connected with a greater power, feelings of elation or joy or of inner equilibrium, calm or peace. Such experiences often take the form of a trance–like or ecstatic experience. Accounts of them are to be found, for example, in Christianity, Hinduism, Sufism and Judaism as well as in primal religions.

Peak and mystical experiences are described as sudden, transient joyful or ecstatic moments, often triggered, for example, by great art or music, the overwhelming beauty of nature, meditation or intense feelings of love. They are generally characterised by a deep sense of well–being and of being fully alive, integrated and in tune with one's self; by an absence of anxieties, tensions, doubts and inhibitions; by feelings of peace, wonder, awe and reverence; by deep feelings of non–judgmental acceptance, love and compassion for others and the world; by profound feelings of oneness or connectedness with the world or the universe (in the most powerful peak experiences, to a point where the individual's sense of self may temporarily dissolve); and by a strong sense of reaching beyond or transcending the self.

Momen (2009) identifies a number of the central characteristics of such mystical experiences. He emphasises that each person's mystical experience is unique and different from those of other people. He points out that such experiences are generally very important to the individuals to whom they happen in a way that other experiences tend not to be. They can be life–changing and transformational. They may also be accompanied at times by a sense of having been called to some form of mission. While they are transient (normally lasting no longer than half an hour), they are generally very intense and energising experiences which demand the individual's attention and respect. They are experienced as having a liberating power, sometimes resulting in a sense of being temporarily freed from the demands of physical reality. They often involve changes in perceptions of time and space to the extent that the experience is perceived as occurring 'outside time and space'. In other words, time may appear to stop and perceptions of space may be distorted. Maslow (1971: 164) called this 'a loss of placing in time and space'. It is often accompanied by an unusual clarity of perception and vision which he described as a sense of 'limitless horizons opening up to the vision'. Sometimes, there is a conviction of having achieved insight or knowledge (or of it having been revealed) which feels authoritative (often referred to as 'noetic') and may be very difficult, if not impossible, to put into words (often referred to as 'ineffable'). Momen notes that although it may be possible to take steps to make the occurrence of such experiences more likely, it is not possible to make them happen. When they do happen, moreover, there is generally a sense of the experience 'taking over', leaving the individual as a passive recipient who is not in control of it.

There are also what Momen (2009) refers to as paranormal religious experiences. These are experiences which lie outside the range of normal human experience and scientific explanation (such as near–death experiences or contact with the dead through mediums) and which are seen as evidence of the existence of the spiritual world. While in the West, many would not regard these as genuine spiritual experiences, they are found in many religions – for example, in Christianity, Judaism, Sufism, Hinduism and in primal religions where they occur in the context of shamanism (a range of beliefs and practices regarding communication with the spirit world).

Finally, both Momen (2009) and Richards and Bergin (2005) outline a number of other kinds of reported spiritual experience which fit less readily into the above categories. These include experiencing the presence, love or forgiveness of the Divine; experiencing feelings of awe and gratitude towards the Divine; hearing what is believed to be the voice of the Divine within one's mind; having an inspirational dream or vision; receiving flashes of insight or inspiration when faced with difficult problems; and spiritual or faith healings

– that is, experiencing positive and long–term improvements in mental and physical well–being as a result of spiritual healing practices such as intercessory prayer, laying on of hands or distance healing.

While there does seem to be a clear distinction between what Momen (2009) calls paranormal religious experiences and other forms of spiritual experience, I am not sure how helpful it is to distinguish between regenerative, charismatic and mystical experiences in the way that Momen does as there appears to be so great an overlap between them. I prefer to think of all of these experiences as mystical – that is, as involving an immediate, direct experience and consciousness of the transcendent, however we may conceive of it. Such experiences, if powerful enough, may lead to a conversion or a confirmation or deepening of existing faith. They may also include a sense of having been 'called' or given a divine commission or of being given some kind of sacred gift. Taylor (2010), a researcher into transpersonal experience, describes such mystical experiences as 'awakening experiences' in the sense that they take us into altered or higher states of consciousness. They have also been called 'glimpse experiences' in the sense that they are viewed as temporary glimpses of a level of consciousness that is beyond the normal or 'mundane' level.

As does Elkins (1998: 83), I see such experiences of the Sacred as existing 'on a continuum of intensity'. Elkins regards such experiences as varying in intensity from low intensity 'poignant moments' such as being overwhelmed by the wonder and beauty of nature; to medium intensity 'peak experiences' which are longer–lasting and more intense and can produce permanent changes in our lives; to high intensity 'mystical encounters' which are so intense, powerful and overwhelming that they may cause temporary 'psychological disorganization' and often initiate a transition from one way of life to another. Taylor (2010) also distinguishes between low, medium and high intensity experiences. His descriptions of low to medium intensity experiences seem to correspond closely to Elkins' poignant moments and peak experiences, while his medium to high intensity experiences would best be described as mystical experiences. In mystical experiences, there is, as he sees it, both an intensification of the characteristics of lower intensity experiences coupled with an awareness of the presence of the transcendent, however it may be conceived.

My own experience of the kinds of spiritual experience James (1985) and Maslow (1968) describe is that they have been much more prominent – both more frequent and more powerful – in the second half of life. While I remember a number of the kind of poignant moments Elkins describes in my late teens and twenties, it was not until my early thirties that I had what I would now recognise as a medium intensity peak experience. This was an intense and profoundly moving experience which occurred at a very difficult time in my life. It was powerful enough to convince me of the existence of something beyond myself and led to a spiritual re–awakening after a period in my life when my spirituality had lain dormant for a time. In my forties and fifties, there have been a number of such mystical experiences. They have varied in intensity and in their impact on my spiritual journey. Each experience has been distinctive and each has affected me in different ways. Most of them have come 'out of the blue' and interestingly, none have occurred in the context of engaging in prayer or meditation.

The following is an account of a powerful mystical experience that occurred shortly after I had watched a film with a number of strong spiritual themes running through it. I was journaling my reactions to the film when it happened and so was able to record the experience very shortly afterwards. The following is an extract from my journal entry:

> I do not know what it is that just happened within me but I do know that I have never felt so alive and so in tune with everything around me. It felt as if my spirit was singing and dancing within me and soaring towards something so far beyond me that I felt raised or lifted up with it. Tears were flowing freely. My whole body was tingling with so much energy that I couldn't contain it. It felt as if it was spilling out of me. It was so intense and intimate and so achingly beautiful. And there was such a strong sense of connectedness, of oneness, of coming home, of being where I belong, of being somehow more fully myself. There was too a deep sense of peace and stillness in my spirit and I wanted more than anything to give myself up to it as fully as I could. And this is the strangest thing – it felt as if I was somehow expanding beyond my conscious self. Part of me was fully aware of my surroundings and part of me was 'out there' but the two were still connected.
>
> I was being held so tenderly by Love and it was so moving, healing, restoring and freeing that I could not stop the tears flowing. I did not want it to end but I knew with certainty that it would and that I needed to immerse myself in it – to surrender myself to it – as fully as I could. It was so beautiful that it is almost hurt to feel it and yet it was not painful at all. It felt as if there was some kind of energy moving around freely within my body, heart, mind and spirit. It touched all of me and reached so far into deep spaces within my being that it is impossible to describe the feeling it brought with it. It

felt as if I was standing on a mountaintop looking out over a place of such incredible beauty that it completely filled my senses.

This experience had such a profound impact on me that I found it hard to engage with everyday life for several days afterwards. The sense of loss I experienced when it ended stayed with me for some time and the memory of it is still fresh in my mind some years later.

What does the available research tell us about such spiritual experiences? In the 1960s and 70s, Abraham Maslow's research into what he termed peak experiences strongly suggested that such mystical experiences are widespread, if not universal (Maslow 1962, 1968, 1970b, 1971). He recognised a parallel between the peak experiences he studied and the mystical experiences that James explored and that have been reported by people across the centuries. His research led him to believe that peak experiences are extremely common and that virtually everyone has a number of such experiences in the course of their lives. He also hypothesised that everyone has the capacity to experience such moments and suggested that in 'non–peakers', they may in some way be resisted or suppressed.

While the process of awakening may for some be the first stage in the journey, for others – and particularly for women – it may be preceded or accompanied by what Christ (1986) calls 'an experience of nothingness'. Writing specifically about women's spirituality, Christ's (1986) description of what she calls the 'spiritual quest' outlines a spiritual growth process which has a number of key elements. She describes the experience of nothingness as a profound sense of meaninglessness, emptiness and powerlessness, something akin to what Elkins (1998) calls an 'existential depression' or an experience of 'the dark night of the soul'. In some traditions, it is spoken of as a spiritual desert experience. It may be triggered by painful or traumatic life experiences or it may come seemingly 'out of the blue'. It may also come more than once in the spiritual journey. Paradoxically, being drawn into such a period of darkness is in itself an archetypal spiritual growth process. Elkins sees it as a form of painful existential crisis – a crisis of being – and believes that it often plays a crucial role in the journey from false self to true self and in the awakening of the conscious self to the transcendent.

The process of questing

The second of these archetypal growth processes is that of questing. The word quest is defined as a long and arduous search for something of vital importance. It is derived from a Latin verb meaning to ask or seek. The concept of the spiritual quest is a common one in many myths (such as the quest for the Golden Fleece in Greek myth), legends (such as the quest for the Holy Grail) and spiritual traditions (such as the North American Indian 'vision quest', the undertaking of spiritual pilgrimages to holy places such as Jerusalem, Mecca or the Ganges and the Zen Buddhist allegory of the search for the ox). Schulkin (2007) argues that human beings have 'an instinct' for the spiritual quest, that undertaking such a quest is 'fundamental to the human condition'. At times, it is a solitary quest. At other times, we may choose to share the journey with others. Moody and Carroll (1997) call this process of questing 'the Search' and see it as the second stage in the spiritual journey. Our task during the process of awakening is, they say, to choose to respond to the Call rather than ignoring or refusing it. Attending to the Call then leads us into the Search. Harris (1989) saw this responding and searching as part of a more encompassing process of 'Dis–Covering' by which she meant the work of bringing into being 'a deeper I' and of discovering the 'deeper world' in which that 'I' is unfolding.

At its deepest level, then, the quest is the search not only for re–connection with the core self or soul, but also for a more profound connectedness with the transcendent. At another level, it is a search for spiritual guidance or teaching and for a particular spiritual pathway and practice to which we are willing to commit ourselves.

The process of letting go

The fourth archetypal growth process is that of learning to let go. As I have already discussed, from a core self model perspective this is primarily a psychological task which requires us to begin to let go of our old way of seeing ourselves and the world and of the self we have constructed in order to survive. Essentially, what we are letting go of is that which stands in the way of our re–connecting with the core self.

It is also a letting go, however, of whatever it is that stands in the way of realising our connectedness with the transcendent. Moody and Carroll (1997) call this stage 'the Struggle' and see it as a struggle of both heart and mind. This is a struggle which may, for example, involve wrestling with the dark side of our nature, letting go of the false self, confronting the death of our dreams, dealing with regret and remorse or learning to still the mind. Harris (1989) saw it as yet another aspect of the process of 'Dis–Covering' and described it as becoming aware of and acknowledging our human brokenness and at the same time, recognising and engaging our power or capacity to face and grow beyond that brokenness.

The process of emerging

At a psychological level this is, as I have already described it, the process of reconnecting with our deepest, innermost self, of allowing this core self to emerge and develop to its full potential as we learn to let go of the survival self that has straight–jacketed its growth. Using spiritual language, we might speak of the birthing of the soul. Slowly, the soul emerges from the shadows where it has lain dormant and hidden and begins to embrace its freedom. Harris (1989) described this as the work of 'unveiling and revealing… the truth of our being' (p. 30). She saw it as being part of the process of Dis–Covering and as involving the two steps of 'finding' (in which aspects of the self are unveiled or revealed) and 're–membering' (the reintegration of what is unveiled or discovered into the newly emerging sense of self). She also identified the further steps of 'Creating' (an ongoing creative process of giving our unique spirituality an authentic form), 'Dwelling' (making sacred the various spaces in our lives) and 'Nourishing' (nurturing our sense of self and spirituality through the practice of various forms of spiritual discipline). I would see all of these steps as part of the ongoing process of emerging.

And as we become more deeply connected with this core self, what also emerges more strongly is our capacity for moving into what Elkins (1998) calls 'sacred consciousness' – an alternative or higher state of consciousness that is qualitatively different from our normal state of consciousness. Christ speaks instead of the development of what she calls 'mystical insight' which enables the 'powers of being' to be revealed (p. 13). Elkins (1998) sees this as an inherent archetypal or universal ability, a potential that all of us have but not all of us seek to develop. Moody and Carroll (1997) call this the stage of 'Breakthrough' and see it as a process of breaking through to the highest level of consciousness – what they refer to as 'transcendent consciousness'. In Hinduism, this would be known as 'samadhi', in Buddhism as 'nirvana', in Zen Buddhism as 'satori', in Sufism, as 'fana'. In Christianity, it might be referred to as 'the peace that passes all understanding'. Elkins (1998) defines it as a level of conscious awareness in which we are more sensitive to, more in tune with the presence of the transcendent, whether within or beyond us. We learn to see and experience the Sacred or Divine in all that exists – in ourselves, in others, in the world around us – and to see ourselves as closely inter-connected with the rest of creation. In other words, we 'sacralize' life (Lynch 2007). We see all of existence as being imbued with the Sacred.

For many people, significant peak and mystical experiences will play an important part in this process of expanding consciousness through taking us temporarily into an altered state of consciousness and giving us glimpses of the transcendent. Rowan (1993) argues, however, that it is important not to overvalue such experiences or to see them as the end–point of the journey. I agree and would add that such experiences are not a substitute for the necessary psychological processes of letting go and of emerging and that they are not in themselves sufficient to bring about the kind of transformational changes that I have described above.

The process of transforming

Harris (1989) argued that as we transform ourselves through this process of awakening, questing, letting go and emerging, so our own personal rebirth begins to ripple out in a way that has the potential to foster the transformation and renewal of others and of the world in which we live. The way of experiencing, seeing, knowing, being and loving that we are learning as we engage with the spiritual journey becomes visible to and inspires others and so a way of life is handed on from one generation to the next. Harris called this process 'Traditioning'. She saw it as the passing on not of laws or teachings or doctrines, but of a specific way of being in the world. This is an expression of what Erikson (1980) called 'generativity' – that is, our altruistic concern for future generations. Similarly, Moody and Carroll (1997) see the final stage of the soul as that of 'the Return'. Significant spiritual breakthroughs leave their mark on us forever but afterwards, everyday life goes on as before. As the Zen proverb puts it, 'Before enlightenment you chop wood and carry water. After enlightenment you chop wood and carry water'. We return to the world, however, deeply changed with knowledge and experience which we can share with others, for example through becoming teachers, guides or mentors or through acts of service to others. In entering into this process of Traditioning, furthermore, we keep on growing and changing as our encounters with others and with the Divine challenge us to move into the next stage of the journey. And so the dance continues.

Factors that shape the journey

The fourth assumption I make is that the way in which our spirituality evolves across the lifespan is dependent on the impact of a number of inter–related factors which impact on our spiritual journeys in various ways. It follows that the particular form our spirituality takes at any point in our life will inevitably be shaped, at least partly, by the complex interaction of these different influences. I would include here such factors as age, gender, temperament and personality; cultural, family and spiritual tradition; and significant life experiences and relationships. These include our spiritual experiences and those deeper spiritual or soul relationships (O'Donohue 1997; Elkins 1998; Benner 2002) which often have a profound impact on the way in which our spirituality evolves. Finally, the work of psychologists like Fowler (1995) and others shows that some aspects of our spirituality are also shaped to a degree by the level of our cognitive, emotional and psychosocial development. In other words, the way in which we develop spiritually is at least partly determined by the extent to which we have dealt successfully with key psychosocial developmental challenges in our lives.

I have already explored the impact of temperament and personality factors and of significant spiritual experiences on the way in which our spirituality is expressed and evolves. There are also, it seems, clear gender differences in relation to religion and spirituality. While there is as yet a dearth of psychological research in this area, the research that has been undertaken so far indicates that women appear to be more religious than men in a variety of ways. Their religious orientation is more likely to be intrinsic rather than extrinsic. In other words, it is more likely to be a fundamental part of their self–concept and way of being in the world (Allport 1969). They also tend to engage in private religious activity more often (Nelson 2009). Hood (2001) maintains that women's spiritual experience is more likely to be mystical in nature and that they report mystical experiences, and particularly powerful ones, more often. Research also indicates that women's spirituality has more of a relational quality than men's in the sense that there is a strong emphasis on emotional and relational connectedness with self, others and the Divine (Nelson 2009; Slee 2004).

In relation to spiritual development, Slee's research into women's faith development suggests that women's developmental pathways may differ in a number of respects from men's (Slee 2004). She identifies three central themes which she sees as reflecting a number of key patterns in women's faith development: the experience of alienation by which she means a profound sense of disconnection from self, others and the transcendent; the experience of awakening or breaking through to 'a new consciousness and spiritual vitality'; and the importance of relational consciousness and connectedness. Clearly, men may also experience existential crises which are similar to women's experience of nothingness or alienation. Slee (2004) does not specifically indicate how she sees women's experience as differing from men's but I suspect that the recurring themes of lack of sense of self or of the giving away of self to others, of powerlessness and paralysis, of self–negation, of imprisonment and of loss of voice that surfaced in her research are more prominent in women than in men. In relation to the process of awakening, Christ (1986) argues that the process of awakening in women may also be qualitatively different from that in men. For women, she maintains, awakening is not so much 'a giving up of self' as a 'coming home to self'. Rather than being surrendered to the transcendent reality, women's selfhood gradually becomes more rooted and grounded in it. Slee (2004) also argues that women's awakening is characterised by a movement away from objective, rational and analytical ways of knowing towards more subjective, instinctive, intuitive and 'bodily' ways as their trust in their own internal locus of evaluation grows and they are able to reclaim ways of knowing that are more natural to them. This is of course a movement that may also occur in men especially in the second half of life, but it is perhaps particularly liberating and empowering for women.

The work of Fowler (1995) and others has focused primarily on the impact of our cognitive, emotional and psychosocial development on the spiritual journey. I have chosen to focus on Fowler's model in some depth as I believe that it offers the therapist some valuable insights into the process of spiritual development from a psychological perspective. Despite the fact that his original formulation of the theory is now thirty years old and that there have been many criticisms of his work, Fowler remains the leading and most significant theorist in this field. His theory has been widely researched, critiqued and debated (Streib 2003) and has had an important impact on some aspects of pastoral and educational ministry. Furthermore, many who encounter his writings find them very helpful in enabling them to make sense of their own spiritual journeys. Jamieson (2002) records his observation that people often have 'a revelatory 'ahh' experience' in encountering Fowler's work for the first time. This is I think particularly true for those who are moving into the later stages of spiritual development and who often find themselves caught up in an intensely painful and disorienting process of transition in their spiritual journeys. My own personal experience has been that Fowler's writings have been a rich resource, both in enabling me to make sense of some aspects of my own spiritual journey and in equipping me to work with others, both as a therapist and as a spiritual companion.

Fowler outlined his stage theory of faith or spiritual development in his book, 'The Stages of Faith', originally published in 1981. The book draws on the results of a large scale research project carried out in the States in the 1970s and articulates what he calls his 'theory of growth in faith' (Fowler 1995: xiii). Fowler offers a broad and inclusive definition of the word 'faith' and it is clear that in using the word 'faith', he is essentially talking about spirituality. Like the theologians Tillich and Niebuhr before him, rather than identifying faith too simply with belief as many have come to do, Fowler (1995) understands faith as a much 'larger', more complex and more mysterious phenomenon. He argues that to reduce faith to a question of belief is a serious error and that there is an urgent need for us to 'reimage' faith. The key 'question of faith', he argues, is not concerned with what we believe, but with what or whom we set our hearts on. Faith, as he sees it, is more a matter of trust, commitment and loyalty rather than a matter of belief. What we believe is no more than our way of understanding and making sense of what we experience as we relate to the transcendent.

At its heart, then, faith involves the search for what Fowler calls 'a center of value and power' that is sufficiently worthy for us to place our trust in and to commit ourselves and our lives to. It is not a separate, compartmentalised dimension of life, but 'an orientation of the total person' (p.14). It is 'a state of being ultimately concerned', a process of determining what Tillich (1957) would call our 'god values' – those values that have 'centering power' in our lives, that sustain us, that give us a sense of direction and purpose, that enable us to find meaning in our existence. Faith is, however, not always religious in its content – in Fowler's terms, the particular 'centering values, images of power and master stories' we choose to commit ourselves to. Nor is it always religious in its context – that is, the environment in which faith develops.

In his later writings, Fowler (1996) offers a more formal definition of faith which articulates more fully how he sees it as operating in our lives. He describes it as 'an integral centering process' that gives us a sense of direction and coherence in our lives; connects us with others through shared trust and loyalties; grounds our personal worldviews and communal loyalties in our awareness of and relationship to the transcendent; and enables us to face and come to terms with the limitations of our existence through a reliance on whatever we believe to be ultimate in our lives. He also views faith as multidimensional. For Fowler, faith includes an affective dimension which centres on our feelings of trust in and commitment and loyalty to the transcendent; a cognitive dimension which is concerned with constructing meaning and making sense of experience; a relational dimension which is an alignment of both the heart and the will and involves trust in and loyalty, commitment and devotion to something or someone Other; and a social dimension. The development of faith is seen as requiring 'community, language, ritual and nurture' (p. xiii) and the way in which our inborn capacity for faith is activated and develops is seen as depending largely on the kind of relational environment we grow up in.

Fowler's research led him to believe that what he calls 'the human side of faith' is capable of being analysed from a developmental perspective. He is very clear that what he is concerned with is the structure and dynamics of faith rather than the content of faith. In other words, what he is interested in exploring are the changes that can be observed in what he calls 'the operations of faith' – that is, in our ways of knowing, judging, valuing and committing in the context of faith (Fowler 1995: 275). He argues that the development of faith, whether religious or non–religious, is a universal phenomenon and that we have an inherent genetic potential to develop this spiritual aspect of our being. It is clear that Fowler views faith as an active, evolving existential process which is dynamic rather than static, and which is characterised by movement and change rather than stability. He also believes that everyone's faith, irrespective of its content, generally develops in the same way through the same stages. He identifies 'seven stagelike, developmentally related styles of faith' (Fowler 1995: xiii) and sees the sequence of these faith stages as a kind of 'rising spiral movement'. What he means by this is that each stage with its new strengths and capacities emerges out of and builds on the previous one, but without denying its value or validity. As we progress through the stages, furthermore, those life issues that faith must confront re–present themselves time and again and are dealt with at increasing levels of complexity (p. 274).

The process of faith development is therefore seen as invariable, sequential and hierarchical and it is here that we see the strong influence of other developmental structural stage theories on Fowler's work – theories such as those of Piaget (1929) on cognitive development, Kohlberg (1984) on the development of moral thinking, Kegan (1982) on the development of the self and lifespan development theories such as those of Erikson (1980) and Levinson (1978). As do other structural stage theorists, he views each stage as a well–defined, integrated phase of development with observable characteristics which mark it out from the others. Each stage, he believes, must be experienced in turn. In other words, there is no possibility of skipping from stage to stage in a random way. The movement from one stage to the next brings with it the development of new strengths and capacities. These build on those already achieved in previous stages and enable us to engage with the particular life issues we face in more complex ways. Interestingly, however, while he does see his description of the various stages of faith development as capable of being generalised and therefore of being tested cross–culturally, he stops short of actually claiming universality.

The seven stages Fowler (1995) identifies are as follows:

> Stage 0: Primal faith
> Stage 1: Intuitive–Projective Faith
> Stage 2: Mythical–Literal Faith
> Stage 3: Synthetic–Conventional Faith
> Stage 4: Individuative–Reflective Faith
> Stage 5: Conjunctive Faith
> Stage 6: Universalizing Faith

Stage 0: Primal faith

This is the faith of infancy. Fowler believes that we all begin our spiritual journey as infants and that this 'pre–stage' of primal or 'undifferentiated faith' underlies all that comes later in the journey of faith development. Such faith has as yet no clear shape. It is vague and indistinct. Essentially, it is a simple prelinguistic 'disposition to trust' that emerges out of our earliest experiences of relational mutuality with our primary caregivers and the basic confidence we develop in them as a result. It is a fundamental trust not only in those who care for us and in the environment they create for us, but also in ourselves and in 'the larger value and meaning commitments ' which are transmitted to us through the care we receive (Fowler 1995: 121). What Fowler (1995) is arguing here is that as we experience our parents' caring and nurturing of us, we begin to sense something of their way of being in and seeing the world and of their trust in and loyalty both to other people and to whatever it is that gives their lives meaning.

Fowler (1996) believes that it is during this stage that what he calls 'the body self' begins to develop. Stern (1985) calls this emerging sense of self 'the core self'. It is at this stage that we begin to experience ourselves as an integrated, boundaried physical whole which is separate and distinct from others. We become aware of having feelings that we relate to this emerging sense of self and aware of our ability to control our own actions. We also begin to have an expectation of the continuity of the self in relation to our environment. There is clearly some overlap here both with my own concept of the core self and with the person–centred concept of 'the organismic self' (Seeman 1983). Another key sense of self that is believed to emerge during this stage is what Stern (1985) calls the 'the subjective (or inter–subjective) self'. We begin to develop the capacity to share our subjective experience with others. Parent and infant share with each other their attention to particular objects or experiences in their environment. They communicate their intentions to each other through familiar postures or gestures. They also share their feelings with each other. This is the first step in the development of our capacity for engaging in mental and emotional intimacy. Fowler (1996: 34) links this emergence of the subjective self explicitly with what he refers to as 'the birth of the soul'. He describes it as 'the awakening of soul intimacy'.

At the heart then of Fowler's first stage of primal faith lies 'the fund of basic trust and the relational experience of mutuality' that emerge, all being well, as its key strengths (Fowler 1995: 121). As our sense of self begins to develop, moreover, so does our capacity for imagination, for ritualisation and for symbolisation and our awareness of and connection with that part of ourselves that Fowler calls the soul. All of these play a vital role in the process of faith development. The key danger in these early months is that as a result of parental neglect, abandonment or abuse, our capacity for basic trust and mutuality in relationships may fail to develop. We may not feel welcomed or at home in the life space into which we have been born. We may not see ourselves, others or our environment as worthy of our trust. We may not begin our lives with that 'ground sense of hope' that Fowler speaks of. And the basic mistrust that emerges may later colour our relationship with the transcendent.

Stage 1: Intuitive–Projective Faith

This is the style of faith that Fowler believes to be characteristic of early childhood, although he argues that an adult version of it may also be found in some primitive societies. It is as Jamieson (2002) puts it, the faith of 'the Innocent'. As our capacity for language, thought and imagination continue to develop, we make the transition to this magical, fantasy–filled phase of faith in which make–believe is not distinguished from reality. There is at this stage a strong tendency to draw on magical explanations of events and to make sense of our experience through the use of powerful images and symbols. At this point, however, we have no capacity to organise such images intellectually into any kind of logical or coherent narrative.

This is also an imitative phase of faith. Our earliest images of the transcendent are shaped primarily by our experiences of parental care and we reach our earliest understanding of the experience of the transcendent through the experience of our primary caregivers – that is, through the stories they tell us, the examples they give us and the patterns of behaviour we observe in them. As religious symbols and language are so widely present in society, this is true of children from both religious and non–religious homes. Fowler (1995: 128 – 9) argues that whether or not they have received religious education, children in Stage 1 draw together the images and fragments of stories that are prevalent in their culture in a way that enables them to construct one or more images of the transcendent.

Fowler sees the key strength of this stage as the emergence of our capacity for imagination, the ability to grasp the experienced world through powerful images and stories that express something of our intuitive understanding of and feelings towards 'the ultimate conditions of existence' (p. 134). The key danger is, he believes, that we are vulnerable to being terrorised by frightening or destructive images (such as images of hell or the devil) or that such powerful images may be used to bring about a conversion experience or to reinforce particular moral codes, doctrinal teaching or taboos.

Stage 2: Mythic–Literal Faith

This is primarily the faith of later childhood, though Fowler (1995) maintains it can also be found quite often in adolescents and in a smaller number of adults. As we develop the capacity for what Piaget (1929) called 'concrete operational thinking' – the capacity for logical but still concrete thinking – so we become increasingly able to distinguish between reality and fantasy. We also develop at this stage the capacity to 'narratize' our experience – in other words, the ability to use stories to give our experiences meaning (Fowler 1995: 136). Such developments precipitate the transition to Stage 2 faith, or as Jamieson (2002) describes it, the faith of 'the Literalist'.

As we encounter the narratives of the faith communities to which we belong, these myths and stories become very important to us along with the moral rules and attitudes that they convey. Because the capacity for abstract thought has not yet developed, however, they are generally absorbed without question. Their symbolism is understood literally. We have not yet developed the ability to step back from the stories we are told, to reflect on them, or to make general or abstract statements about their meaning. Consequently, there is in this style of faith a strong dependence on the literal interpretation of sacred texts, often accompanied by a lack of deeper reflection on faith stories. Beliefs and convictions are deeply held and in the absence of doubt and questioning, faith results in a strong sense of security. Belonging to a faith community becomes increasingly important and we are likely to be deeply influenced by the authoritative teaching and rules we encounter in that context.

Fowler sees the emergent strength of this stage as the rise of narrative and the emergence of story, drama and myth as ways of making sense of and finding meaning in our experience. The dangers, he believes, lie in 'the limitations of literalness' and in the over–reliance on the principle of reciprocal fairness and justness in making sense of how the world works. This can, he maintains, give rise either to an extreme, over–controlling form of perfectionism or as a result of neglect, abandonment or abuse by significant others in the child's life, a deep and pervading sense of 'badness'. He also sees this over–reliance on reciprocal fairness as one of the key factors which precipitate the eventual transition to the next stage of faith development.

Stage 3: Synthetic–conventional faith

Fowler (1995) believes that this third stage of faith typically begins to emerge in adolescence but that it is also the stage at which many adults permanently settle. He sees this stage as being precipitated both by the adolescent's developing awareness of conflicts and clashes between differing authoritative stories (such as the Genesis creation story in the Bible and the theory of evolution) and by the emergence of what Piaget (1929) called 'formal operational thinking'. This is the capacity for abstract and hypothetical thinking which makes it both possible and necessary to reflect on how we make sense of such clashes between competing stories.

It is, as Jamieson (2002) describes it, the faith of 'the Loyalist'. It is 'synthetic' in that we have a need at this stage to synthesise or draw together the conventional stories, beliefs and values we have absorbed into some form of integrated, coherent whole. It is conventional in the sense that it is essentially conformist. It is characterised by a strong dependence on and loyalty to our faith community and to external authorities, an absence of doubt and questioning and a lack of critical examination of or reflection on our system of beliefs and values. Thinking and understanding tend to remain dualistic or black and white. Convictions are deeply held, resulting in a strong sense of security and a high level of commitment.

As the adolescent's social horizons continue to widen, other spheres of influence such as peer groups, work, popular culture and faith communities become important in shaping development. An increasing number of 'significant others' have the potential to contribute either positively or negatively and sometimes in conflicting ways to the process of identity and faith formation. At this stage, furthermore, spiritual authority is generally not seen as residing within the self. It is located either in significant others such as parental figures or in the recognised leaders of the faith communities to which they belong. Fowler (1995) argues that the expectations of these significant others can have a very powerful impact on the course of faith development. Indeed, one of the key dangers in this stage is that we become overly dependent on what Parks (1990) calls 'the tyranny of the they'. Fowler argues that while adolescents generally see themselves as making their own choices and commitments and developing their own strong convictions, it is much more likely that their values and convictions have, as he puts it, 'largely chosen them' (Fowler 1995: 154). This clearly has links with Rogers' concept of the locus of evaluation (Rogers 1951). At this stage of cognitive development, Rogers might argue, our locus of evaluation in relation to our faith tends to be externalised rather than internalised. In other words, we are likely to be more dependent on others' judgments and perceptions rather than on our own. At this stage, we do, however, become capable of reflecting on our own thinking and ways of experiencing. This makes it possible for us to step outside the flow of our life experience and to begin to see it as a whole.

We also begin to move away from literal interpretations of stories or scriptures and a literal understanding of the symbols that are meaningful to us. Such symbols are related to as if they were inseparably connected with that which they symbolise. They are honoured as if the symbols themselves were sacred. Any attempt to demythologise the symbol – that is, to strip it of its mythical element and to understand it from a rational perspective – is therefore seen as an attack on the Divine itself. In terms of images of the transcendent, Fowler (1995) argues that the adolescent generally thinks of the transcendent as a significant Other – as a personal transcendent being with personal qualities such as the capacity for unconditional love and acceptance, understanding and faithfulness. There is often, therefore, a discomfort with the concept of immanence – the presence of the Divine within. Fowler maintains that the 'religious hunger' of the adolescent is for a personal god who knows and is deeply accepting and affirming of his or her emerging identity and personal myth.

He sees this capacity to form a personal life story or myth as the emergent strength of Stage 3. It enables us to develop and maintain a sense of our own identity, to find a sense of direction and purpose in our lives and to make sense of and find meaning in our experiences. The influence of Erikson's work is evident here. The primary psychosocial task of Erikson's fifth psychosocial stage of adolescence is that of forming a personal identity and its related virtue is that of loyalty or fidelity (Erikson 1968). He believed that there is a strong connection between identity and religion and emphasised the importance of our developing what he called 'an existential identity' which he saw as being separate from other aspects of our identity (Erikson 1958). The primary existential questions at this stage are 'Who am I?', 'What can I be'? and 'What do I believe?'. Erikson recognised that for many people, the religious resources of their spiritual tradition play an important role in the process of answering these questions. The formation of a stable and positive sense of identity in adolescence enables us to identify with and commit ourselves to a particular ideology which fits with our way of experiencing and making sense of the world. The failure to do so can result in the development of what Erikson calls 'a negative identity' which is essentially a reaction against or rejection of a particular ideology or community (Erikson 1968).

Fowler believes that the key danger of this stage is that we may internalise (and even hold as sacred) the expectations and evaluations of others to such a degree that we later fail to develop the capacity to trust our own judgements and to act autonomously. Alternatively, experiences of significant betrayal in the context of our relationships with others may damage our capacity to trust and enter into an intimate relationship with the transcendent.

Stage 4: Individuative–reflective faith

This is, as Jamieson (2002) describes it, the faith of 'the Critic'. As young adults who are developing the capacity for critical judgement and a growing trust in our own experiences and perceptions, we begin to choose and 'own' our faith for ourselves, to take greater personal responsibility for it. It is 'individuative' faith in that our thinking is becoming more independent of the views and expectations of others and therefore less dependent on external authorities. In other words, our locus of evaluation gradually becomes more internalised (Rogers 1951). It is 'reflective' faith in that we become increasingly caught up in a process of doubting and questioning, of critically examining and often distancing ourselves from previously held belief and value systems. We may begin to challenge the accepted traditions and practices of the faith communities to which we belong and to become frustrated with a leadership style which requires us to remain dependent and unquestioning. We may develop the capacity to appreciate and celebrate diversity in belief and practice rather than feeling threatened by it.

There is also at this stage what Fowler (1995: 180) calls 'a demythologization' of the symbols and rituals which enable us to relate to the transcendent. In other words, we seek to demystify the symbols and rituals we had previously seen as being sacred in themselves. We come to recognise the symbol as a symbol and to analyse it from a rational perspective rather than simply trusting in and relying on its sacred power and inherent truth as we had done in the past. There is of course loss in this. Tillich (1957) argued that when a symbol is stripped of its mythical element and its mystery in this way, it becomes what he called 'a broken symbol' and inevitably loses some of its power to enable us to relate to the transcendent.

Fowler (1995) believes that there are a number of factors which may contribute to the movement towards Stage 4 faith. For example, we may become aware of serious clashes and disagreements between different sources of authority or witness officially sanctioned leaders making significant changes in policies or practices which were previously regarded as sacrosanct and inviolable. We may encounter experiences and perspectives which cause us to question the way in which our beliefs and values have been formed and have changed over time and to recognise their relativity – in other words, their dependence on the psychological, social and environmental context in which they were formed. Frequently, this is precipitated by the young adult's experience of leaving home, either physically or emotionally, or in later life by significant changes in primary relationships through, for example, bereavement, divorce, children leaving home or changing jobs.

Fowler views the emerging strength of this stage as the capacity for critical reflection both on our own sense of identity and on our worldviews and ideologies. He argues, however, that in its greatest strength, lies its greatest danger – that is, an undue level of confidence both in the conscious mind and in the capacity for critical thinking. At this stage, we tend to pay too little attention to the influence of unconscious processes on our perceptions and behaviour and may also be too quick to assimilate others' 'realities' and perspectives into our own worldview. This is particularly likely where coming face to face with the relativity of our own perspective is too disturbing.

Stage 5: Conjunctive faith

For a significant number of people, this is the faith of midlife. The word 'conjunctive' means serving to connect, join together, combine or unite and Fowler uses it to indicate that moving into this stage of faith involves reuniting what has become separated in earlier stages of the journey (Fowler 1996). Jamieson (2002) terms it the faith of 'the Seer'. Here he draws, I think, not so much on the concept of the seer as a prophet or visionary but on the wider meaning of the word as 'one who sees'.

As we move into early midlife, Fowler (1995) maintains, we may find ourselves feeling an inner restlessness, a growing dissatisfaction with the certainty, clarity and 'neatness' of our Stage 4 faith outlook or a sense of 'sterility and flatness' in the personal meanings we have held dear. We may also begin to recognise that we are not one self, but many selves. We may become aware that we are more than our conscious selves, that there are powerful elements of our being that are largely unconscious, whether personal, social, cultural or even archetypal in origin (archetypal in the Jungian sense of being inherited or derived from the past collective experience of the human race). We may begin to recognise that such unconscious elements have the capacity to shape our choices and behaviour in both constructive and destructive ways. We may find ourselves listening more attentively to the unsettling inner voices of our 'deeper self' and as a result, needing to re–connect with and 'rework' our past and the personal myths we have constructed for ourselves.

It seems to me that there are strong links here with the process of becoming a person that Rogers described and with aspects of his description of the fully functioning person (Rogers 1967; 1980). Fowler's references to connecting with 'the deeper self ' and to the necessity of re–working our personal myths are strongly reminiscent of Rogers' conceptualisation of the journey of becoming as being one of re–connecting with the true or organismic self. They are also reminiscent of Jung's concept of individuation, a process that he saw as taking place principally in the second half of life (Jung 1960). Furthermore, Rogers' image of the fully functioning person (Rogers 1967, 1980) includes references to a deep desire for authenticity, a growing capacity to engage deeply in the process of becoming more fully oneself, a strong feeling of connectedness with and compassion for others and both a longing and capacity for deeper and more intimate interpersonal relationships.

According to Fowler, any of these developments may open up the possibility of moving towards Stage 5 faith. At this stage, he believes that we come to 'a way of seeing, knowing and committing' that moves beyond the rational, logical and analytical thinking that characterises Stage 4 faith. He uses the term 'dialogical knowing' to speak of a kind of knowing that is conscious of the oneness and inter–connectedness of everything; that is open to dialogue with that which we seek to know; that involves an 'I–Thou' rather than an 'I-it' relationship with the known (Buber 1958)[1]; and that values and recognises the wisdom inherent in things as they are rather than seeking to control or modify them (Fowler 1995). Elkins (1998) speaks of this kind of knowing as entering into a form of 'communion' with that which we seek to know. It is a more subjective, intuitive, intimate and mystical way of knowing.

This kind of knowing is accompanied by a growing awareness that truth is both complex and multidimensional and with this, comes a greater openness to the truths to be found in other religions and faith traditions. There is a growing realisation that the stories, doctrines and symbols of our own spiritual tradition offer us a truth that is inevitably partial, incomplete and sometimes even distorted, limited as it is by our own particular experience of the transcendent and by our own interpretation of the teachings we have encountered. At this stage, therefore, we become more open to meaningful encounters with spiritual traditions which may be very different from our own in the hope that such encounters may both enrich our understanding of our own truth and at the same time, challenge aspects of it which may need refining or correcting.

There is within this a developing ability to recognise our own limitations and to be open to hearing the wisdom of others. Fowler is at pains to point out, however, that this does not involve an uncritical or total acceptance of the other's truth; nor does it imply a lack of real commitment to our own faith tradition or some form of 'wishy–washy neutrality'. Indeed, at this stage our own spirituality is fully owned and deeply rooted. It is also founded on a high level of confidence in the transcendent reality towards which our own spiritual tradition points. Consequently, we are able to open ourselves up to the perspectives of others in a principled way, using our own experience of reality to test alternative truth claims. We are also ready to consider balanced evaluations of our own tradition by those from other traditions. We begin to recognise that others' perspectives have the potential both to enrich our own understanding and to correct distortions within it. This opens the way to genuine and serious inter–faith dialogue based on mutual respect, non–defensiveness and what Fowler (1996) calls 'a kind of epistemological humility'.

This has certainly been my own experience of embracing interfaith study and dialogue at this stage of faith. I have found this a profoundly enriching experience which far from weakening or 'diluting' my own spirituality, has strengthened it immeasurably. It has, if anything, deepened my loyalty to what Moore (2002) calls 'the soul of my religion', the essential core of it to which I have always been strongly drawn. Certainly, it has changed my understanding of the Divine and of the spiritual life. It has challenged my way of interpreting sacred texts and writings and made me aware of layers of meaning in the myths, symbols and rituals that speak to me that I had not recognised before. Sometimes that has been an unsettling process. At other times, however, it has been liberating and exciting as my understanding and appreciation of my own spiritual tradition has expanded beyond measure. It has also challenged my prejudices, ignorance and misunderstandings in relation to other faiths and enabled me to recognise and value not only what we have in common, but also our differences.

Another related feature of this stage is our growing ability to deal with uncertainties, paradoxes and the tension of opposites and to live with mystery and 'unknowing'. It is a faith that has learnt 'to live the questions'. It is also a faith that has moved beyond the demythologising strategy of Stage 4 faith. Once again, Fowler (1996: 65) argues, we become more receptive to myths, symbols and rituals. Instead of seeking to deconstruct and analyse them, we begin to recognise their multidimensionality and to enter into them in a way that can illuminate our lives and experience.

Finally, Fowler (1987) argues that there is in the Conjunctive faith stage a readiness for and openness to a deeper level of intimacy which flows out of a heightened awareness of our interconnectedness and interdependence and creates a profound longing for a deeper relatedness with both others and the transcendent. The work of Erikson also seems relevant here. Hoare (2002) argues that Erikson saw religion and spirituality as becoming much more of a continuing focus in midlife. Erikson (1968) saw the primary psychological task of this stage as that of achieving what he called 'generativity' with its associated virtue of care. He defined generativity as 'primarily the interest in establishing and guiding the next generation' (Erikson 1980: 103) and emphasised that it is not only expressed through parenthood, but also through other forms of creativity and altruistic concern. Altruistic care for others is a quality or virtue that is strongly linked with spirituality and religion and Nelson (2009) points out that recent research indicates that that the principal characteristics of highly generative persons – such as hope, trust, faith and altruism – often have their basis in a spiritual orientation in life.

Fowler (1995) sees the emerging strength of this stage as the capacity to recognise that our personal meanings are relative, partial and inevitably distorted apprehensions of the transcendent reality, that in the words of Paul from 1 Corinthians 13 in the Bible, 'For now, we see through a glass, darkly.' The danger, he believes, is that because of our new grasp of the complexity and paradoxical nature of truth, we may become trapped in what he calls 'a paralysing passivity or inaction' which can lead in turn either to complacency or cynicism.

Stage 6: Universalizing faith

According to Fowler (1995: 198), Stage 5 faith is 'paradoxical and divided'. On the one hand, we become more acutely and painfully aware that we are living in a world that desperately needs transforming, that we are part of a fractured, divided human family, that the absence of justice and peace and the failure to love have a devastating impact on too many people's lives. We experience a deep yearning to see the world radically changed. We are gripped by a vision of the world as 'an inclusive community of being' in which we are able to embrace more fully our essential inter–connectedness and inter–dependence. On the other hand, we are also motivated by the need to preserve ourselves and our well–being and perhaps also to preserve the flawed socio–economic system in which we live in the belief that the alternatives that are open to us are likely to be even worse. In Stage 5, therefore, we are caught in the midst of these conflicting loyalties.

Fowler (1995) believes that in a very small number of people, this inner tension eventually drives them towards what he calls 'the radical actualization of Stage 6' (p. 198). Issues of justice, peace and love become all important to them to the point that they are willing 'to sacrifice the self' in order to pursue the vision that fires them. This involves a process of 'decentration from self' (Fowler 1987) – in other words, a letting go of the preoccupation with the survival, security and significance of the self to the extent that it is no longer the central focus of their lives. Fowler sees this kind of self–emptying as the fruit of becoming more fully grounded in and aligned with the transcendent. At this stage, there is also, as Fowler sees it, a stronger emphasis on unity, interconnectedness and the importance of community. Moreover, the Stage 6 concept of community becomes still more inclusive to the point that it is seen as extending well beyond the particular human systems and cultures within which we live out our lives (Fowler 1996). There is, furthermore, a deep compassion and concern for the growth and well–being of all others, including those who have in the past been experienced as opponents or enemies.

Again, Fowler's thinking relates here to that of Erikson and others. Erikson (1968) saw the key psychosocial task of later life as being that of developing what he called 'ego integrity' and its related virtue of wisdom. Developing ego integrity as Erikson saw it is about achieving a sense of fulfilment and satisfaction with one's life and being willing to accept and face death with equanimity. He saw religion as being of primary importance in old age in promoting such integration and enabling people to deal with the ultimate concerns of human existence. Other theorists such as Peck (1968) have expanded Erikson's concept to include an acceptance of what has happened throughout the life course; the belief that life is purposeful and makes sense; the belief that all life experiences, whether positive or negative, have a value in facilitating our learning and growth; the realisation of our interconnectedness with all others; an understanding of our place in the ultimate scheme of things; and the capacity to transcend the self.

Fowler (1995) believes that Stage 6 is reached only by a few people later in life and cites Gandhi, Mother Theresa, Thomas Merton and Martin Luther King as examples. He is also at pains to point out, however, that people who reach this stage of faith development are by no means perfect or 'fully functioning'. He recognises that even the greatest of visionaries have their own particular weaknesses and blind spots and gives the example of Gandhi's unfair treatment of his wife and sons.

He sees the emergent strengths of this stage as the depth of commitment and vision it gives rise to and the capacity to let go of the need to preserve and protect the self and the present order. He does not explicitly identify any specific dangers or limitations of this stage, but I suspect that one of the key dangers may lie in the Stage 6 radical activist's tendency to ignore threats to the self and to the people who are closest to them. As in the case of Gandhi's relationships with his immediate family, it appears that to some extent, their needs and well–being may well have been sacrificed 'for the greater good'.

Movement from stage to stage

The research carried out by Fowler and others suggests that very few people progress through all seven stages of faith development and that people can 'equilibrate' or settle for long periods of time or even permanently at any stage from Stage 1 onwards. For example, Stage 1 faith can be found in adults in some very primitive societies and Stage 3, principally found in adolescents, can also be found in a significant percentage of adults from the early twenties onwards. Perhaps partly because of this, Fowler is at great pains to make it clear that people at later stages of faith development are in no sense holier or more spiritual than those at earlier stages and that the faith stages should not be seen as some kind of 'achievement scale' by which to measure people's worth (Fowler 1995:114). He points out that people need 'time, experience, challenge and nurture' in order for their faith to develop in the ways he describes and contends that each stage has its proper time for ascendancy. He does, however, also make the claim that from a psychological perspective, later stages are 'in significant ways more adequate' than earlier ones (p. 101).

Fowler believes that the readiness for stage change is dependent on a number of key factors – in particular, our level of biological maturation and the stages of psychosocial, cognitive and moral development we have reached. Consequently, while he does not see the seven stages as being rigidly tied to chronological age, he does believe that, at least in relation to the earlier stages, there are minimum chronological ages below which a particular stage change would be very unlikely. Fowler maintains that movement between one stage and the next is generally triggered by life events, crises and challenges which threaten the equilibrium of our current stage of development. Assuming that we are psychologically ready to move towards the next stage, these crises and challenges may push us into transition. Osmer and Fowler (1993) outline four different types of crisis which may trigger movement:

> developmental crises: crises which occur as an inevitable consequence of progressing through the human developmental sequence. These are the common stresses and problems that are related to negotiating the transition period between one stage and the next.

> situational crises: crises which are triggered by disruptive events or relationships which impinge on the normal developmental process (for example, the death of a parent, a divorce, a life–threatening illness). Such crises may potentially impede development either in short–term, reversible ways or in more profound, longer–term ways with the result that certain parts of the personality cease to grow over a long period of time.

> crises of social pathology: crises which are triggered by destructive social pressures or influences which inhibit normal development (for example, racism, sexism and other forms of social oppression).

crises of theological inadequacy: crises which arise as a result of the process of encountering and assessing alternative theories or frameworks for understanding human nature and development. This inevitably impacts on our existing theological framework and may be deeply unsettling.

The experience of transition

In his later writings, Fowler (1996) explores what he calls the 'textures of transitions' in much greater depth. He begins by distinguishing clearly between structural stage changes and the process of conversion. Conversion, he argues, is concerned with making changes in the content of our faith – changes, for example, in the master stories we embrace, in our core values, in the images and symbols that are important to us. Stage changes may, he believes, occur without conversion as conversion can occur without a stage change. Conversion can both precipitate and be precipitated by a stage change or the two may occur concurrently. Finally, conversion can sometimes block or help us avoid the pain of a stage change. While stage changes do not necessarily involve a radical change in the content of faith, however, Fowler (1995) believes that they always require 'a reworking' of that content as we move from one faith stage to another.

He maintains that structural stage changes occur in the following key areas:

> in the way we think
> in the way we form and hold our world views
> in the way in which we relate to external faith authorities (such as our faith communities) and the truths they proclaim
> in our ability to see and respect other people's viewpoints
> in the way we understand and respond to symbols
> in the way in which we make moral judgements
> in the extent to which we draw social boundaries around our faith communities
> in the extent to which the self has evolved

Fowler (1996) describes transitions from one stage to another as often being protracted, painful and disturbing and consequently, sometimes abortive. Drawing heavily on the work of Bridges (1980), he sees people in transition as going through three key phases. The first of these is the phase of endings, the phase that sets the process of change in motion. Fowler (1987) argues as does Bridges that each ending phase we enter into involves 'a symbolic death' which is characterised by four key interrelated aspects or phases:

the experience of disengagement: the giving up, breaking or loss of a meaningful connection to one or more aspects of the world as we have known it – aspects which are crucial to our sense of self

the experience of disidentification (which Fowler describes as 'the internal side' of disengagement): the loss of our previous ways of defining ourselves

the experience of disenchantment: the collapse or letting go of at least some part of the way in which we have made sense of the world and our experience, and of the assumptions, beliefs and values we have previously held

the experience of disorientation: the sense of losing our bearings as the maps we have previously depended on to chart our journey no longer seem relevant or meaningful and we are essentially cast adrift.

Once we have become disoriented, we are on the edge of what Bridges (1980) called 'the neutral zone', the second phase of the process of transition. The experience of the neutral zone has been characterised in a number of different ways: as a 'time out of time' and 'a place that is no place' (Bridges 1980); as a wilderness experience; and as a 'sojourning in the interstices of the world' (Fowler 1987). It is an experience that Fowler believes has similarities with that of 'the dark night of the soul' that St John of the Cross (2003) described. Fowler (1987) argues that we are generally ill–prepared by our culture for what he calls 'the attentive waiting' of the neutral zone. In our 'quick fix' societies with their strong emphasis on the avoidance of pain, unknowing and inaction, there is little room for the patient waiting that is necessary at this stage in the process of transition. Consequently, we rarely give ourselves the time we need to listen to the promptings of our spirit and the voice of our soul. If, however, we are able to allow the process to unfold and to bear its fruit, then in time we begin to move into the third phase of the process. Bridges (1980) calls this the phase of 'new beginnings'. This is, Fowler (1987) maintains, the phase of 'reentry and reintegration'. It is perhaps only then that we can begin to see the neutral zone in a more positive light, to see it in the way that Bridges (1980) does as a time of 'fruitful emptiness' and to value the new insights and perspectives it has brought us.

Research indicates that the transition from Stages 3 to 4 is the most difficult transition to make and this has certainly been my own experience. It is often a deeply disturbing and unsettling process which may in part explain Fowler's findings that many adults do not ever reach this stage and many others only arrive at it in their mid–thirties or forties. It seems to me that there are other factors that may also be important here such as the extent to which we have developed a basic trust in ourselves (Erikson 1968), the extent to which we have developed an internalised locus of evaluation (Rogers 1951) and the extent to which we have developed a strong sense of our own personal identity (Erikson 1968). Another key factor may be the security of our adult attachment style (Bartholomew 1990). There is some empirical evidence that those of us who have a secure attachment style are generally less threatened by the possibility of changes in our spirituality (Nelson 2009). Furthermore, the transition from Stage 3 to 4 often requires a process of disengagement from the faith community to which we have been deeply committed. This is partly because most faith communities have little or no understanding of this process of faith transition and therefore tend to misunderstand it or to see it in a negative light. Consequently, they are at best unable to offer those who are in transition the support and resources they need. At worst, they may even be dismissive or rejecting of those who are going through this process. Fowler (1995) argues that when we are in transition, we have a strong need for the personal position we are moving towards to be accepted and respected and for the reflective process we are engaged in to be understood and supported by our significant others. For those who are insecurely attached and who fear abandonment and rejection, therefore, the potential consequences of making the transition between Stages 3 and 4 may simply be too costly.

I have, I believe, engaged with this Stage 4 reflective process at two different points in my life – firstly, in late adolescence when I left home both emotionally and physically, and secondly in my late thirties when I began to find myself feeling straight–jacketed by the largely Stage 3 faith community in which I had become involved some years earlier. The first experience involved a temporary conversion (that is, in Fowler's terms, a change in the contents of my faith) from a Christian to a humanist philosophical worldview. It also precipitated, however, a prolonged period of searching for my own 'path to the sacred' as Elkins (1998) would call it. In my early thirties, this eventually led to a re–conversion experience and interestingly, a temporary but short-lived reversion to Stage 3 faith.

Both experiences fit Fowler's description of Stage 4 faith very closely. In both periods of my life, I found myself beginning to question 'the givens' of my earlier faith and to experience doubt and uncertainty where previously there had been deep conviction and security. I found myself grappling with inconsistencies in the faith stories I was exposed to and with aspects of doctrine and teaching which did not fit with my own personal experience and to which I could no longer give assent. Lynch (2003) describes this process as one of 'losing my religion' - a form of words with which I can readily identify.

Both Stage 4 experiences were unsettling and disturbing, but the second more profoundly so – something that also echoes Fowler's research findings.

Going beyond Fowler

While the insights offered by Fowler's theory have been welcomed by many, his work has also attracted a number of serious criticisms (for example, Dystra and Parks 1986; Parks 1990; Astley and Francis 1992; Streib 2003). Many of these, I believe, are at least to some degree justifiable. This process of critical reflection has led to a number of developments in Fowler's thinking as evidenced by his later writings (Fowler 1996; Fowler et al 2004). At the same time, it has also generated a number of alternative stage models of faith development which have sought to address those aspects of the theory which are perceived as more problematic.

Many of the criticisms levelled at Fowler's theory have also been applied to structural stage theories in general. Firstly, it has been argued that the linear view of development that the theory proposes is an over–simplification of what is essentially a highly complex process that is much less linear in people's experience than the theory would suggest. For example, May (1987: 168) argued that while there may be different 'levels' of faith, they are not necessarily experienced sequentially and are probably better viewed as 'representative dimensions of spirituality rather than phases one must go through in sequence.' Similarly, Worthington (1989) believes that in relation to adult spiritual development, rigid stage models are not flexible enough to portray the variability in the developmental process. He maintains that more flexible models which take into account both the complex interaction between cognitive, emotional and relational factors and the impact of life events may provide a better understanding of the way in which spirituality evolves in adulthood. Secondly, the theory has been criticised for placing too much emphasis on the role that cognitive processes play in shaping faith development and paying too little attention to the affective and imaginative elements of faith and to the role of the unconscious (Streib 2003). A related criticism is that it pays too little attention to the dynamic interplay between faith structure and content in the process of faith development. It is clear that Fowler (1995: 273) does recognise what he calls 'the structuring power' of specific faith content and that he is aware of the importance of the inter–relationship between structure and content. Nevertheless, relatively little attention is paid to the complex interaction between them in the shaping of an individual's unique spiritual journey.

Thirdly, it has been argued that the model fails to recognise the degree to which the development of individuals is shaped by their social and cultural context and that it is therefore very unlikely that it will be universally applicable across all cultures. His critics point to the fact that his empirical basis was too restricted, drawn mainly as it was from middle class Americans. To date, there have been around thirty empirical studies that have replicated Fowler's findings (Slee 1996; Streib 2003) and a small number of studies that have sought to assess the applicability of the theory to other faith traditions and cultures. While these have generally suggested a reasonable degree of cross–cultural validity, they have also indicated that the theory may not be entirely free of cultural bias in relation to some specific stage descriptors (Streib 2003). Both Slee (1996) and Streib (2003) conclude therefore that the research evidence is as yet too weak to determine the extent of the theory's cross–cultural validity.

Fourthly, it has been criticised for being too andocentric – that is, for not taking into sufficient account gender differences in patterns of thinking and behaviour and for generalising typically male patterns of thought to the whole population. Slee (2004) points out that the developmental theories Fowler draws on in his work are in the main the work of male theorists whose models of development are themselves predominantly andocentric. While she recognises that Fowler does pay some attention to research on the identity formation and development of women in his work, she contends that his model does not adequately reflect the findings of this research. Furthermore, while she welcomes his later proposal to include a concept of 'relational knowing' in his description of Stage 4, she argues that what is needed is a 'wholesale reworking of the stage sequence' to reflect this aspect of women's patterns of faith. She also points to empirical evidence that suggests that his stage descriptions may be biased against women, something that Fowler himself acknowledged as a possibility (Slee 1996).

As a result of such criticisms, a number of alternative models of spiritual development have been articulated, the majority of these in response to Fowler's work. Some of these such as Peck's four stage model (Peck 1990a, 1993) Helminiak's five stage model (Helminiak 1987) and Liebert's six stage model (Liebert 2000) are essentially alternative linear or structural stage models. There have also been attempts to move away from what Friedman et al (2009) describe as 'vertical' models of spiritual development with their value–laden assumption that some stages of development are higher or lower, less or more 'adequate' than others. Some theorists have attempted to develop what might be called 'non–linear' models of spiritual development. For example, in an attempt to move away from models based on ascending stages, Streib (2003) identifies five different religious styles, loosely based on some of Fowler's stages. His model is derived from what is known as the 'milestone model' of development proposed by Loevinger (1976). It views the developmental path of each style as a rising curve that descends after reaching its peak but persists on a lower level as subsequent styles reach their peaks. Streib believes that this perspective reflects the nature of religious styles development more accurately and captures more fully the 'multi–layeredness' of religious styles at any point in the lifespan. Another similar model is Mabry's (2006) inclusive faith styles model which he describes as 'non–developmental and non-hierarchical'. On the basis of his research, Mabry identifies six broad faith styles, each of which is regarded as being of equal value. He recognises that people often 'migrate' from one faith style to another but also that such migration is not random. In other words, people are unlikely to migrate to styles that are very different from their existing style other than through a very slow, incremental process of change.

In conclusion, while there is clearly more work to do in refining and researching Fowler's stage theory, I would agree with Slee (2004) that we should not completely jettison the theory as some have argued. She maintains that, while there may be significant omissions and distortions that need to be addressed, it offers a particularly comprehensive understanding of faith development which has not yet been rivalled. Nelson (2009) adds that it has given us a clearer understanding of some of the universal features of faith, that it has enabled us to become more aware of the inter–connectedness of spiritual development and other developmental processes and that it gives us the possibility of making comparisons of people's faith development, both within and across diverse groups of people.

What we can learn from Fowler's approach is, I think, that there do appear to be observable patterns in our spiritual journeys – patterns that seem to resonate with many people and that they often find helpful in enabling them to negotiate the sometimes turbulent waters of spiritual transition. People do appear to progress through a number of phases in their spiritual development, although these phases may not be as hierarchical and the process not as uni–directional as structural stage theories suggest. The way in which they do so, furthermore, does appear to be shaped to a degree by the extent to which they have dealt successfully with other developmental challenges in their lives.

Rebecca – a woman in transition

In an attempt to draw all of this together and to demonstrate its relevance for therapeutic practice, I intend to draw on my work with a client whom I shall call Rebecca. This client entered therapy because, as she put it, she felt she had lost touch with the person she really is and wanted to find her again – a very unusual entry statement. She had been experiencing what she described as a mild depression since she had turned forty and talked of wrestling with low self–esteem and a growing sense of unhappiness and frustration with the direction her life was taking. At the end of our first session, she voiced her awareness that it seemed in part to be 'a kind of a spiritual thing' to her but at this point, she found it difficult to put into words exactly what she meant by that statement.

As Rebecca's story unfolded over the next few sessions, it became apparent that her feelings of depression and low self–worth partly stemmed from a difficult childhood. In her early teens, her father and mother had divorced after years of significant marital discord which Rebecca felt had impacted badly both on herself and her older sister. Living in a house 'full of tension, anger and tears' had left its mark on her as had her experience of being badly bullied at senior school. When her father left the family, moreover, her mother entered into another relationship very quickly and within a year, she had to adjust to her mother's remarriage. Her relationship with her stepfather proved to be a very difficult and stormy one. She felt he had little time for her and that she was 'in the way'. She also saw her mother as continually 'taking his side' in the many arguments that ensued. At the same time, her relationship with her natural father, which until then had generally been a positive one, was also suffering. He had moved out of the area following the divorce and within eighteen months, had also remarried. She saw him infrequently because he lived so far away, and she had felt that the relationship was gradually 'slipping away' from her.

Another important element of Rebecca's story was that since her mid–teens she had struggled with a fear that she might be gay. She had had a number of short term relationships with men in her twenties but had always felt that she was 'going through the motions' and doing what was expected of her. She had never felt sexually attracted to a man and acknowledged that she had had 'a significant crush' on a number of women at varying times in her life. Because of her Christian faith and her church's negative position in relation to homosexuality, she had never allowed herself face her fears but was dogged by a persistent feeling that there was 'something missing in her life'. She had not had a partner for over ten years.

As therapy progressed, furthermore, it became apparent that Rebecca was also struggling with her Christian faith. She had started going to a charismatic conservative evangelical church with a friend of hers in her mid–teens and had been a practising Christian since then. For many years, her faith had been a source of some comfort to her and belonging to a tight–knit, caring and supportive Christian community had given her a sense of belonging and that she 'mattered'. More recently, however, she had been feeling that her faith was 'slipping away' from her too. Her use of the words 'slipping away' here seemed highly significant. She acknowledged that her relationship with God had always been a somewhat distant one and that she had never seen herself as having a close personal relationship with him. Recently, she had also been wrestling internally with aspects of her church's teaching and with some of the doctrines of her faith that no longer seemed to make sense to her or to fit with her own experience of life. She had always struggled with charismatic prayer and worship, but now no longer felt able to pray at all and was finding the style of worship in her church almost impossible to engage with. This was a source of considerable distress to her. Indeed, she had come to the point of no longer being sure who or what God was to her. She had not felt able to discuss this with anyone, however, because she saw it as 'her problem' and as evidence of her inadequate faith.

Moreover, one of her friends, Aisha, was a practising Hindu. She felt strongly attracted to this woman whom she saw as 'deeply spiritual' in a way that she was not. She could not come to terms with her church's dismissiveness of her friend's faith and there were, furthermore, aspects of Hinduism to which she was beginning to feel strongly drawn. Through the conversations she was having with Aisha, she was coming to recognise the difficulty she had always experienced in relating to a male God and her growing anger and frustration with the religious patriarchy that was so predominant in the version of Christianity to which she had been exposed. She had on several occasions tried to open up a conversation with people in her church about her questions and concerns but felt that she had effectively been silenced. She had also been strongly advised to distance herself from Aisha whom she felt was being seen as 'a bad influence' on her.

From the point of view of Fowler's faith development model (Fowler 1996), Rebecca was in transition between stages 3 and 4, the most difficult transition to make. Partly triggered by her relationship with her Hindu friend which had a strong spiritual dimension to it, she was also experiencing what Moody and Carroll (1997) would term 'the Call'. Spiritually, she was awakening in a way that she had not done before. She had a strong sense that she needed 'to go deeper' spiritually, but at the same time, was questioning some of the principal tenets of her spiritual tradition. This was a very difficult, confusing and distressing time for her. She no longer felt 'at home' in the church to which she belonged which resulted in a deep sense of loss. She felt that she had 'lost her way' and was in danger of losing her faith but, at the same time, had a curious and inexplicable sense of excitement that 'something important' was happening in her spiritual life and that she needed to pay attention to it. From a Rogerian point of view, however, her journey through this transition was being hampered by her lack of openness to and trust in some aspects of her own experiencing and by her largely externalised locus of evaluation.

Rebecca was also deeply troubled by her sense that she had 'lost touch' with herself. As we explored this together, it became clear that in part, what she was experiencing was a call to reconnect with her core self or soul. She was embarking in midlife on what Rogers (1967) would have called the process of becoming, what Jung (1973) would have called the process of individuation, what Moody and Carroll (1997) would call 'the Struggle' and what, in spiritual language, we might refer to as the birthing of her soul. In the midst of this, she was also experiencing a profound longing for a deeper relationship with God. As a result of her childhood experiences, Rebecca's adult attachment style (Ainsworth 1985) was a fearful one. From a core self model perspective, this form of insecure attachment rests on a belief system in which the beliefs about both self and others are predominantly negative. This is a position that essentially says 'I am not OK and neither are you'. Her image of God (whom she had conceptualised as male) was largely shaped by aspects of her relationships with the significant men in her life and was one of a distant, unloving and controlling God who would not tolerate anything less than perfection. Her constant fear was that she would not be able to live up to God's expectations and that in the end, God would abandon her.

Her image of herself was similarly negative. She saw herself as inadequate, as not 'good enough for God' and because of this, as not worthy of his attention or love. Her adult attachment style was also reflected, therefore, in the nature of her relationship with God. From an Eriksonian point of view (Erikson 1968), her basic trust both in herself and others and therefore her capacity for intimacy were under–developed and this was impacting not only on her relationship with others, but also on her relationship with the transcendent.

In conclusion

It seems to me that in order to accompany Rebecca on her journey in a facilitative way – a journey in which the psychological and the spiritual are inextricably interwoven – it is necessary to attend to all of the dimensions of her being, including the spiritual. An understanding of the growth processes at work in her psychological journey needs to go hand in hand with a similar depth of understanding of the growth processes that were energising the movement in her spiritual life. We need a map of the journey of becoming that recognises that it is profoundly spiritual in nature, that it is not possible to separate the psychological and the spiritual and that to attempt to do so risks impeding a process that involves and affects us at every level of our being.

As we listen to people's spiritual stories, we may be able to identify aspects of their journeys that resonate with our own and to observe key themes and patterns that surface over and over again. Models can be helpful in enabling us to make sense of our experience and of the way in which our journey is unfolding, but they should not be allowed to direct the course that our journey takes. Every spiritual journey is unique and when we encounter another's spiritual journey, whether as therapists or spiritual companions, it is, I believe, best to come to it afresh and without presuppositions for more often than not, it will confound our expectations and surprise us. As Griffith and Griffith (2002: 49) put it, we need to adopt 'an intentional uncertainty about "what ought to be"…' in order to allow what is to emerge.

Chapter 5 notes

1. Buber (1958) distinguished between an 'I–It' and an 'I–Thou' relationship. In an 'I–It' relationship, the other is related to as an object to be analysed, contemplated, observed, reacted to or used. In an 'I–Thou' relationship, the other ceases to be an object and we are drawn into a deeper, more intimate relationship or communion between two 'thous'. Elkins (1998: 70 - 74) argues that such 'I–Thou' encounters 'touch the sacred'.

2. Momen (2009) defines mysticism as a religious orientation that emphasises both 'a direct intuitive knowledge' of the transcendent and the process of attaining union or unity with this ultimate spiritual reality.

6: Creating sacred space

I felt it shelter to speak to you.
Emily Dickinson 1891

Sally's story

Sally and I had been working together for some weeks. Together we had been exploring the impact on her of her parents' dysfunctional relationship which had often led them to be emotionally abusive and even physically violent towards each other in front of her when she was a young child. In the previous session, I had offered her the opportunity to do some creative work with stones and shells in order to help her explore her perceptions of and feelings about her relationships with her parents. She had found this very helpful in enabling her to access some of her deeper feelings about what she had experienced as a child and we had agreed to continue working in this way in the following session.

At the start of this session, she indicated that she wanted to continue working with the stones and shells. We had set aside those she had been using previously and she placed these on the table in front of her. I asked her how she would like to work with them today. For a short while, she sat silently looking at them and occasionally moving them around as if uncertain how to proceed. Then suddenly, she picked up a shell from the basket that I remembered her picking up but rejecting the week before. It was a beautifully shaped and coloured shell, but it had what looked like a large, ugly black growth attached to it.

She sat quietly fingering the shell for a few minutes and I noticed her eyes beginning to fill with tears. It felt important for me not to intrude in any way at this point so I said nothing. Then she picked up a sharp–edged, flat stone from the basket and began to chip away at the black growth. For the next half hour, she worked almost frantically at chipping away as much of the black growth as she could. She was crying most of the time. From time to time, she would look up and our eyes would meet for a few seconds. Neither of us said anything. At one point when she looked up, there were tears in my eyes too. She looked momentarily surprised but then held my gaze for longer this time. It was as if there was no need for either of us to say anything because we both knew and understood what was happening for her. The communication between us at such moments felt all the more powerful because it was wordless. Eventually, her sobbing began to subside and she stopped working at the shell. She looked at me again and smiled briefly through the tears. I felt an overwhelming urge to reach out to her so moved forwards and briefly rested my hand on hers. Then we both sat in silence for a few minutes before she began to talk about what had happened for her. This process was so profoundly important to her that she took the shell home with her in order to continue to restore it to its former shape and beauty. I believe it symbolised very powerfully for her the journey of becoming in which she was engaged.

What Sally needed in order to be able to grow through the pain she had experienced was not primarily my theoretical knowledge and understanding though there were times when I was able to use that understanding to enable her to make sense of her experiences in a different way. It was not primarily the skills I had developed as a therapist though they undoubtedly had a part to play in enabling me to convey my understanding of the world as she saw it. What she needed most of all was a relationship, a relationship between two people reaching out to each other as vulnerable human beings, a relationship in which she felt accepted and valued for who she is, a relationship in which she felt safe enough to risk being herself and facing her pain. She needed someone to be there with her in the darkness, in the confusion, in her fear and anger, in her despair. She needed to be met where she was and to be held as she allowed herself to experience and express the feelings that had been locked inside her for so long. She did not need my experience or my professionalism or my therapist persona; they would simply have 'got in the way'. She needed someone who was prepared to risk something of herself in the encounter. First and foremost, however, I believe she needed to feel loved.

Over the years, what I have learnt about therapy, both as therapist and client, has convinced me that it is, as Rogers (1957b) first asserted, the experience of a particular quality of relationship which is in itself therapeutic; that it is my 'way of being' as a therapist that is far more important than my 'way of doing'; that it is from the encounter between myself and my client as two human beings that the potential for growth and healing emerges. In other words, they have led me to believe that, 'The relationship is the therapy…' (Mearns and Thorne 2000: 85). If as a therapist I offer people my theoretical knowledge and understanding, I may at best enable them to analyse or make sense of their experience in a different way, to understand better why they feel or react the way they do. They may gain insight, become more self–aware, feel enlightened and that may in itself be experienced as helpful. If what I am offering people is no more than a blend of skills and techniques, I may at best facilitate their exploration of their frame of reference (or 'mental map') and communicate something of my understanding of it. I may enable them to become more aware of the way in which they make sense of their experience, to explore alternative perspectives, to identify possible solutions to the problems they face. And that too may be helpful to a degree.

The application of theory and techniques, however, does not in itself enable people to embrace the deeper levels of personality change that Rogers (1967) talked about. It does not in itself facilitate the process of 'becoming a person' that he described so powerfully – the move towards letting go of the masks we wear, of becoming more open to the full range of our own experiencing, of learning to trust what Rogers called our 'organismic' or true self and to rely on our own internal locus of evaluation. This is change at a profound level. It is a transforming experience. It is a liberating experience. It is about leaving behind aspects of what Laing (1977) called our 'first social identity'. In the context of our early experiences and relationships, 'We learn to be whom we are told we are' (Laing 1977: 95). In the process of becoming a person, we discover – or perhaps, more accurately recover – who we truly are. I believe that what enables people to embrace this process of 'relaxing into being' (Thorne 2003b: 6) is the experience of a relationship in which they feel safe enough to risk a real and meaningful encounter with the story they are living and ultimately, with themselves.

Therapy, moreover, is not just about embracing change and growth. It is often about finding emotional healing or as Benner (1990) describes it, 'recovering from past hurts'. Clients often come to therapy because they have been deeply wounded and are seeking release from the feelings of hurt and anger that threaten to overwhelm them. The application of theory and techniques does not in itself bring about the kind of emotional healing they seek. What they need is someone who is willing to share their pain, to be fully present with them as they face the depth and intensity of the feelings they fear, to sit with them in the darkest places in their innermost being. Cassidy (1988) calls this 'sharing the darkness.' Benner (1990) believes that it is only in relationship that we are able to experience fully the healing of such emotional wounds. Writing from a Christian perspective, he reflects on the biblical command to 'carry each other's burdens' (Galations 6: 2) and on the mysterious way in which the sharing of the burden does in itself seem to lighten the load.

Benner (1990) sees this willingness to share the other's pain as 'the essential curative core' of the therapeutic relationship. This certainly fits with my own personal experience. The most profoundly healing encounters I have had have indeed been encounters in which very little has been said by the listener; in which 'being' has been far more important than 'doing'; in which it has been my awareness of the other's presence with me at a profound level that has enabled me to find healing through facing and moving through the pain. They have been encounters in which I have experienced being met and held by the other's being as I have felt safe enough to allow painful feelings to surface and find expression.

Finally, at its deepest level when the client and I are working together with 'the raw material' of being (Elkins 1998), when therapy becomes what I would call 'soul work', I am seeking to create a space that is so profoundly safe that the soul – the very core of our being – can risk disclosing itself, can risk the intense vulnerability of being seen and known. This does not happen quickly or easily. Kirkpatrick (2005: 7) speaks of 'the sacred privilege of seeing others in the truth of their nakedness' and recognises the depth of courage needed by both therapist and client in order to make such an encounter possible. Enabling the client to enter into such a soul–to–soul encounter also involves, I believe, achieving a particular quality and depth of relationship which I would call the experience of soul love, a concept I will return to later.

As a core self therapist, the most fundamental assumption that I make about the process of both psychological and spiritual growth is that people begin to heal, change and grow when they are offered a particular quality of relationship, a relationship characterised by 'the core conditions' as they have come to be known (Rogers 1957b). I believe that it is this quality of relationship that is in itself both therapeutic (that is, having the power to heal – and maieutic – that is, having the power to facilitate change and growth (Clinebell 1984). It follows from this as Johns (1996: 3) argues that it is the therapist's self that is his or her 'principal tool/instrument.' What I bring to the counselling relationship of the person I am – what I experience, what I think, what I feel, how I react to the other – is far more important than any theoretical knowledge or understanding I may have or any skills or techniques I may have acquired.

In this chapter, I will begin by revisiting Rogers' original 'core conditions' hypothesis (Rogers 1957b) before moving on to articulate what I mean by the concept of soul love and the role I see it as it playing in both the therapeutic and maieutic process. It was in 1957 that Rogers published his landmark paper entitled 'The necessary and sufficient conditions of therapeutic personality change'. In this paper, he described six conditions which he believed must be present in any therapeutic relationship if constructive personality change is to take place (Rogers 1957b). I will briefly explore each of these in turn, reflecting on them from a core self model perspective.

In psychological contact

Firstly, Rogers (1957b) maintained that client and therapist must be in 'psychological contact' with each other. What he was arguing is that both client and therapist must be able to form what he called 'a minimal relationship' with each other. In other words, both client and therapist must to some degree be aware of and impacted by each other's presence, even if only at an unconscious level. When two people find themselves sharing the same space and make eye contact or verbal contact with each other, they are making a psychological connection with each other, however brief and minimal this may be. They are recognising each other's presence and communicating that awareness to each other. This is the most basic level of psychological contact. I prefer to use the term 'psychological connection' as I think it reflects more accurately the belief that what is needed is not only mutual awareness of each other but also the communication of some form of recognition of each other's presence. I would therefore want to expand and reword Rogers' first condition in the following way:

> Client and therapist experience at least to some degree a basic psychological connection with each other. Each is aware of and acknowledges the other's presence.

At a deeper level, however, making a psychological connection involves far more than simply communicating a recognition of the other's presence. It involves a willingness to be available to each other, to be receptive to each other, to be responsive to each other. It entails an openness to enter into a meaningful encounter with each other. At its deepest level – that which Cameron (2003) calls 'subtle contact' – it involves a readiness to move towards intimacy, towards a deeper, more profound level of relating to each other in which barriers are lowered, masks are removed, vulnerability is embraced and we become fully present to each other. There is no sense in this encounter of psychological distance, of holding each other at bay, of needing to defend ourselves from each other or from aspects of each other's experiencing. It is as if one soul reaches out and touches the soul of the other. Rogers (1980: 129) describes this as the meeting of two 'inner spirits.' I would call it a 'soul–to–soul connection', a meeting of two souls. When two people encounter each other at this level, a deeper level of healing and growth becomes possible.

The experience of incongruence

In stating this second condition, Rogers was arguing that for therapy to be effective, the client must be 'in a state of incongruence' with the result that he or she is aware of feelings of vulnerability or anxiety (Rogers 1957b: 222). How was he using the term 'incongruence' in this context? When we are in a state of incongruence, we are experiencing something that does not fit with one or more aspects of our self structure or belief system. If, for example, I do not see myself as a possessive person, but I become aware of experiencing possessive feelings in a particular situation, there is clearly a mismatch between what I am aware of in myself and what I believe to be true about myself. My perception of or assumptions about myself are being challenged by my experience and the awareness of this mismatch is to a degree unsettling or disturbing. It generates feelings of vulnerability or anxiety and motivates me to want to resolve this inner tension. Elkins (1998) speaks of the client not being 'anchored in her own being' and therefore experiencing a sense of disequilibrium.

Merry (1999) argued, however, that there may be another motivational factor that draws people into therapy. He believed that people whose level of vulnerability and anxiety is not high enough to create such an uncomfortable tension within themselves may sometimes choose to enter therapy simply because they value the process of self–discovery that it entails and believe that it will enrich their lives. This is a perspective I share and it certainly reflects my own reasons for entering therapy later in life. From a core self model perspective, I would also want to add that it is often the recognition of being out of touch with or disconnected from aspects of our core self that motivates us to seek further growth. Particularly in the second half of life, a decision to enter therapy can sometimes be made not because we are experiencing some form of psychological distress, but because we are responding to the subtle inner prompting of the actualising tendency which is always gently pushing us towards growth and becoming.

I would therefore want to expand and reword Rogers' second condition in the following way:

> The client is experiencing a degree of psychological tension, discomfort, pain or disequilibrium as a result of being in a state of incongruence and/or of disconnection from his or her core self. Alternatively, the client has come to recognise and value the benefits of being engaged in an ongoing process of personal growth and development.

Rogers (1957b) then moved on to describe three conditions which he believed must characterise the therapist's way of being and experiencing if constructive change is to occur. These have come to be known as 'the core conditions' – congruence, unconditional positive regard and empathy. [1]

The quality of congruence

In stating his third condition, Rogers (1957b: 223 – 4) argued that in order to be perceived as trustworthy and dependable, the therapist must be 'a congruent, genuine, integrated person' within the counselling relationship.

When we are being congruent, we are able to be authentic, real and natural in our relationship with the client. We are not distant or emotionally detached. We are not hiding behind a defensive mask or putting on a polite front or hiding behind a professional role. We are 'at home' in ourselves, comfortable 'in our own skin', capable of being fully and freely all that we are in each moment. We are in touch with all aspects of our own experiencing, whether positive or negative. We are fully acceptant of and therefore open to the flow of the perceptions, attitudes and feelings we are aware of in ourselves as we interact with the client and where therapeutically beneficial, we are willing to express them. It is very clear from this that what Rogers was describing is essentially a way of being in relationship.

I agree with Lietaer (2001) when he argues that it is clear from Rogers' definition of congruence that it has two dimensions, both an inner and outer dimension. The inner dimension for which Lietaer uses the term 'congruence' relates to our capacity as therapists to access the full flow of our own experiencing. The outer dimension refers to our willingness, if appropriate, to express or communicate aspects of ourselves – our perceptions, attitudes or feelings – to the client, whether verbally or non–verbally. Lietaer calls this outer aspect 'transparency', a word that Rogers himself also used. Brazier (1993 cited in Wyatt 2001) makes a similar distinction between what he calls 'implicit congruence' – that is, awareness of therapist experience that is not explicitly communicated to the client – and 'explicit congruence' where this awareness of experience is explicitly expressed in the relationship. Mearns and Cooper (2005: 128) develop the concept of explicit congruence even further. They draw a parallel between this aspect of congruence and Bugental's (1976) concept of 'expressivity'. They argue that this involves the willingness of therapists to make some aspects of themselves known to the client, to share with the client openly and honestly some of who they are and some of the facets of their own experiencing. This requires, as they see it, a willingness to 'reach out' to the other.

McMillan (2004) points out that the quality of being real, genuine and without façade that Rogers spoke of is only meaningful in the context of a relationship. He argues too that it does not make sense that Rogers intended the counsellor to be in a state of congruence of which the client may be totally unaware. This is a perspective I share. Rogers himself repeatedly referred to the willingness of the therapist to express attitudes and feelings, both through words and behaviour, where appropriate (for example, Rogers 1966, 1967, 1980). Furthermore, in his later writings, he extended the third and sixth conditions of his hypothesis further through arguing that the therapist's congruence must be communicated to and perceived by the client, at least to a minimal degree (Rogers 1967, 1973; Rogers and Sanford 1984).

Lietaer (2001) points out that it is possible to be both congruent and at the same time, minimally transparent within a relationship. My experience of being in therapy, albeit briefly, with a psychodynamic therapist was that she was indeed minimally transparent within our relationship. I saw her as professionally distant and impassive. She showed little if any sign of emotion, even when I was at one point in considerable emotional distress. Neither did she disclose anything of her own experience to me at any point in the process, either verbally or non-verbally. I perceived her as withholding her self from our encounter and consequently, found her very 'difficult to read'. I had little sense of being met by another genuine human being. It is entirely possible that this therapist was inwardly fully congruent within our relationship – in other words, that she was open to and aware of the full range of her experiencing. It is also possible that internally, she was experiencing both unconditional positive regard and empathy for me. However, because she was not sufficiently transparent within the relationship, I had no way of knowing or sensing whether these three fundamental qualities were present or not. The core conditions were neither communicated to me nor perceived by me and therefore Rogers' sixth condition was not met. I did not feel at any point, as Rogers (1967) put it, 'fully received'. Consequently, at times I felt unsafe and became increasingly aware that I was withholding the more vulnerable parts of myself from the therapist. Within a relatively short time, I withdrew from the relationship.

The quality of unconditional positive regard

In this fourth condition, Rogers (1957b: 225) argued that the therapist must experience a degree of unconditional acceptance and prizing of each aspect of the client's being and must feel a warmth and caring for the person which is non–possessive and respectful of the separateness of that person. The term 'unconditional positive regard' was first introduced by Standal (1954) and then adopted by Rogers shortly afterwards. A number of other words and phrases have also been used to capture something of this quality. Rogers himself spoke of 'respect', 'acceptance', 'liking that is not conditional', 'a total prizing' and 'a non–possessive caring'. Others have used such alternative terminology as 'consistent valuing' (Mearns and Thorne 1999), 'unconditional acceptance' (Schmid 2001a), 'openness towards the other' (Lietaer 1984) and 'non–possessive warmth' (Lietaer 2001).

Writing from the perspective of what he calls 'encounter philosophy', Schmid (2001a: 50 – 51) uses the term 'acknowledgment'. Acknowledging the other, as he sees it, goes far beyond simply being aware of them. It involves both a deeper appreciation and valuing of the essence of the other as a 'precious' being of worth and dignity and a willingness to be 'open for' the other in the uniqueness of his or her being. He makes it clear that unconditionality lies at the heart of this therapeutic quality and that it is, '...an active and proactive way of deliberately saying yes to the Other as a person.'

It is clear from this that offering the client unconditional positive regard involves far more than a surface–level acceptance which essentially says, 'Whoever you are is alright with me.' I find myself, as others have done, wanting to qualify such words as acceptance, valuing or prizing by using adjectives such as 'fundamental', 'deep', 'complete' or 'total' in order to capture their meaning in this context more fully. What makes it possible for us to hold such an attitude towards our clients? Schmid (2001a) believes that our capacity to do so rests on and is an expression of our fundamental trust in the other and in the actualising tendency. I agree but I believe it also reflects and expresses the person–centred assumption that the innermost core or essence of our human nature is positive.

What has struck me forcibly about Rogers' (1967) description of the continuum of personality change is how central acceptance is to the process, not only the therapist's acceptance of the client, but also the client's acceptance of him– or herself. We cannot allow ourselves to experience fully or express to others what we cannot accept in ourselves. To risk doing so also risks the rejection we most fear. We cannot open ourselves up to the possibility that we may have perceived things inaccurately in the past or have made the wrong assumptions if we cannot accept our own limitations and growing edges. We cannot accept the measure of responsibility we bear for the problems we are experiencing if we judge ourselves harshly for the mistakes and poor choices we may have made in the past. It seems to me that at the heart of this process of change and growth lies our capacity for compassionate self–acceptance. And if that is true, then the compassionate and loving acceptance of all that we are by the therapist must also be central to the process of change. Paradoxically, acceptance is the beginning of change.

If I were to reword Rogers' fourth condition, I would substitute the words 'acceptance' or 'positive regard' with the word 'love' in the following way:

> The therapist experiences a degree of unconditional love for the client.

This is because I believe the term 'unconditional love' captures much more fully the experience Rogers and others have tried to describe. I am of course not the first person to talk about the importance of love in therapy. Indeed in his earlier writings, Rogers himself used the word 'love' on occasion when talking about therapy and was one of the first people to do so (for example, Rogers 1956 cited in Kirschenbaum and Henderson 1990a). Indeed, Kahn (1997: 39) argues that while Rogers seldom acknowledged it openly, what he was describing was essentially 'a therapy of love'.

Thorne (1991) points out that there is very little reference to the concept of therapeutic love in the large body of professional literature on counselling and psychotherapy. This is an observation also echoed by Peck (1990: 186) who ventures the opinion that therapists seem to be 'embarrassed by the subject of love'. Peck goes on to suggest a number of reasons as to why this might be so, attributing it amongst other things to our tendency to confuse romantic and 'genuine' love; the marked emphasis on what can be readily observed and measured in scientific disciplines such as psychotherapy; and the strong tradition in the psychoanalytic approach of the distant, emotionally detached therapist – the so–called 'blank screen' – who views any feelings of love towards the client as part of the problem rather than part of the solution.

Given the potential danger to a therapist's professional reputation of voicing beliefs that are deemed to be unscientific and untestable and to have no place in rigorous scientific analysis, I have found it heartening and somewhat surprising in researching this book to discover how often prominent and experienced theoreticians and practitioners in the field have been willing to testify to the therapeutic value of love. A number of other person–centred writers such as Patterson (1974), Thorne (1991), Schmid (2001a) and Hawkins (2010) have allowed themselves to draw on the word 'love' in their writings. For example, Thorne (1991: 180) maintains that when we are able to offer clients the kind of therapeutic relationship that Rogers described, essentially what we are offering them is an experience of being loved. Hawkins (2010: 24) speaks similarly of love being 'the root and heart of the therapeutic endeavour'.

It is, furthermore, not only person–centred therapists who do so. For example, the psychoanalyst Ferenczi claimed that love is the 'indispensable healing power' in therapy (Ferenczi 1956 cited in Halmos 1965: 49). Peck (1990: 187) believes that if therapy is to be effective in bringing about healing and growth, 'it is essential for the therapist to love a patient'. Yalom (1991: 227) emphasises the importance of being 'lovingly present' and makes reference to the power of 'psychotherapeutic eros'. Elkins (1998: 176) sees love as being 'the most powerful healer of the wounded soul' and Wosket (1999: 41) believes that her ability as a therapist rests on her 'capacity to love.'

The quality of empathy

In this fifth condition, Rogers (1957b) argued that therapists must experience and be able to communicate to a degree an accurate, empathic understanding of the client's unique way of perceiving reality. They must possess the capacity to enter into the client's own private world, to 'walk in the other's moccasins' as Native American Indians might say. They must be able to see the other's world as if it were their own and to arrive at an accurate sensing of the other's feelings and meanings in the moment.

It is very clear from this that in responding empathically to the client, therapists are more concerned with understanding clients' internal frames of reference – that is, their particular way of perceiving themselves and their experience – rather than with their own perspective or frame of reference. At the same time, it is, however, vital as Rogers (1959) points out that the therapist does not become 'lost' in or overwhelmed by the client's frame of reference. In empathising with the client, therefore, the therapist must always maintain what he called the 'as if' condition. Schmid (2001b) argues that this 'as if' quality is crucial because it distinguishes empathy from identification – that is, failing to hold the boundaries between self and other, feeling in the same way as the other feels and 'dissolving' or become 'wrapped up' in the other's emotions. It also distinguishes it from 'interpretation' by which Schmid means the judging, evaluating or analysing of the other's self and experience and consequent 'objectifying' of the other.

It is also apparent that empathy involves far more than the use of one or more techniques or communication skills such as paraphrasing or reflecting. It is quite possible to be a competent technician – that is, to be able to make what Mearns and Thorne (1999) call 'stock reflective responses' competently – without necessarily being empathic. They argue that empathy cannot be fully encapsulated in one single empathic response or even a series of such responses, that it is an ongoing process of 'being with' the client (p. 39). Rogers (1980) expressed a similar viewpoint when he argued that empathy is a 'way of being' – or more accurately as Schmid (2001b) points out 'a way of being with' – rather than a listening technique. I agree for it seems to me that our capacity to empathise rests on an implicit valuing of the uniqueness and legitimacy of each other's being and experiencing, on a recognition of and deep respect for our essential 'otherness'. It rests also on both a desire and a willingness to cross the distance between us, to 'bridge the gap', as Schmid (2001b: 62) puts it, between our respective inner worlds.

The sixth condition

Lastly, Rogers (1957b) argued, it is not enough for the therapist to be congruent in the relationship and to experience acceptance of and empathy with the client. The client must also be able to perceive what the therapist is endeavouring to communicate, at least some degree. In other words, these aspects of the therapist's experiencing have to be communicated effectively to the client.

In relation to this final condition, Rogers' initial formulation of it makes reference to 'achieving the communication' of the core conditions at least to some degree. I have reworded it in the following way:

> The client perceives, at least to a minimal degree, the therapist's unconditional love, congruence and empathic understanding.

This reflects the fact that it is the client's experience and perception of the therapist's ability to live the core conditions in his or her way of being that is of fundamental importance here. I am not speaking here of communication skills. I am speaking of a way of being self and of being with others which is shaped by the depth of my desire and commitment to embrace the three core conditions as fully as I am able and to live them out in all areas of my life.

In re-stating Rogers' core conditions hypothesis, I have also changed the order in which the three core conditions are stated, placing unconditional love before congruence and empathy. In so doing, I am in effect identifying unconditional love as the primary therapeutic agent. What then of the other two therapeutic conditions – empathy and congruence? Am I downplaying the significance of these two other core conditions or failing to acknowledge the inter–relationship between the three? I believe not. The core conditions of empathy and congruence are, I think, of fundamental importance to the process of constructive change. Not only do they play their own part in the process, but as Wilkins (2001) points out, they also 'provide the context' in which the therapist's love becomes believable. In other words, it is the experience of the therapist's empathy and congruence that enables the client to begin to receive and trust the unconditional love that is being communicated. Mearns and Thorne (2000: 86) argue that it is not possible to separate out the three core conditions of congruence, empathy and unconditional positive regard, that it is 'in their dance, in their intricate interweaving', that their full therapeutic power lies. I agree, and yet at the same time, it is my contention that it is the experience of unconditional love that is of primary importance in this therapeutic triad.

To what extent has Rogers' core conditions hypothesis been borne out by the research conducted so far? It is beyond the scope of this book to provide a detailed analysis of the relevant research findings but what seems clear from Cooper's (2008) comprehensive overview of the current state of research is that, as Rogers predicted, the quality of the therapeutic relationship is closely associated with therapeutic effectiveness. This is true not only for relationally–oriented approaches such as person–centred therapy, but also for those that have traditionally placed less emphasis on the quality of the therapeutic relationship such as cognitive–behavioural therapy. The research also indicates that therapists' ability to communicate the core conditions effectively is closely associated with positive therapeutic outcomes and that relational factors are more important than therapeutic techniques in determining the outcomes of therapy (Cooper 2008). As Cooper puts it, the facts do indeed appear to be friendly.

In what specific ways, however, does the experience of a therapeutic relationship bring about psychological growth and change? In other words, what are the actual mechanisms of the change process?

The role of the actualising tendency

To 'live deep' (Thoreau 1995) is to become and at the heart of this process lies what Rogers (1951) calls 'the actualising tendency' or, using spiritual terminology, what I would call the spirit. Understanding the process of change begins then with understanding the role the actualising tendency plays in bringing it about.

Rogers (1951) argued that the actualising tendency is the only force on which the therapist can ultimately depend and that the source of positive change and growth lies in the actualising tendency itself. Indeed, this reliance forms the basis of the therapist's fundamental trust in the client's own internal resources for growth. This capacity is released – that is, it becomes actual rather than potential – in what Rogers called 'a suitable psychological climate'. The experience of such a suitable relational climate, it seems, leads us to discover within ourselves the capacity to draw on what it offers us in order to move towards growth. Merry (1999) talks of such therapeutic relationships 'promoting' the actualising tendency and enabling it 'to find expression'.

As we have seen, however, if the individual's psychological climate has not been sufficiently nurturing, the actualising tendency may become constricted. Barrett–Lennard (1998: 75) argues that the actualising tendency needs both 'a tolerant environment and essential nutrients' – both physical and psychological – in order for it to function optimally. If the individual's psychological environment is in some way inadequate or hostile, the actualising tendency continues to operate but can as a result become deeply buried under layers of defences, hidden behind façades or in some way warped and distorted.

The role of the therapist

Like Rogers, May (1958) also saw therapy as a creative process which is primarily concerned with facilitating that which is emerging or becoming within us. He argued that our natural state as human beings is one of being involved in an ongoing process of becoming and that problems in living arise when this natural process becomes blocked or inhibited.

Wilkins (2003: 75) refers to the actualising tendency as 'the actual agent of change' and to the therapeutic relationship as 'the active facilitator' of change. This is, I think, a helpful distinction to make. The task of the therapist then is to create positive movement in the client's psychological environment (Thorne 1991), to create a different psychological 'climate' in which the client can begin to rediscover the person he or she actually is (Mearns and Thorne 1999). Merry (1999) drew a direct parallel between the work of the therapist and the work of a gardener. Both, he argued, are concerned with creating the right conditions for growth and development. Using the analogy of the growth of a plant, all plants need certain resources (water, light and nutrients) to grow and fulfil their potential. If they are partially deprived of these resources as they are developing, their growth will at best be stunted. The good gardener attempts to create the conditions in which the plant's inherent capacity for growth can be fully realised. However, it is the plant's inborn capacity for growth that is the source of the growth. Similarly, the therapist attempts to offer clients the resources they need for growth, to create those conditions in which the actualising tendency can operate freely and without distortion. Clinebell (1979) offered an alternative image of the counsellor as a liberator who enables people to find the freedom to be themselves and to live life to the full. Writing from a Christian perspective, he saw counsellors as 'co–creators of wholeness' who essentially co–operate or align themselves with the work of the spirit in bringing about growth and change (Clinebell 1984).

Writing also from a spiritual perspective, Elkins (1998: 184 – 9) draws on the image of the therapist as midwife in his exploration of the process of therapeutic change. The therapist, he argues, acts as a midwife 'to the new self that is trying to be born' (p. 189). He believes that the experience of a therapeutic relationship characterised by the core conditions sets in motion the ontological process of becoming. Indeed he views the core conditions themselves as ontological, as having to do with being. He argues that at a deeper level, empathy is not just a matter of entering into the world of the other as he or she experiences it and attempting to see things from within their frame of reference. It is essentially a process of attuning ourselves to the other's innermost being. As we do so, their core self – the essence of who they really are – begins to emerge. Similarly, he believes that the experience of being unconditionally accepted also facilitates this process of becoming. It is when we feel accepted just as we are in that moment, that we find the freedom to change and grow. This is, as Elkins (1998: 184) recognises, a paradox which he believes to be in itself 'an ontological dynamic'. Finally, Elkins (1998) points out that congruence is also ontological in nature. When as therapists we are being fully congruent and transparent in the therapeutic relationship, the client's emerging being will inevitably 'resonate and respond', no matter how disconnected the client may be from this core self (p. 185).

The impact of the therapeutic relationship

Drawing both on his own clinical experience and on research, Rogers (1959, 1980) outlined a number of specific ways in which he saw the therapeutic relationship – and particularly, the experience of empathy – as bringing about growth and change.

Firstly, it dissolves feelings of alienation and isolation from others. When someone empathises with us, we feel understood. We see ourselves and our world as 'making sense' to someone else and consequently, we no longer feel so estranged from others or so alone. Even if only temporarily, we find ourselves feeling deeply connected with another human being. Secondly, it helps to strengthen our sense of our own personhood or identity. Laing (1965: 139) argued that the development of a sense of identity 'requires the existence of another by whom one is known.' Similarly, Buber (1951) spoke of our human need 'to be confirmed' by another as who we are and who we have the potential to become. Empathy, Rogers (1980) argued, provides that confirmation. When someone empathises with us, they recognise and honour our existence, our dignity, our individuality and our uniqueness. They are conveying to us that our story matters, that what is important to us matters, that we matter. They are as Kirkpatrick (2005) puts it 'mattering' us which in time enables us to matter to ourselves. They are in a powerful way affirming our selfhood.

Thirdly, the experience of empathy enables us to feel unconditionally accepted, valued and cared for and eventually to begin to accept, value and care for ourselves. There is clearly a strong link here between the impact of empathic understanding and of unconditional positive regard. Rogers (1980) argues that it is not possible to empathise fully and accurately with another's inner world unless you are able to encounter that person and their world without evaluating and judging them. It is not possible unless you are able to accept and value that person and their experience, and unless 'you, in some sense, care' (p. 152). True empathy, he said, is 'always free of any evaluative or diagnostic quality' (p. 154). The experience of such empathy enables us to feel unconditionally accepted rather than judged or evaluated and thereby increases the level of our own self–acceptance – and I would add, self–love.

Fourthly, the experience of empathy enables us both to access and explore a wider range of our experiencing in an uninhibited way and to risk revealing that experience to another. As we experience another's understanding, we become more able to listen accurately to and empathise with ourselves, and particularly to listen to our 'visceral experiencing' (in other words, our 'gut sense') and to our 'vaguely felt meanings' (Rogers 1980: 159). Our experience has in a sense been validated by the other's empathy. Our openness to the richness and complexity of our own experience gradually increases and we become less likely to defend ourselves against those aspects of our experience that may be confusing, unsettling or even threatening or that we may view as in some way unacceptable. This inevitably increases the level of our self–awareness and our self–reflective capacity. It also enables us, I believe, to begin to move towards processing our experience with a kind of non–judgemental curiosity. Rogers (1980) spoke of this eventually freeing the full flow of our experiencing. Furthermore, the experience of empathy also encourages us to take the risk of sharing what we are discovering about ourselves with the other as the fear of being misunderstood or rejected gradually dissolves. It therefore increases both self–exploration and self–disclosure. As a result of our willingness to be more open and vulnerable with each other, our feelings of isolation and alienation are further lessened and our capacity for intimacy is released.

Fifthly, it enables us to experience a wider range of our feelings (including those that have been in the past either denied or distorted in our awareness) and to express them more freely, both verbally and nonverbally. As the feelings we are able to risk expressing are received with empathy and acceptance, others that we would previously have found too threatening or unacceptable are gradually allowed into awareness. Slowly, we become more able to risk the expression and sharing of these more difficult feelings as our trust in the other's ability to receive and hold them continues to grow. More of the feelings we express, moreover, are about ourselves or aspects of our experience rather than about others and their experience.

In addition, empathy enables us to perceive ourselves, others, our environment and our experiences more accurately and in a more differentiated way. What Rogers (1980) is saying here is that it enables us to be more aware of the richness and complexity of our experience and 'to symbolise' it more accurately. Our perceptions become more realistic and more objective. We also become more concerned with seeking what he called 'exactness of symbolisation' – in other words, with finding exactly the right words to capture our personal meanings.

Empathy also enables us to become more aware of the incongruity between certain aspects of our experience and our belief system and to tolerate the anxiety this generates. As our openness to our own experiencing increases and as we become more accepting of it, so does our awareness of the incongruence between some elements of our experience and our existing perceptions and beliefs. The therapeutic process itself often temporarily increases the level of incongruence the client is experiencing and thereby results initially in an increase in anxiety levels and defensiveness. In a sense, the existing belief system is 'under threat' from the therapeutic relationship and its impact may at first be strongly resisted. The more distorted the belief system is, the stronger the resistance is likely to be. Rogers (1959: 240) argued, however, that where such threats are empathically understood in the context of an accepting environment in which we experience the therapist's unconditional positive regard, we become in effect more able to tolerate the anxiety this process generates without resorting to defensive strategies.

Furthermore, the experience of empathy enables us to develop a greater trust in our own locus of evaluation and organismic valuing process. As we experience another's acceptance and empathic understanding of our experience and their consistent trust in our own internal resources, so our trust in our own capacity to evaluate our experience grows. We become more able to respond to our experience on the basis of our own organismic valuing process and to have faith in our ability to make judgements and decisions that are right for us. I believe that the experience of the therapeutic relationship also enables us to become aware of the extent to which our current belief system has been internalised from others and of the extent to which we have been dependent on their evaluations rather than our own. It also enables us to take the risk of beginning to question the evaluations of others where these do not fit with our own. This then makes it possible for our belief system to begin to reorganise as it starts to assimilate those aspects of our experience which we have previously defended against. It is as we begin to admit previously denied or distorted experience into our conscious awareness and to trust our own locus of evaluation that our existing belief system gradually begins to re–structure in order to take into account this new information. The new structure that emerges, moreover, is likely to be increasingly congruent with our experience as we deny less of that experience to our awareness. In other words, as we become less judgemental of our own experience, it becomes less threatening to us and we become correspondingly less defensive. I would also want to add that the experience of a therapeutic relationship enables us to become aware of those life strategies we have been using which are not constructive or which inhibit growth and to understand how these were (and perhaps still are) working for us. Such awareness and understanding is, I believe, the beginning of behavioural change.

What is interesting about Rogers' (1959) account of the way in which change occurs in the therapeutic process is that there is no reference to the impact of the therapist's congruence on the client. The emphasis here is clearly on the importance of unconditional positive regard and empathy. It is very clear, however, that that the therapist's capacity to be congruent became more important to Rogers later in his professional development (Rogers 1973, 1974). As we have seen, it was also around this time that he amended his statement of the core conditions hypothesis by adding the condition that the counsellor's congruence must also be communicated to the client, at least to a minimal degree (Rogers 1973). Later he also argued that 'in the ordinary interactions of life' – that is, between partners, friends, colleagues, teachers and students – congruence may be the most important quality in that it enables us to begin to relate to each other in 'a climate of realness' (Rogers 1980: 160).

I believe that the communication of the therapist's congruence to the client is also of fundamental importance to the process of therapeutic change. Firstly, it is important in its own right because by being both congruent and transparent in the relationship, the therapist is effectively creating that 'climate of realness' of which Rogers spoke. He or she is effectively modelling an authentic way of being which invites the client to risk more of his or her own authentic being in the encounter. Indeed, Rogers (1967: 167) observed that as therapy progresses, there is in the client a gradual movement 'away from façades', a growing tendency – albeit cautious and tentative at first – 'to move away…from a self that he is not.'

Secondly, along with empathy, it enables the client to receive and trust the unconditional positive regard the therapist is communicating. Like both Bozarth (1998) and Wilkins (2000, 2003), I would argue that what Rogers called unconditional positive regard and what I would call unconditional love is the most powerful core condition in the therapeutic process. However, both empathy and congruence play a vital role in enabling the client to receive and trust this love in a way that might not otherwise be possible.

Rogers (1959: 249) maintained that in order for unconditional positive regard to be effectively communicated, 'it must exist in a context of empathic understanding'. Like Wilkins (2000), I would, however, want to argue that in order for unconditional positive regard to be fully experienced by the client, it must also exist in a context of congruence.

Each of the core conditions is then important in its own right. Each has its own specific role to play in the therapeutic process. However, I believe, as do Mearns and Thorne (2000) and Mearns and Cooper (2005), that their therapeutic potency lies in their 'mutually enhancing integration', in the way in which they operate together to create a relational climate of incredible safety.

Beyond 'the core conditions hypothesis'

Just over twenty years after he first articulated what has come to be known as 'the core conditions hypothesis', we find Rogers (1980: 129 – 30) making reference for the first time to the concept of therapeutic presence in seeking to describe some of his experiences, both as a therapist and as a group facilitator. He had come to recognise that there were times when something qualitatively different seemed to happen in his encounters with others. It seemed to him that at such times, it was his 'presence' itself that was therapeutic for the client. In these moments, he felt himself to be in a slightly different state of consciousness and to be in closer touch with a deeper, more intuitive part of himself. At times, he also had a sense of his 'inner spirit' connecting with the inner spirit of the client. Rogers was clearly speaking here of experiences which he believed to be spiritual in nature. Presence as he described it is fundamentally a transcendental phenomenon, a reaching beyond self and other in relationship 'to become part of something larger.' Indeed, he goes on to describe these experiences as spiritual and mystical.

Writing some ten years later, Thorne (1991) corroborated Roger's experience of these moments of presence through his description of 'the quality of tenderness'. He described tenderness as 'a state of being' during which his awareness seemed sharper and his understanding of the client deeper and more intuitive. At such times, he would experience a strong sense of aliveness and well–being, of 'physical vibrancy', of being profoundly energised, both physically and sometimes sexually. There were often intense feelings of joy and of being caught up in a 'stream of love'. In his later writings, he uses the phrase 'quality of presence' and calls such experiences 'magic moments' (Thorne 1998: 46).

Thorne (1991) makes it clear that he is not suggesting that he now sees Rogers' three core conditions as necessary but insufficient or that this

162

fourth quality needs to be added to them in order to enhance their effectiveness. What he suggests is that where this quality of tenderness is present in the encounter between two people, 'something qualitatively different may occur' (Thorne 1991: 74). There is in these moments, he believes, the potential for reaching a greater wholeness of being and of recognising what he calls 'the liberating paradox'. He describes the ability to grasp this paradox as the ability to embrace the world of 'both–and' rather than the world of 'either–or'. In other words, as a result of this experience, we become capable of living with the paradoxes within our being – for example, the fact that we are both strong and weak, that we feel both love and hate. We also come to recognise that they are 'not contradictory, but complementary, not paralyzing but releasing.' (p. 78). This is ultimately, I think, about reaching, however momentarily, a place of utter self– and other–acceptance and a recognition of the incredible beauty of the human soul.

Thorne believes that if both client and therapist are able to trust 'the working of tenderness', the experience of it can lead to a number of things happening – for example, a sudden release of emotion, an overwhelming need for physical contact or a desire to speak about things of the spirit. Furthermore, his experience is that it invariably results in significant changes in the client's self–perception and can also lead to marked changes in attitudes and behaviour.

Both Rogers and Thorne seem to be describing the same phenomenon as Mearns (1996) does when he talks about the experience of 'relational depth'. Mearns and Cooper (2005: xii) define the term 'relational depth' as 'a state of profound contact and engagement between two people, in which each person is fully real with the Other, and able to understand and value the Other's experiences at a high level.' For me, there is something missing from this definition and I want to offer a slightly broader one which emphasises the important of unconditional positive regard more fully. I believe relational depth to be a level of profound connection and engagement between two people within which moments of particularly heightened and intense inter–connectedness may occur. In such a relationship, each person is able to be fully real and transparent with the other and to experience and communicate both a high level of understanding and valuing of the other's experience and a deep unconditional acceptance of and love for the totality of the other's being.

Again, I prefer to draw on the word 'connection' rather than 'contact' because I believe it captures the quality of the experience more accurately. It stresses both the mutuality of the experience and the sense of oneness that is often experienced in such moments. This definition also acknowledges, as do

Mearns and Cooper (2005), that the term 'relational depth' can be used to refer both to a particular quality of relationship – an enduring sense of deep connectedness between two people – or to specific moments of in–depth encounter between two people. My assumption is that such 'magic moments' as Thorne (1991) describes them are much more likely to occur in the context of a relationship which both parties would describe as relationally deep. What has struck me about such experiences is the affinity they seem to have with Maslow's description of peak experiences (Maslow 1962) and with James' description of mystical experiences (James 1985). Consequently, I wonder whether they might usefully be thought of as relational peak experiences.

I too have experienced such moments of presence and tenderness, both in my work with students and clients and in the context of other close personal relationships. I can, furthermore, identify strongly with all of what Rogers, Thorne and others have described. The experience does feel to me to be a profoundly spiritual one. It is also a very beautiful one. There is a strong sense of 'treading on holy ground', of having entered a sacred space, of a deep connectedness with both the other and with the Divine. Such moments feel somehow timeless and are often wordless. The quality of our relating does feel both intense and intimate and I too often find myself feeling moved to tears or laughter. There is a strong feeling of being fully at peace and 'at home' in myself and an ability to respond spontaneously and intuitively to the other which seems to flow from the innermost part of myself. Often, there is a deep longing for physical contact which I am learning to trust and not to be afraid of. I find myself feeling unusually alive, energised and spiritually uplifted. Finally, the love that I experience in those moments does indeed feel infinitely tender.

Writing from a psychoanalytical perspective, Stern (2004) describes such encounters as 'moments of meeting' and speaks of 'a 'mutual interpenetration of minds'. Buber (1958) would be more likely to talk in terms of 'I–Thou meetings' or 'genuine dialogue'. This 'I–Thou' relationship involves an opening up to and loving affirmation of the other's being. It involves my meeting the other as they actually are in the moment rather than as I have assumed or imagined them to be. It is an unpredictable and therefore risky encounter into which I am required to enter fully and vulnerably.

Cooper (2005) conducted a qualitative research study into therapists' experiences of relational depth. His participants characterised such encounters with their clients in a number of ways. They described themselves as experiencing high levels of empathy (often in the form of embodied empathy) and greater perceptual clarity; high levels of congruence – a sense of being there for the other as a person, of acting more intuitively and spontaneously and of bringing more of self into the encounter; a deeper acceptance and prizing of the client (sometimes described as love); a feeling of being totally immersed in the work, free from distractions, and deeply engaged with the client; 'a lightness of being'; feelings of being fully alive, energised, excited and stimulated; feeling deeply moved, touched or impacted by the client; feelings of profound connection, closeness, intimacy or togetherness which are often wordless; high levels of mutuality in the relationship and a strong sense of 'co–openness', 'co–transparency' and 'co–acceptance'; feelings of awe and wonder at the beauty of the other's being; and changes in perception of time. There is clearly a high degree of overlap between these varying therapeutic perspectives on the experience of relational depth. Rogers, Thorne, Mearns, Cooper and others, appear to be talking about the same phenomenon. What then of the client's perspective?

A small research study carried out by Knox (2008) suggests that clients may experience something very similar. They spoke of feeling profoundly safe and held even when feeling intensely vulnerable; of feeling genuinely accepted and cared for; and of feeling known and completely understood, as well as or better than they knew themselves. They described an awareness of being very open with the therapist and of both therapist and client being unusually aware of each other's thoughts and feelings. They also talked of experiencing the therapist differently and of seeing the therapist as offering something more than they would have expected from a professional relationship. They felt trusted by the therapist and used such words as 'real', 'warm', 'solid', 'fearless', 'trustworthy' and 'present' to articulate their perception of the therapist at such times. They spoke of being responded to in a human, compassionate way from the core of the therapist's being and of experiencing the relationship as deeper or 'on a different level'. They used words such as 'special', 'rare', 'meaningful', 'dynamic' and 'intense' to capture the quality of their meeting or encounter with the therapist at such times and saw these encounters as 'having their own energy'. They also described a feeling of mutuality and equality – a lack of power differential between client and therapist – and a sense of what Knox calls a 'bi–directional flow' between them.

When asked by Knox to describe the impact of such experiences of relational depth, moreover, clients described the experiences as powerful, memorable, meaningful, facilitative, enabling and healing. They spoke of them as 'moments of change' or 'catalysts for change', either in themselves or in the therapeutic relationship. In relation to changes in themselves, they described becoming more open and able to share and verbalise their innermost feelings. They felt more validated in themselves and more connected with themselves. They spoke of feeling more real, more solid, more human and more whole.

They also experienced themselves afterwards as feeling more alive, more energised, more at ease and more positive. Their sense of self–worth increased as did their self–confidence and they reported improved relationships with others.

The experiences of therapists like Rogers, Mearns, Cooper and Thorne and the recent research findings of Cooper, Knox and others (Knox et al 2012)[2] fit very well with my own personal experiences of meetings at relational depth, both within and outside the context of the therapeutic relationship. As part of drawing our relationship to a close, I often ask clients to identify what they regard as the most important and helpful aspects of our relationship and our work together. Where I perceive our relationship to have been one of relational depth, the client invariably describes it similarly and highlights exactly the same 'moments of meeting' that I would also have identified as being particularly significant.

Research into the experience of relational depth is still in the early stages and such findings will need to be replicated with larger and more representative groups of clients and therapists. There are also many unanswered questions. For example, are the changes reported temporary or lasting changes? What kind of impact do such experiences have on the ending of the relationship? Might it be much harder for clients to let go of such relationships, particularly where there are no other relationships in their lives in which they experience such a depth of connectedness with others?

What is becoming clear, however, is that both therapists and clients who experience such encounters of relational depth view them as highly significant and therapeutic. Such experiences generally stay with them and are often seen as 'something to hold on to'. Mearns and Thorne (2000) talk of such relationships and moments as offering the client 'something really special'. I believe that, in part at least, this 'something really special' is a particular kind of love that I have come to think of as soul love.

From relational depth to soul love

What kind of love am I talking about when I use the term 'soul love'? I would argue that the experience of presence, of tenderness, of relational depth that Rogers, Mearns and Thorne and others have talked about flows out of a particular quality and depth of loving. This kind of love has, I believe, a number of special characteristics which set it apart from other forms of love.

Agape love

Soul love is first and foremost a profoundly unconditional and unselfish form of love which, both in early Greek philosophy and in the Jewish–Christian spiritual tradition, is known as 'agape love'. Greek philosophy distinguished between four kinds of love – storge (the natural affection that exists, for example, between family members); philia (the bond of love that exists between friends); eros (passionate, sensual and sexual love); and agape (a non–possessive, unconditional and self-transcending love that is deeply committed to the growth and fulfilment of the other). Agape is a love that is self–giving rather than self–seeking. It is non–possessive rather than jealous and controlling. It is primarily concerned with seeking the good of the other rather than with meeting our own needs. It is unconditional, undiscriminating love rather than love that is dependent on the other being loveable. It is also endlessly patient and trusting of the other's capacity to grow rather than giving up easily on the other. If we compare this kind of love with Roger's (1967) description of the experience of unconditional positive regard – a quality that he explicitly linked with agape love (Rogers 1956) – the overlap between the two becomes very clear. Schmid (2001a: 59) describes it as 'personal love' and is also clear that in using the word 'love' in the context of therapy, he is not talking about what the Greeks called eros, storge or philia. Nor is he talking about love 'in a religious sense' though it is unclear exactly what he means by the latter.

This kind of love also seems very similar to Maslow's concept of Being or B–love. Maslow (1968: 42 – 43) defined B–love as 'love for the Being of another person' and characterised it as non–possessive, generous, altruistic, unselfish, 'unneeding', nurturing, pleasure–giving and primarily concerned with the other's self–actualisation. B–love, he said, is 'welcomed into consciousness' and is 'completely enjoyed'. He saw it as 'a richer, "higher," more valuable subjective experience' in which there is little or no fear of or hostility towards the other. It is also a kind of loving which makes possible what he called 'B–cognition'. B–love, he claimed, enables us to see the uniqueness of the other more clearly, to recognise potential as yet not fully realised, to see and receive the other as they truly are. Similarly, Benner (2002) notes that such soul love is characterised by a depth of knowing of the other that sees beneath what he calls 'the outer garb of persona'. It begins with 'an absence of idealization' (p. 68). It is grounded in the capacity to see the other realistically, to recognise the other's strengths, gifts and unrealised potential but at the same time, to be keenly aware of his or her limitations and growing edges. Such awareness does not, however, lessen the degree of love, acceptance and respect that is offered to the other. Such soul love comes as close to fully unconditional loving as is humanly possible. This kind of love, Maslow (1968: 43) argues, is the kind of love that 'creates' the other.

The kind of love that the Greeks called agape is of course not just central to person–centred theory and practice and to the Christian tradition. It is also a key concept in all of the other major world religions. Oord (2007) argues that, to varying degrees, all of the world's major religious traditions emphasise the primacy of love. In Judaism, for example, 'chesed' which is translated variously as steadfast love or loving kindness or faithfulness, is seen as an attribute of perfection. Undertaking an act of chesed is viewed as the ultimate way of emulating God. There is an emphasis both on the unconditionality of chesed and on the absence of any selfish motivation. In Buddhism, metta, similarly translated as loving kindness, is one of the ten Buddhist perfections or virtues. It is seen as having three aspects: the application of metta in our everyday behaviour towards others; metta meditation which is seen as a way of radiating metta throughout the universe and of achieving samadhi (a form of higher consciousness); and metta as a total commitment to the philosophy of universal love. Metta actively promotes the well–being of all beings (again reflecting unconditionality) and is viewed as having strong healing power. In Hinduism, bhakti, the way of love, is seen as one of the paths or yoga which can unite us to Brahman. Bhakti may take different forms depending on whether it is being expressed in the context of our relationship with Brahman or with others. Hinduism also shares with Buddhism the concept of karuna which means compassionate action. Finally, the concept of love as a form of ideal ethical action is also present in Islam.

The core assumptions of person–centred theory and practice thus echo the wisdom to be found in the world's major spiritual traditions. They both assert the primacy of unconditional love.

A passionate love

Soul love is also, I believe, a profoundly passionate and personal love. Here, I am using the word 'passionate' in its wider sense. I am referring to a love that is imbued with longing and deeply felt. Agape love is often characterised as universal rather than particular, as impersonal and detached rather than personal and deeply involved, as a dispassionate act of will rather than a feeling. While agape love may be something most of us need to grow into and while that process may initially involve the making of a conscious and deliberate choice to extend love to the other, the concept of such love as a dispassionate act of will is not something that fits with my own personal experience. Nor does it fit from a Christian perspective with biblical images of God or portrayals of Jesus' way of being. Divine love is both universal and inclusive (agape) but also deeply personal, particular and suffused with longing and passion (eros).

Sheldrake (1994: 2-3) notes that in traditional Christian spirituality, agape and eros have often been viewed as two distinctive forms of love – a 'lower' form (eros) and a 'higher' form (agape). It seems to me that it is more helpful to view eros and agape as two different qualities of love rather than as two distinct forms of love and to recognise that they can and often do co–exist, both in human and divine love. Furthermore, there is, I think, a danger in divorcing agape from eros. As Sheldrake (1994: 3) points out, 'It is all too easy for a so–called universal, disinterested agape love to be simply uninterested and well–protected. A gift of everything but myself.'

I would certainly not wish to be the object of such impersonal, detached, dispassionate love and I doubt that the experience of receiving it could ever bring about significant healing or growth. I see soul love as a powerful fusion of both agape and eros. Here I am also drawing on the deeper layers of meaning of the word 'eros' that go beyond the purely physical and sexual – that is, eros as an expression of spirit, of the life force that energises and vitalises our existence; eros as a source of creativity and passion; eros as an expression of the drive towards union with the transcendent. Elkins (1998) argues that it is often eros that first impels us to enter into the kind of 'I–Thou' relationships that Buber (1958) described and that also provides the creative energy that helps to sustain and develop them. He believes that erotic energy is present in most, if not all, intimate relationships including friendships – and I would add, therapeutic relationships.

A hospitable love

Soul love is a deeply hospitable love. Drawing on the biblical concept of hospitality, Nouwen (1996: 88) maintains that the development of a therapeutic relationship requires us to create what he calls 'an empty but friendly space'. At its deepest level, hospitality is about 'creating space for the other' in which others can experience the freedom to be themselves (p. 69). He uses a range of words to capture something of the quality of the space he is describing – open, free, empty, friendly, safe, fearless, inclusive, receptive, responsive, affirming, supportive, understanding, compassionate and non–judgmental. He sees this level of hospitality as requiring 'the full and real presence of people to each other' (p. 89). Clearly, there are strong parallels here between Nouwen's concept of hospitality and the three core conditions identified by Rogers.

I experience this kind of loving hospitality as an invitation to enter a profoundly safe and sacred space; a space in which I am welcomed, met and embraced just as I am in each moment of my encounter with the other; a space into which I can pour all of who I am and what I am experiencing without fear of judgement or rejection; and a space in which I can discover the freedom to follow my own path and to find my own way back to my self.

A graceful love

Soul love is also a 'grace–filled' love. The Christian concept of grace is a notoriously difficult concept to define as it is used in a variety of different ways in different contexts. Strictly speaking, there is no single Old Testament word for grace, though theologians have linked the concept with a number of Hebrew words used to describe the nature of God – for example, the Hebrew words 'chesed' and 'raham' (translated as mercy or compassion). The New Testament Greek word which is normally translated as 'grace' is 'charis'. Literally translated, it means 'gift'. In its broadest sense, Christian theologians generally use the term 'grace' to refer to God's gifts to humanity (including life itself, creation, God's acceptance of and benign goodwill towards humanity and his revelation and communication of himself to the human spirit). Biblical passages such as the New Testament parable of the prodigal son (Luke 15: 11 – 32) are seen as teaching the concept of grace.

Drawing all these strands together then, we find the word 'grace' linked with such concepts as loving kindness, compassion, mercy, forgiveness and faithfulness. We also find it linked with such words as free, unmerited, undeserved. Again, there are clear parallels here with the Rogerian concept of unconditional positive regard.

A reverential love

Soul love is a reverential love. Dictionary definitions of the word 'reverence' generally refer to feelings of profound awe and respect. The word is also linked with such words and phrases as 'venerating', 'honouring' and 'holding sacred' and I would also want to add the words 'awe' and 'wonder'. We are perhaps used to and more comfortable with using the word 'reverence' in the context of our relationship with the Divine. I agree, however, with O'Donohue (2000: 110) when he argued that we need to 'retrieve our capacity for reverence' not only for the Divine, but for life and for others. He believed that every human being is a profoundly sacred presence in the world and that it is not possible to be fully present to others without revering their unique presence. Similarly, Kirkpatrick (2005: 7) argues that unless we approach our encounter with the other with something of this sense of awe and reverence, we are not likely to be invited into 'the deepest recesses of another soul'.

The African greeting 'Sawubona' which means 'I see you' captures this beautifully. When the indigenous people of certain African tribes approach each other, they stand facing each other, looking directly into each other's eyes for a few seconds. They then voice the greeting 'I see you' and the response 'Ngikhona' or 'I am here' before continuing on their way. This is, I think, an act of recognition at the level of soul. Inherent in it is the belief that until I am recognised and honoured by others, until I am 'seen' in this profound way, I do not fully exist as a person. By recognising or as Rogers (1967) might say, receiving each other in this way, we bring each other into being.

A compassionate love

Soul love is a deeply compassionate love. A typical dictionary definition of the word 'compassion' will refer to a deep awareness and sympathy for the suffering of another coupled with a desire to relieve that suffering. The word 'compassion' is, however, derived from the Latin words 'pati' and 'cum' which together mean 'to suffer with'. To be compassionate therefore means to enter into another's suffering or to suffer with that person.

Compassion is of course an important concept and value in many world religions. For example, in 'The Essence of the Heart Sutra', His Holiness the Dalai Lama (2005) explicitly links the concept of compassion with loving kindness and argues that genuine compassion requires both wisdom (understanding the nature of suffering) and loving kindness (a deep level of intimacy and empathy with the other). Writing in a Christian context, Nouwen et al (1982) see compassion as a deeper, more profound emotion than pity or sympathy. They point out that the Greek word 'splangchnizomai' appears twelve times in the Gospels and means 'to be moved with compassion'. Literally, it means 'to be moved in the guts', the guts being regarded at the time as the centre where our most powerful and intense emotions are located. It is related to the Hebrew word for compassion – 'rachamim' or tender, compassionate love – which in turn comes from the word 'rechem' meaning 'womb'. Indeed, Nouwen et al (1982) describe compassion as 'a movement of the womb of God.'

Compassion speaks to me of a more intimate solidarity with those who are suffering. It goes beyond a simple awareness and understanding of or concern for the suffering of others to a willingness to enter into that suffering and to be fully present with them in the pain they are experiencing. It is about 'getting into the black pit' with them and simply being there as they find their way through the pain to a place of healing. The title of Cassidy's (1988) book 'Sharing the Darkness' expresses this very well. In it, she writes about the spirituality of the carer and describes it as 'a spirituality of presence, of being alongside, watchful, available; of being there' (p. 5).

If we compare this to Rogers' description of the experience of empathy, the relationship between the two concepts becomes clearer. There is a strong parallel here between the ability to 'enter into' the client's world as he or she experiences it and the ability to 'enter into' the client's suffering and I believe it is possible to think of compassion as an aspect of – or perhaps, more accurately, an extension or expansion of – empathy. Indeed, Wosket (1999: 213 – 4) sees compassion as 'a higher order form of empathy' that requires 'true intimacy' between therapist and client.

A tender love

Soul love has, as I have experienced it, a particular quality of tenderness. Thorne (1991) points out that the word 'tender' is a multifaceted one with many layers of meaning. Etymologically, the adjective is linked with the Latin word 'tener' meaning tender, delicate or soft and with the Latin verb 'tenere' meaning to hold or support.

Relational tenderness is very difficult to define or depict adequately in words. It is associated amongst other qualities with warmth, care, affection, vulnerability, sympathy, soft–heartedness, mercy, compassion, kindness, protectiveness, gentleness and sensitivity. It may perhaps be more easily and powerfully captured in visual images or through stories. For me, it is encapsulated very well in the story of Jesus' encounter with the prostitute portrayed in the Gospel of Luke in the Bible (Luke 7: 36 – 50). It is, I think, clearly evident not only in Jesus' loving response to the prostitute but also in her actions towards him.

Tenderness is a central concept and value in a number of the world's major religious traditions. The Bible makes direct reference to it a number of times. Tenderness is, for example, seen as an attribute of God (Exodus 34: 6 – 7; Luke 1: 78). Additionally, in both Colossians 3.12 and Ephesians 4: 32, we are urged to 'clothe' ourselves with tenderness. In Islam, two of the key attributes of Allah – 'Al-Rahman' (the beneficent) and 'Al-Raheem' (the merciful) – are both derived from the root word 'rahmat' which means, amongst other things, tenderness of heart. In Buddhism, tenderness is closely linked with two of the so-called 'limitless qualities' – those of loving kindness and compassion – and in Hinduism, the Divine Mother (the motherly aspect of Brahman) is seen as full of tenderness.

My own experience of such loving tenderness has been one of my emerging self being received and held with infinite care, gentleness and sensitivity. At such times, I have sensed in the other an acute awareness of and openness to the depth of my vulnerability, a determination to tread with gentleness and sensitivity and a willingness to wait patiently for that which is surfacing within me, however long it may take. It is, however, the other's embracing – perhaps the word 'enfolding' captures it best – of the darkest and most wounded places in my being, of the parts of myself of which I am most afraid and most rejecting, that brings with it the greatest measure of healing.

An intimate love

Lastly, soul love is characterised, I believe, by the capacity for a particular quality and depth of intimacy which I call 'soul intimacy'. What I mean by this is the capacity to engage intimately with the other at the level of soul. The word 'intimate' has its origins in the late Latin verb 'intimare' – to make known to someone else – which was itself derived from the Latin 'intimus' meaning innermost. We can of course be intimate with each other on a number of different levels – for example, emotional, intellectual, physical, sexual and spiritual. I believe that the experience of soul love creates a profoundly sacred space between two people which makes it possible for one person to open up to the other at the level of soul, at the level of our innermost being.

The most growthful relationship I have ever experienced in my life has not been in the context of therapy, but in the context of an intimate friendship – what Kirkpatrick (2005) and O'Donohue (1997) refer to as a soul friendship or anam cara relationship, 'anam cara' being the Gaelic term for soul friend. In this relationship, I have experienced to a greater degree than in any other in my life the kind of soul love that I have been describing. It is a love that is deeply committed to my growth and fulfilment as a person, that is profoundly accepting and valuing of all of who I am, that has no expectations and makes no demands of me, that receives what I offer of myself with tenderness and compassion and a depth of understanding and 'holding' that is very rare. Consequently, I have been able to risk a level of openness and vulnerability within the relationship which has deeply surprised me. I have felt safe enough to 'bare my soul', to share my innermost thoughts and feelings, no matter how difficult or painful, knowing that they will be fully and sensitively received. The extent of the growth, both psychological and spiritual, that I have experienced as a result has also taken me by surprise. Kirkpatrick (2005: 50) voices the belief that such love 'creates persons'. Talking of friendship, O'Donohue (1997: 41) describes a true friend as someone who awakens you 'in order to free the wild possibilities within you.' Both of these have been true for me. I would speak, I think, of being loved into becoming.

As I have explored these many characteristics of soul love – its unconditionality, its deep commitment to the other's well–being and growth, its passion, its hospitality, its gracefulness, its reverence for the other, its capacity for compassion, its tenderness and its depth of intimacy – what I have become aware of is how strongly interwoven these different strands are. Their potency and creative energy lies, I think, in their coming together. It does indeed create in Mearns and Thorne's words, 'something really special' (Mearns and Thorne 2000) and as Rogers (1980) himself recognised, it has the power to make possible profound healing and growth.

In conclusion

I would argue that at its best, therapy is nothing more than and, at the same time nothing less than, a highly skilled and disciplined expression of soul love. It is skilled in the sense that the therapist has developed and honed natural relational skills that all of us have to some degree. It is disciplined in the sense that it must always remain true to its essential nature and purpose – that of enhancing the other's well–being and facilitating their growth. It rests on and flows out of our natural human capacity and desire to love unconditionally, passionately, compassionately and tenderly; out of our willingness to be as fully present and real in our encounters with others as we are capable of; and out of an attitude of profound reverence for the sacredness and beauty of the human soul, the essence of who we are as persons in the process of becoming. This is the kind of love that enables us to embrace the freedom to be who we are, or perhaps more accurately, who we are becoming. It is the kind of love that enables us to create the sacred space that is needed for the soul to risk disclosing itself to another soul. In so doing, it makes possible the most profound of connections between two people – spirit to spirit and soul to soul. It is, I believe, this kind of soul love that 'creates persons'.

Chapter 6 notes

1. For a more in depth exploration of the three core conditions, see Mearns and Thorne (2013), Bozarth and Wilkins (2001), Haugh and Merry (2001) and Wyatt (2001).

2. For a more in-depth exploration of the concept of relational depth, see Mearns and Cooper (2005) and Knox et al (2012).

7: A spiritually oriented approach

…the best of therapy sometimes leads to a
dimension that is spiritual.
Rogers (quoted in Baldwin 2000: 33)

A spiritually–oriented approach

Barbara is a woman in her late fifties who has recently received a diagnosis of aggressive breast cancer. She sits opposite me, sobbing intermittently, as she struggles to tell her story and to allow herself to begin to feel the pain, the fear and the anger that threatens to overwhelm her. She does not yet know if the treatment she is receiving is going to work and she is not ready to die. She is afraid of so much – that her second husband of only a few months will not cope well without her, that she will not survive long enough to attend her daughter's wedding or to welcome her first grandchild into the world, that her dying will be more painful and traumatic than she can bear. And she is intensely angry. She is angry at the unfairness of it all, angry at the insensitivity of some of those who are caring for her, angry at not being listened to by her family and friends who cannot cope with her distress, and angry at herself for not doing something long before she did about the lump she had been aware of for some time.

What she cannot risk voicing as yet is that she is afraid of death and of what lies beyond; that she is angry with a God that she is not sure she has ever really believed in; that somewhere deep inside her she believes she is being punished for not being a good enough person; and that she is struggling to make sense of and find meaning in her suffering. The words remain unspoken though the need to utter them is strong. She is unsure that it is acceptable to speak about such things in therapy. She cannot trust that they will be heard and understood and not ignored or dismissed. And so, for the moment, they remain locked inside her, part of her pain that she does not feel able to share, even in a space as safe as this one.

What does it mean to be a spiritually–oriented therapist? First and foremost, it means that we must be prepared to take the spiritual dimension of human existence seriously. However important spirituality may be in our own lives, whatever our own spiritual beliefs might be, we have to recognise that spirituality will come into the room, perhaps more often than we might suppose. And when it does emerge in our work with clients, we have to be willing to give it the same level of attention and respect as we would any other aspect of our clients' lives and experience. We have to learn to listen for the spiritual, to become attuned to it, to recognise it for what it is when it surfaces in less obvious or explicit ways, and perhaps even to offer it space, to invite it into the room when our intuition tells us that it may already be present. We have to develop what I would call a spiritual sensitivity, to turn on 'our spiritual radars' as Pargament (2007) puts it. We also have to be prepared to work in a focused way with the spiritual and existential issues clients often bring into therapy.

In working with Barbara, this involved recognising that her twice repeated statement that 'none of this makes any sense' strongly suggested a possible underlying spiritual agenda. Consequently, having reflected back her statement, I chose to follow it with a response that offered her a tentative invitation to talk about her struggle to make sense of her experience and about the deepest, most difficult questions it had raised for her. This was all the opening she needed. It gave her permission to bring her spirituality into the room and the assurance that she would be held and supported as she did so.

Secondly, the spiritually–oriented therapist will bring to the therapeutic relationship what is sometimes referred to as 'a beginner's mind', a mind that is stripped of its assumptions, its fixed ideas, its dogma, its prejudices, particularly in relation to spirituality. What is needed is an attitude of non–judgmental openness to and acceptance of clients' spiritual experience and the meaning it holds for them; a willingness to learn from them when their spirituality is foreign to us; and a keen awareness that when spirituality comes into the room, we are treading on sacred ground. Talking about the things of the soul takes us into a place of intense vulnerability. There is, as Pargament (2007) argues, no room for spiritual intolerance here, whether it is caused by 'spiritual rejectionism' – that is, the assumption that spirituality is inherently problematic or pathological – or by 'spiritual exclusivism' – that is, the assumption that there is one absolute truth and only one way in which to approach it. He notes that, at its extreme, exclusivism can lead to a failure to value and respect alternative paths to the sacred, an intolerance of any forms of spirituality other than our own and the rejection of potential solutions, coping strategies or spiritual resources that are not consistent with our own spiritual orientation. Because of the narrowness of their spiritual perspective, moreover, exclusivists may only be able to work effectively with clients who share their own spiritual orientation. They may even be at risk of breaching their own ethical codes of practice if they fail to respect the diversity of human spirituality or attempt to impose their own spiritual worldview on others.

Pargament (2007) acknowledges, however, that exclusivism need not lead to spiritual intolerance if it is balanced by humility, compassion and an openness to paradox. What he is saying here is that exclusivists need to be able to balance their position with an awareness that their understanding of truth may be partial or imperfect, with a capacity to value and respect others' search for the Sacred when it differs from their own and with a recognition 'that many things can be true at the same time' (p. 188 – 9). Such an attitude of non–judgmental acceptance does not mean that we cannot challenge aspects of clients' spirituality when it is clear that they are in some way destructive and damaging, either of themselves or others. But it does mean that such challenges must always be offered with the utmost sensitivity and in the context of a profound respect for the client's deeply held spiritual beliefs and values and for their right to choose their own spiritual pathway, however different it may be from our own.

Thirdly, the spiritually–oriented therapist will bring to the therapeutic process an awareness of the complex inter–connectedness of all aspects of our being, including the spiritual, and an understanding that spirituality is often subtly interwoven with the psychological problems clients face. Whatever shape it may take, our spirituality cannot therefore be labelled, boxed and relegated to the back of the therapeutic shelf as irrelevant or unimportant. It is profoundly relevant. Our spirituality has the potential to impact either positively or negatively on both our physical and mental health and well–being in a variety of ways. In extreme cases, moreover, spiritual problems can have potentially serious or even life–threatening consequences. For example, one Christian client I worked with – a pastoral care worker – came into therapy in order to help her recover from severe burnout. She had driven herself to the point of collapse as a result of her own extreme interpretation of a passage in Galatians which she regarded as a biblical command to 'crucify the self'. Another client had chosen to give in to her husband's highly abusive sexual demands (at times tantamount to rape) because of her strongly held religious belief (based on a passage in the book of Ephesians in the Bible) that she should submit to him as 'the head of the wife'.

Pargament (2007) argues, furthermore, that psychological and spiritual distress often 'go hand in hand' and that there is a complex interaction between psychological problems and spiritual problems which is not always easy to disentangle. He points out that aspects of our spirituality can give rise to or exacerbate the psychological problems we are wrestling with and conversely, that our psychological problems have the potential to impact adversely on our spirituality. In the same way, though our spirituality can sometimes act as a resource in enabling us to cope better with the problems in living we face, it can also be a source of resistance which impedes the therapeutic process and may even sabotage our growth or healing.

Lindsay came into therapy when she was in her early twenties. She was struggling with intermittent bouts of depression, accompanied by suicidal thoughts and self–injury. When her emotional distress became unbearable, she would binge–eat in order to dull the pain. Lindsay had been repeatedly sexually abused by her uncle as a child and then raped by a boyfriend in her late teens. She had told no one about what had happened to her, fearing that she would not be believed or that she would be blamed. She had a strong Christian faith and as she found the courage to tell her story and face her pain in therapy, she decided to take the risk of telling the pastor of the church she was attending in order to ask for his prayer support. While he was very supportive of her, his response was to give her a verse from the Bible (Isaiah 43: 18): 'Forget the former things; do not dwell on the past'. He also urged her to trust God's healing rather than rely on therapy to solve her problems. Tragically, Lindsay chose to end her therapy at this point. Some two years later, she returned. Nothing had changed or been resolved. The injunction not to dwell on the past had become a source of resistance which had effectively caused her to bury her distress for a second time. And sadly, the fact that the prayer ministry she had received had not enabled her to heal and to move on from her painful past had left her feeling that her faith was too weak and that she was inadequate as a Christian.

Fourthly, the spiritually–oriented therapist will bring to the therapeutic relationship a broad knowledge and understanding of spirituality, both religious and non–religious. This does not mean that we need to be an expert on all forms or expressions of spirituality. It does, however, imply a willingness to expand our existing knowledge and understanding of human spirituality as the need arises in our work and an openness to learning from experience, both our own personal experience and that of our clients. West (2000) maintains that all therapists, irrespective of whether they see themselves as having a personal spirituality, should have some degree of knowledge about the major religious and spiritual traditions within their society, about ways of mapping people's spiritual development and about the kind of spiritual issues that people may encounter on their spiritual journeys. Pargament (2007: 190) echoes this when he argues that, because of the rich diversity of religious and spiritual experience, personal spiritual maturity is not in itself sufficient to equip a therapist to work with the spiritual dimension of experience. He believes that the spiritually–oriented therapist must be prepared to look beyond his or her own spiritual tradition and to develop what he calls 'a well–integrated professional spiritual perspective'. He sees what he calls 'spiritual illiteracy' as a significant problem for the therapist.

Given the important role that spirituality plays in many people's lives and in the problems in living they face, such 'spiritual illiteracy' would indeed seem to be a serious shortcoming and one that has important implications for therapist training and supervision. This is an issue I will return to later.

Fifthly, the spiritually–oriented therapist will bring to the therapeutic relationship an awareness of the complex inter–weaving of our psychological and spiritual journeys. As we have seen, the journey towards the soul or core self – the process of becoming that Rogers (1967) described – is both a psychological and a spiritual journey. Soul lies at the heart of both journeys and therefore connects them both. Spirit energises both journeys and therefore directs them both. It inspires us not only to become but also to transcend or reach beyond our core self in whatever way is meaningful for us. It follows then that therapy is at its deepest level both a psychological and a spiritual process.

In addition, the spiritually–oriented therapist will bring to the therapeutic relationship a high degree of self–awareness and authenticity in relation to his or her personal spirituality and an understanding of how that spirituality might potentially impact, both positively and negatively, on the therapeutic process. Our spirituality is an inherent part of who we are. We cannot leave it behind us when we walk into the room with our clients. It will be there whether we intend it to be or not. And it will shape every aspect of our work with the client whether we intend it to do so or not. Consequently, there is a responsibility on our part as therapists to engage in an ongoing process of examining our own evolving spirituality and its relationship with our practice. We need to develop our awareness of those core assumptions and beliefs that are fundamental to our own personal spirituality and of the ways in which they may manifest themselves in our therapeutic work. We need also to be aware of how our personal spirituality is being impacted and changed, as it inevitably will be, by our encounters with our clients. Pargament (2007) sees this spiritual self–awareness as 'an antidote' to the potential for coercion in therapy. It helps to protect us against the danger of failing to respect clients' autonomy and right to choose their own spiritual path or of seeking to impose our own spiritual worldview or values on them. He also sees it as paving the way for therapists to develop a greater authenticity or congruence in relation to their spirituality.

Some time ago, one of my supervisees presented an issue in supervision around her concern for her client's spiritual well–being. Her client was struggling with her previously strong Christian faith to the extent that she had started to explore alternative spiritual paths and the therapist, whose own spirituality was exclusivist in outlook, was finding it very difficult to sit with her client's emerging spiritual journey. She was fully aware of the importance of respecting her client's autonomy and was working very hard to ensure, as far as possible, that her own spiritual perspective would not intrude unhelpfully into the therapeutic process. At the same time, she was aware of how uncomfortable she felt whenever the client moved into an exploration of her disillusionment with Christianity and of a growing sense of being incongruent in some of her interactions with the client. On one occasion, moreover, she had been aware of deliberately changing the subject when the client began to talk about her sense of being increasingly drawn to Buddhism as a spiritual path.

Having talked her dilemma through in supervision, she recognised that she could not be sure that her exclusivist perspective did not constitute a threat to the therapeutic alliance and consequently, that it was in the best interest of her client to be congruent with her about the difficulty she was experiencing. On doing so sensitively and respectfully in the next session, the client then disclosed her own awareness of the therapist's struggle. She had been aware of the change of subject – something she felt had happened on more than one occasion – and had come to the conclusion that the therapist disapproved of the direction she was taking. This had been painful for her as she valued her relationship with the therapist highly and did not want to walk away from it. As a result, she had reached the decision not to bring issues relating to her spirituality into the room again. In this situation, the therapist's decision to be congruent had a very positive impact on her relationship with the client, taking it to a depth it had not reached before. Both client and therapist were able to talk through the tension they had been experiencing in the relationship very openly and honestly and to reach a place of mutual respect for the differences in their spiritual orientations. This enabled them not only to continue to work together effectively, but also to open up further meaningful dialogue about the client's spiritual journey.

Finally, the spiritually–oriented therapist will bring to the therapeutic relationship the capacity to create what I have called 'a sacred space'. What does it mean in practice to offer the client such a space? Firstly, it means creating a space that is acceptant of the client's spirituality whatever shape it might take; a space in which the client's deeply personal sacred story can be told and honoured, however different it might be from that of the therapist; and a space in which the client's spiritual experience and beliefs can be freely explored without fear of ridicule, judgement or condemnation. Pargament (2007) argues that spiritually–oriented therapy is not 'grounded in religious authority or legitimacy.' Instead it is grounded in a commitment to enable clients to discover and live out their own spiritual truths as they perceive and experience them. When we are able to offer such 'soul hospitality' (Benner

2002), we respond to the invitation to enter the other's sacred places and meet the other on his or her own sacred ground.

Secondly, it means developing the capacity for what Kirkpatrick (2005) calls 'soul listening.' Soul listening, as I see it, is the art of listening to each other at the level of soul and as such, is an expression of soul love. This goes far beyond a superficial 'surface listening'. It involves the creation of a profoundly safe and intimate sacred space in which the speaker feels fully heard, received and honoured at the deepest level of his or her being. It is the gift of the tender, loving presence of one person to another, a reaching out of soul to soul and spirit to spirit, an entering into a mysterious and profoundly spiritual I–Thou encounter between two souls who are both engaged in their own unique ways in the process of becoming a person.

When I listen at the level of soul, I am listening, as Jackson (2003) puts it, from the depths of my own soul into the soul of the other. I am listening with awe and reverence for the voice of the other's soul, attuning myself to the profound mystery and sacredness of the other's innermost being. I am creating a space that is so profoundly safe that the soul – the very core of our being – can risk disclosing itself. Such soul listening is, I believe, a profoundly spiritual and creative process. Kirkpatrick (2005) sees it as 'spirituality in action' on behalf of the other. Jackson (2003) also sees it is a spiritual act or practice and regards it as having the capacity not only to bring the other's soul 'into life', but also to deepen both the client's and the therapist's capacity to experience the presence of the transcendent.

In conclusion, the effective spiritually–oriented therapist will have a well–developed sensitivity or attunement to the spiritual; a knowledge and understanding of spirituality which extends beyond their own personal spirituality; a profound respect for and valuing of others' spiritualities which goes deeper than tolerance; an openness to learn from and be changed by their encounters with clients; a high level of self–awareness, genuineness and personal integrity in relation to their spirituality; a recognition of the profound inter–connectedness of body, mind, soul and spirit; an understanding of the subtle interweaving both of psychological and spiritual problems and of the psychological and spiritual journey; and the capacity to create a sacred space in which the client's evolving spirituality can be fully received.

Opening the door

One of the questions therapists often ask is, 'How do you bring spirituality into the room?' It is not uncommon for them to express concern about taking the initiative to open up a dialogue about such a sensitive aspect of the client's experience and about the risk of introducing their own agenda rather than following the client's. Griffith and Griffith (2002) point to Kahle's (1997) research which surveyed over 150 therapists and found that while 98 per cent were willing to talk about spirituality if the client introduced the topic, only 60 per cent were willing to introduce the topic of spirituality themselves and only 42 percent were willing to initiate a conversation about God. The principal concerns that inhibited therapists from initiating discussions about spirituality were fears about imposing their belief systems on the client, concerns that any religious differences between them and their clients might create a barrier between them and strong convictions that dependence on God effectively disempowers people. These are all genuine concerns which need to be taken seriously. However, as Griffith and Griffith (2002) argue, there are ways of guarding against these risks.

It has been my experience that spirituality often comes into the room, either explicitly or implicitly, without my having to invite it in. Occasionally, some aspect of the client's spirituality may be presented as a problem that the client is seeking to address. A young Christian woman in her early twenties who has come to therapy to talk about her experience of being sexually abused by her father as a child, tells me of her inability to relate to God as father and of the distress this causes her. A middle aged woman who has experienced a number of major tragedies in her life speaks openly of her struggle to understand how a loving God could have allowed such things to happen to her and to those she loves and of her inability to 'rejoice in her suffering' as she believes the Bible commands her to do.

Alternatively, the client's spirituality may also emerge naturally and almost incidentally as part of the story the client is telling or it may surface more subtly in the client's use of language or images. For example, as she is telling me the story of her intensely painful early childhood, my client makes a brief reference to 'someone up there having it in for me' and then changes the subject somewhat abruptly. While some might argue that such 'throw away lines' are nothing more than figures of speech and would dismiss them as unimportant or irrelevant, my experience tells me that more often than not, they are in fact the client's way of 'setting the stage' for a spiritual dialogue as Pargament (2007) puts it. They are in a sense an invitation to the therapist to enter into the client's sacred space. Our task is simply to respond to the invitation gently and tentatively and by doing so, to 'open the door', as Griffith and Griffith (2002) put it, to a deeper exploration of the role that spirituality plays in the client's life.

In this case, simply reflecting back the client's statement was enough to enable her to bring into the room her image of God as a punitive, vindictive judge and executioner – an image akin to that of 'the Cosmic Sadist' that Lewis (1966) spoke of in his reflections on the experience of bereavement following the death of his wife. I did not make the assumption that she would want to talk further about this aspect of her spirituality but offered her the space to do so if she felt it would be helpful. The invitation was initially declined and it was not until several weeks later that she chose to take it up. I suspect that had I not reflected back her statement and offered the opportunity to make it a focus of our work together, it might never have resurfaced. Pargament (2007: 18) describes this as 'the process of making the implicit explicit'. What is hinted at or expressed obliquely is heard and attended to. What is difficult to acknowledge or express is given the space to emerge in its own time and in its own way.

What though if there are no such invitations? What if spirituality does not enter the room either explicitly or implicitly? Do we have the right as spiritually–oriented therapists to bring it into the room when it is not already there? Are there other ways of 'opening the door' which do not risk making assumptions about what is important to the client and relevant to the problems they are facing or which do not risk imposing our own agenda on the client?

Orienting the client to therapy

It seems to me that one of the simplest ways of opening the door to the spiritual dimension in therapy is to do so as part of the process of orienting the client to the process of therapy. In the pre–therapy literature which therapists and therapeutic agencies give to their clients, they generally offer a brief description of their therapeutic approach and list the problem areas that clients often bring to therapy or that they are open to working with as therapists or agencies.

Other than in the case of pastoral or transpersonal approaches to therapy, rarely does such pre–therapy information make explicit reference to the spiritual dimension of human experience or list spiritual problems or concerns as possible areas of focus. It seems to me that this is a missed opportunity to signal to clients in an unthreatening way that their spirituality is a valid focus in the therapeutic process and that the therapist is open to working with this dimension of their being and experience. To make this explicit in pre–therapy information perhaps goes some way towards dispelling the perception that therapists tend to be dismissive of spirituality and effectively gives clients permission to talk about their spiritual lives when it would be helpful to them to do so.

Making a spiritual assessment

Another way of opening the door to the spiritual is that of making some degree of assessment or evaluation of the client's spirituality as part of the therapeutic process. Richards and Bergin (2005) note that while it has become increasingly more common over the past twenty to thirty years for therapists to conduct comprehensive assessments of the client's background and functioning, it is relatively rare for these assessments to include any form of exploration of clients' spirituality and the role it plays in their lives.

They argue strongly that making what they call 'a religious–spiritual assessment' is of vital importance in enabling the therapist to gain a deeper empathic understanding of clients' ways of making sense of the world, of life and of their experience as they perceive it. This is of course therapeutically important in its own right as Rogers (1967) asserted. It is also, however, essential if we are to develop the capacity for what Augsburger (1986) calls 'interpathy' or cross-cultural empathy. As Lartey (2003) puts it, interpathy is 'what needs to happen when empathy crosses cultural boundaries.' It is also what needs to happen when empathy crosses religious or spiritual boundaries. If we are to avoid what Richards and Bergin (2005) call 'religious insensitivity and bias', if we are to tread softly in the client's spiritual world, then we need to be prepared to enter into that world with the utmost respect, no matter how strange or alien it might seem to us, and to seek to understand it. Pargament (2007: 202) echoes this when he argues that spiritual assessment is essentially a process of becoming familiar with or 'getting to know' the spiritual dimension of the client's being.

Richards and Bergin (2005) and Pargament (2007) also identify a number of other reasons for making a spiritual assessment. Firstly, it helps the therapist to determine how healthy the client's spiritual orientation is and whether it is impacting positively or negatively on his or her life and functioning. It enables the therapist to assess the relevance of clients' spirituality to the problems in living they are presenting and to determine whether their spirituality is part of the problem or may potentially be part of the solution. It can also bring to the surface unresolved spiritual problems or concerns that clients may wish to address in the context of therapy. Finally, it may help to indicate whether and how best to address the spiritual dimension of the client's being and whether there are any specific spiritual interventions that may be helpful. In addition, making a spiritual assessment can be another way of inviting the client's spirituality into the room. It sends a clear signal that the client's spirituality is not 'out of bounds'; that the therapist is interested in and values the client's search for the Sacred, however it might manifest itself; and that therapy can offer a safe space in which the client is free to explore his or her own unique spirituality as it is evolving. Sadly, this will often be a safer space than the client's own religious community.

Pargament (2007: 225 – 6) identifies a number of key areas to consider when making such an assessment: the history of clients' spiritual journeys and how they might see their future journey; how clients experience and image the transcendent; what spiritual pathways are nourishing and supporting of their spirituality; and how their spirituality impacts on their life and well–being. He sees these questions as focusing not so much on the 'whats' of spirituality – such as whether clients believe in the existence of a transcendent reality, pray or attend a spiritual community – but on the 'whys', 'wheres', 'whens' and 'hows' of spirituality. He emphasises that such evaluative questions are not questions that therapists pose directly to the client, but questions that they need to be asking themselves as part of the process of developing their understanding of the client's spirituality.

If we accept the value of making some form of spiritual assessment, how might we best think of this process and what might it look like? As a person–centred therapist, I am somewhat ambivalent about the term 'spiritual assessment' because so often the term 'assessment' carries with it the assumption that the therapist has the knowledge and expertise required to make an accurate 'diagnosis', in this case of the client's spirituality. Particularly in relation to such a complex, multifaceted and mysterious phenomenon as spirituality, this is, I think, a dangerous assumption. Consequently, I find it more helpful to think of the process as a form of sacred inquiry. I do not see this as an end in itself or as a separate or distinct stage of the therapeutic process. Instead, I see it as a process that should always be woven naturally into the fabric of the wider therapeutic dialogue and that emerges gradually out of the unfolding relationship between therapist and client. Thinking of it in this way reminds me of the extreme sensitivity that is needed to enable clients to give voice to the innermost part of themselves. It reminds me that to be invited into this sacred and often hidden centre, I have first to earn a level of trust which is deep enough and secure enough to allay the client's fears and reservations. It reminds me that undertaking this exploration will take time, that it cannot be rushed, that I need to see it as a process that will evolve and deepen as the therapeutic relationship between me and my client evolves and deepens.

This process of sacred inquiry is, I think, close to Pargament's (2007) concept of an 'implicit spiritual assessment' which involves, as he sees it, two key elements. The first of these is the therapist's attunement to the spiritual, the 'spiritual radar' that enables us to listen for the client's spiritual language, to notice changes in the 'spiritual temperature' in the room and to be alert to the emergence of spiritual themes and processes, however subtly these may be evidenced. The second is the therapist's use of what he calls 'implicit spiritual questions' that in some way hint at the spiritual dimension rather than pointing to it directly. He recognises that some clients may be unwilling to disclose aspects of their spirituality, particularly at an early stage in the process when trust has not yet been established. Alternatively, clients may not recognise their experiences, values or beliefs as spiritual ones or may be unaware of the wider significance of spirituality in their lives. He identifies a range of open–ended questions which make no assumptions and are inclusive enough for clients to respond to them whatever the shape of their spirituality. He notes that such questions avoid the mentioning of religious institutions and practices or of higher powers, but draw instead on what he calls 'psychospiritual language' by which he means, 'psychologically meaningful concepts' that in some way encourage spiritual exploration (Pargament (2007: 217 – 18). Some of the implicit spiritual questions I have found most helpful are the following:

> What resources you/gives you hope/enables you to cope when you are going through a difficult time?
> What gives your life meaning/gives you a sense of purpose?
> What are you searching for in life?
> What are your deepest longings?
> What makes you feel more fully alive?
> How do you make sense of/find meaning in this experience?
> How has this experience affected you/changed you at the deepest level?

My experience tells me that such psychospiritual questions are responded to more readily and freely when they emerge naturally out of the flow of the ongoing conversion rather than being introduced separately. Generally, invitations to spiritual exploration should not come 'out of the blue' but in response to what is already surfacing in the room, however subtly that might be. Moreover, the particular question asked will depend on what is already beginning to emerge. For example, one of my clients who had been feeling mildly depressed for some months was exploring a general dissatisfaction with life that had begun to surface within her in mid–life. She articulated a persistent feeling of 'wanting more' than life had offered her so far. I reflected back the deep existential longing that was being expressed and asked her what it was she was searching for. At this point in her journey, she had no clear sense of what 'the more' was and was very clear that she wasn't 'religious or anything like that'. She was, however, able to voice her growing conviction that 'there must be more to it than this' and that there was 'something missing' in her life that she could not quite identify. This led to a very fruitful exploration of the spiritual awakening she was experiencing. Another client who had been going through a very difficult and traumatic time in his life spoke of his struggle to cope with his feeling of being 'overwhelmed by the enormity of it all' and his surprise that it 'had not finished him off'. The question I posed on this occasion was around what it was that had given him the strength to live through his experiences. This question opened up a dialogue about the importance to him of his religious faith, an aspect of his experience which had not explicitly surfaced before then, in part because he had not seen it as appropriate to talk about it in therapy.

Making an explicit spiritual assessment

Pargament (2007) also advises making a more explicit spiritual assessment – something he sees as a two stage process. The first stage involves making what he calls 'an initial spiritual assessment' at the start of therapy. This entails asking a number of basic questions which are designed to assess the role that religion or spirituality plays in the client's life; the extent to which the client's spirituality is aligned with a particular religious or spiritual tradition and community; the extent to which the client conceptualises the problem in spiritual terms and sees his or her spirituality as having been impacted by the problem; and finally, whether the client's religion or spirituality is a potential resource that the client might draw on in resolving the problem. While I can see the potential benefits of this, I also have some reservations about asking clients such explicit spiritual questions, however inclusively they are worded, at such an early stage in the therapeutic process. Having indicated in the pre–therapy information I give to clients that I am open to working with spiritual issues and concerns, I prefer to wait and see what emerges naturally as the client's story is revealed, while at the same time remaining alert and responsive to signs that the spiritual may be entering the room. If at some point I were to introduce a question focused on spirituality, it would be much more likely that I would draw on an implicit rather than an explicit one. Furthermore, if such questions did result in clients disclosing an aspect of their spirituality, I would consider it important to ask them whether they saw it as relevant to the problems that concern them and whether they would find it helpful to explore their spirituality in greater depth as part of the therapeutic process.

The second stage of the assessment process that Pargament (2007) describes is that of undertaking a more in–depth assessment of the client's spirituality. Should the initial assessment indicate that the client does see spirituality as playing an important part in his or her life and that it may be relevant to the presenting problems, Pargament (2007) advises making a more thorough, focused assessment. He recognises that spirituality is expressed more easily through the medium of stories and sees the assessment process as one of enabling clients to tell the story of their spiritual journey. This requires the therapist to draw on what he calls open–ended 'evaluative questions' which are designed to place the client's particular spiritual story within a larger spiritual framework. The framework he has developed (pp. 222 – 3) covers four key areas:

> 'taking a history and a future' – exploring how the client's spirituality emerged and developed and how they might see it unfolding in the future

> 'sacred destinations' – exploring the client's spiritual goals and what Pargament (2007) calls their 'spiritual trajectories' through life

> 'sacred pathways' – exploring the breadth and depth of the client's spiritual pathway(s), how effective they are in enabling them to reach their destination and how well integrated they are into the rest of their lives

> 'spiritual efficacy' – exploring how at ease the client is with their spirituality, how they see their spirituality as growing and how it impacts on their general health and well–being.

Again, Pargament emphasises that drawing on the 'evaluative questions' he identifies is not a matter of conducting a formal structured assessment but of weaving them naturally into the therapeutic dialogue.

Other practitioners have developed a much more structured approach to making a spiritual assessment. For example, Richards and Bergin (2005) describe what they call a 'multilevel, multisystemic assessment strategy' developed in the context of their theistic approach to psychotherapy. This is a much more structured and directed process which involves a semi–structured intake interview and may include the use of a client intake questionnaire such as Ellison's spiritual well–being scale (Ellison 1983). As a practitioner who is fundamentally person–centred, I feel much more at home with Pargament's approach than with that of Richards and Bergin. To my mind, Pargament's emphasis on allowing the process of sacred inquiry to take shape naturally as the client tells his or her own sacred story and weaving it into the wider therapeutic dialogue is more compatible with person–centred philosophy and practice and avoids some of the risks and dangers inherent in making a more structured and explicit spiritual assessment.

The use of spiritual interventions in therapy

In the context of spiritually–oriented therapy, the general purpose of spiritual interventions is that of enhancing the client's psychological and spiritual growth and general well–being. More specifically, spiritual interventions can be used to achieve a variety of different therapeutic goals. For example, they may be used as a way of enabling clients to re–connect with and nurture their core self or soul (Elkins 1998). They may also be beneficial in helping clients to recognise and address aspects of their spirituality which are inhibiting the resolution of their problems or in enhancing their ability to draw effectively on the spiritual resources of their own tradition in coping with the difficulties they face (Pargament 2007). The use of spiritual interventions is not, however, a defining feature of a spiritually–oriented approach. It is quite possible to work effectively with the spiritual issues and concerns that clients may bring to therapy without drawing on any specific spiritual interventions or practices. Furthermore, there are spiritually–oriented therapists who would never incorporate such interventions into their practice and would argue that, because of the associated risks and dangers, it is inappropriate to do so. There are also others who might be prepared to draw on some forms of spiritual intervention in certain circumstances, but would do so relatively infrequently and with some degree of caution.

What does the research tell us?

What seems clear from the available research is that many spiritually–oriented therapists are open to drawing on spiritual resources in their work. Moreover, even in the context of mainstream therapeutic approaches, it is much more common than we might expect. The research indicates that therapists from a range of different orientations and spiritual traditions draw on a wide variety of spiritual resources and practices in their work. These include various forms of prayer, meditative and contemplative practices, sacred texts and other spiritual writings. They may also engage in discussing or teaching religious or spiritual concepts or seek to facilitate such spiritual healing processes as forgiveness (Pargament 2007; Richards and Bergin 2005; West 2000). In addition, a number of other spiritually–oriented techniques such as active imagination (Jung 1973), guided imagery (Rowan 1993)[1], Inner Dialogue or dialoguing with the Higher Self (Whitmore 2004), spiritual journaling, yoga and other body–focused practices are also used, primarily in the context of transpersonal therapeutic approaches.

Furthermore, survey studies undertaken in the USA indicate that surprisingly high percentages of contemporary therapists (including pastoral counsellors, clinical psychologists and psychiatrists) will now incorporate spiritual interventions into their practice alongside more traditional therapeutic techniques. The percentages range from 30 to 90 per cent depending on the group surveyed and the specific intervention in question (Richard and Bergin 2005). Unsurprisingly, higher percentages of therapists who describe themselves as religious or spiritual in outlook use such interventions. They also tend to draw on a wider range of them (Raphel 2001; Shafranske 2000). Richards and Bergin (2005) conclude from these findings that, at least in the USA, the use of such spiritual interventions is a significant and growing phenomenon. A similar picture also seems to be emerging from research undertaken in Britain over the past twenty years (Gubi 2002, 2004, 2008; Rose 1996, 2002; West 1998).

Richards and Bergin (2005) point out that the majority of spiritual interventions drawn on in therapy can be traced back to some form of religious or spiritual practice originally developed in the context of one or more of the world's major wisdom traditions. Sometimes these practices are integrated with psychological techniques or are adapted in some other way with the result that they are used differently than they would normally be in a religious context. For example, in the context of a biblical counselling approach[2], clients might be asked to read, reflect on or even memorise a particular passage from a sacred text as a means of enabling them to modify specific beliefs that are impacting adversely on their psychological or spiritual well–being. Hurding (1992) refers to this as a 'prescriptive' use of scripture. At other times, spiritual practices are drawn on in much the same way as they would be in religious settings. For example, clients might be encouraged to engage in a particular form of meditative practice in order to help them cope more effectively with the levels of stress they are experiencing.

Richards and Bergin (2005) argue that research into the physical and psychological benefits of such spiritual practices as prayer and meditation provide good general support for their use in therapy. For example, there is both a wealth of anecdotal evidence and a growing body of empirical evidence that suggests that the process of engaging in prayer can impact on us positively, both physically and psychologically as well as spiritually. An increasing number of research studies have been conducted into the effects and benefits of various kinds of prayer. In exploring the benefits for the pray–er of engaging in prayer, Gubi (2008: 35 – 7) offers a thorough overview of much of the available research and summarises some of the key benefits which have been identified by those engaged in the practice of various forms of prayer. He reviews the work of a wide range of writers and researchers who in turn draw both on their own and other's self–reported experiences of prayer. It is clear from this work that many people believe themselves to be benefiting from engaging in personal prayer, both physically and psychologically as well as spiritually.

There is also a large amount of empirical evidence that such spiritual practices as contemplation and meditation can have significant beneficial effects on both mind and body. For example, Baer (2003) conducted a review of the empirical research relating to the use of mindfulness meditation, a form of meditation that has been derived from Eastern meditation practices. While she recognises that these studies often have significant methodological flaws, she concludes that interventions based on mindfulness meditation may not only improve general psychological functioning but may also help to alleviate a range of mental health problems. Similar benefits have also been observed as a result of engaging in Transcendental Meditation (TM), a concentration–based approach to meditation which requires the focusing of attention on one particular stimulus such as a single word (or mantra) or an object (Alexander et al 1991). Interestingly, their review of the empirical literature suggests that the positive benefits are greater when transcendental or mystical experiences occur during the practice of TM. In similar vein, Wachholtz and Pargament (2005) found that when the focus of the meditation had some form of spiritual content (in this case, meditation to a spiritual phrase such as 'God is love'), the beneficial effects of the practice were again substantially increased.

Another recent strand of research has emerged from the field of neurobiology. Using such techniques as electroencephalography (which records and analyses the electrical activity of the brain) and brain imaging (studying the structure and functioning of the brain through electronic imaging such as MRI scanning), the short and long term effects of particular meditative practices on the brain have been studied scientifically. While this research is, relatively speaking, still in its infancy, an increasing number of studies have found positive evidence that the practice of particular forms of meditation, both religious and non–religious, results in a number of neuroelectrical and neurochemical changes in the brain (Cahn and Polich 2006). For example, some studies which have focused on changes in brain wave patterns during meditation (such as Travis 2001) have provided evidence that during the practice of meditation, there are increases in Alpha, Theta and high Beta brain waves. These are strongly associated with a heightened sense of relaxation, peace, emotional equanimity and general well–being. Other studies have suggested that meditation may lead to increased levels of serotonin and melatonin in the brain. These are neurotransmitters that positively influence mood and behaviour in a variety of ways (Mohandas 2008).

In relation to drawing on sacred texts in therapy, Richards and Bergin (2005) believe, as does Pargament (2007), that such interventions can be therapeutic, and that there is some empirical evidence that suggests that they are. They acknowledge, however, that to date, there is little if any conclusive evidence that this form of intervention has beneficial effects. Pargament (2007) identifies a number of studies which suggest that where sacred texts are integrated into therapy, improvement may be more rapid. As Richards and Bergin (2005) point out, however, where such interventions have been used as part of an overall therapeutic approach, it is generally not possible to determine how much of its effectiveness can be assigned to their use.

Finally, Richards and Bergin (2005: 305 – 9) also offer a review of the available research relating to the effectiveness of therapeutic approaches that are spiritually–oriented. They conclude that the preliminary evidence from outcome studies suggests that spiritually–oriented therapies and interventions may be at least as effective as and sometimes more effective than their secular equivalents when working with religious clients and that spiritually–oriented approaches may be effective with a range of presenting problems and client populations. While such research does appear to provide some support for the use of spiritual interventions in therapy, it is, however, important to recognise that it is in its infancy, often tends to be methodologically weak and therefore cannot be regarded as in any way conclusive.

How then might spiritually–oriented therapists validly draw on spiritual resources and interventions in their work? The choices therapists make in relation to the issue of drawing on spiritual interventions are likely to depend not only on their own spiritual tradition where relevant, but also on their therapeutic orientation. The decisions they make will also depend on the way in which they weigh up the potential benefits and dangers or risks of incorporating such interventions into their work with clients.

The use of spiritual interventions in therapy is indeed controversial and there are undoubtedly a number of pitfalls, dangers and ethical issues that therapists need to be aware of in drawing on them in their work. I intend to look in a little more detail at the use of prayer and sacred texts in therapy as these are two of the most frequently used resources. In so doing, I offer a set of practical guidelines for the use of spiritual interventions which I see as being consistent with person–centred practice. I believe that adhering to such guidelines both increases the likelihood of spiritual interventions being effective and minimises the risks and dangers inherent in their use.

The nature of prayer

Before considering whether prayer has a valid role to play in the therapeutic process, it is important to explore what we understand and mean by the word 'prayer' and to recognise that the word will mean different things to different people. Concepts such as prayer are notoriously difficult to define and for those who engage in prayer, no definition can hope to capture what they experience as lying at the heart of prayer – its fundamental essence – which is profound, mysterious and deeply personal. Something is inevitably lost in the process of definition. James (1985: 464) offered an inclusive definition of prayer. He saw prayer as '...every kind of inward communion or conversation with the power recognized as divine.' Here it is clear that prayer is being seen primarily as a relational act. When people are asked to describe how they make sense of their experience of prayer, there are a number of key words that surface repeatedly – words like connection, communication, communion (in the sense of intimate fellowship), conversation, encounter, awareness and experiencing. Rose (2002: 3 – 4) points out that in most of its forms, prayer both 'assumes the existence of "an other", however that other is defined' and 'implies relationship' with the other, however that relationship is experienced. Gubi (2008: 17, 26) echoes this in his succinct but inclusive definition of prayer as a process of encounter, connection or communication with what he calls 'transcendent otherness'. Prayer, as he sees it, is 'I' engaging directly with 'Other'.

In religious contexts, this 'Other' is generally conceived of as some kind of non–physical force, entity or being and is experienced as being greater than or beyond the boundaries of the self. From a Christian perspective, for example, prayer may be seen as the channel or medium through which the self relates to a personal God. In other contexts, however, the 'Other' may be differently defined. For example, prayer may be seen as a means of connecting with our spiritual centre – our soul, our 'Higher or Inner Self' or our 'Inner Light' as the Quakers call it. Alternatively, it may be seen as enabling us to tap into the source of love, compassion and wisdom that resides within the self. In some schools of Buddhism, for example, prayer is primarily seen as a practice designed to awaken these inherent capacities rather than as a process of communication with something that is seen as existing separately from the self. Prayer may also be experienced in a variety of different ways, even within the context of the same religious tradition. When talking about how Christians may experience prayer, for example, Gubi (2008: 26) identifies a range of different experiences such as a sense of connectedness and intimacy with the 'other', an experience of the absence of the 'other', a contemplative gazing at the 'other' or a waiting in silence on the 'other'.

Prayer and the therapeutic process

For some therapists, prayer may form a very important part of their everyday life and experience and one which they may naturally want to draw on in their work. In the late 1990s, Rose conducted a research project into the inter-relationship between prayer and the counselling relationship (Rose 2002: 8). She made a detailed qualitative study of eleven therapists from a variety of faith backgrounds. This was focused on the ways in which therapists draw on prayer as part of their work. She was interested in why they pray, how they pray, what they pray for and how they make sense of their practice and experience of prayer in the context of the counselling process. She found that five of her respondents (not all of whom described themselves as actively religious) regularly prayed before a session, six prayed silently in sessions, six named their clients in prayer outside the context of the therapy session and three prayed overtly in sessions.

Similarly, West (1998) conducted a study of nineteen British Quaker therapists, seeking to identify the ways in which their spiritual beliefs impacted on their practice. He found that around four fifths of his respondents engaged in some kind of spiritual preparation, often involving a form of prayer, and almost three quarters prayed for their clients, sometimes during sessions. In addition, Gubi's (2004) survey of both mainstream and pastoral counsellors indicated that for a significant number of practitioners (around 50 per cent of mainstream counsellors and 80 per cent of pastoral counsellors), prayer formed an important part of their therapeutic practice. A smaller percentage (ranging between 6 and 16 per cent) were using prayer overtly with their clients.

It is clear from this research that a significant number of therapists who have a religious or spiritual outlook do draw actively on prayer in their work with clients and that they do so in a variety of different ways. Rose (1996; 2002) outlines a range of ways in which therapists may use one or more different aspects of prayer in the context of their work. The prayer–related behaviours most commonly identified in her research were praying when feeling anxious, asking for help for oneself as therapist, contemplating or meditating on clients and their problems, praying silently in the session, naming clients in prayer and praying before sessions. In addition, Richards and Bergin (2005) and Pargament (2007) highlight the practice of encouraging clients to draw on various forms of prayer as a spiritual resource. Rose (2002) and Gubi (2008) also explore the way in which therapists see the role of prayer in relation to their practice. Many therapists see prayer as a way of resourcing or nurturing themselves in their work – for example, as a way of centring or stilling themselves before a session or 'recharging their batteries' afterwards; as a way of developing their ability to be fully present or to connect with the client at a deeper level; or as a way of deepening their awareness and understanding of what is going on, both within the client and themselves.

Some therapists may also engage in praying for the client, either outside the context of the therapy session or during the session itself in which case it generally takes the form of silent prayer. This may be done with or without the client's knowledge and consent. They may see this practice in various ways – for example, as a way of enhancing the therapeutic relationship, facilitating the process of growth and healing or in some way accessing or 'channelling' divine power. For example, Clinebell (1984) talked of using prayer 'on behalf of' the client. He described using what he called a 'right–brain method' which involves imagining the presence of a warm healing light surrounding both the therapist and the client. Clinebell saw this as a form of intercessory prayer which can be done both during the session and between sessions.

Finally, a small number of therapists choose to engage in praying overtly with or for the client during the session itself. Often this will take place at the beginning or end of sessions and will involve, for example, asking for God's presence and guidance, 'lifting the session to God' or praying that what is necessary will surface during the session. Sometimes, the client will voice the prayer while the therapist prays silently. Sometimes both will voice a prayer or will engage in silent prayer together. This may be seen as a form of listening prayer which enables both counsellor and client to 'to tune in' to God.

For example, an important aspect of Tournier's dialogue counselling is what he called moments of 'silentiotherapy'. Tournier believed that it is vitally important for the counsellor to be sensitive to the 'inner dialogue' with God that takes place both within the counsellor and the client. He described moments of spontaneous silence in the counselling session where, as he saw it, God was clearly speaking directly to the client and he believed that this inner dialogue may be taking place even when the client does not believe in God and '... thinks he is wrestling only with himself.' (Tournier 1957: 159 – 69) He saw these moments as sacred and as being enhanced by his own silent meditation at the time and he argued that such silences 'can become the highest form of personal communion, real communion, especially if we both feel we are in God's presence' (Tournier 1965: 217 – 219).

Using sacred texts and writings in therapy

All of the world's major religious and spiritual traditions have one or more sacred texts or scriptures that their adherents view as sacred or holy and that they draw on as a source of spiritual insight and wisdom. In relation to the Western theistic religious traditions such as Christianity, Islam and Judaism, many, though not all, believe such writings to be God's direct revelation of himself to human beings. For example, Jews may believe that God revealed himself and his law to the prophet Moses and that this revelation is recorded in the Torah. Similarly, Muslims may believe that Allah revealed himself to the prophet Mohammed through the angel Gabriel and that his eternal words are recorded in the Qu'ran. For Christians, the key sacred text is the Bible, a collection of sacred writings by a range of authors which is seen by many as being 'God–breathed' – in other words, literally the word of God.

Not all Eastern world religious traditions view their sacred texts in this way. For example, in Hinduism, there are two kinds of sacred writings: Sruti (or hearings) which include the Vedas and Upanishads and which are viewed as the wisdom of holy men revealed to them by the gods; and Smriti (or memory texts) which are essentially collections of stories passed down from generation to generation and eventually recorded by men of wisdom. In Buddhism, there are a number of different sacred texts – the Tripitaka or sacred writings of Theravada Buddhists which contain both stories of Buddha and the teachings of Buddha and his followers and many other sacred texts which contain stories, rules for living and other sayings.

Richards and Bergin (2005) point out that religious people may engage with these sacred texts and writings in many different ways. Some will view their tradition's sacred texts as divinely inspired and therefore infallible. Others will see them as the fallible writings of human beings and therefore as subject to errors and misunderstandings. Some will study their sacred texts daily while others rarely if ever actually read the original sacred texts themselves but rely instead on the teachings and interpretations of their spiritual tradition and leaders. Some will engage with sacred texts in order to deepen their understanding of their tradition's theology and doctrines; some will derive comfort, insight, meaning, guidelines for living, a sense of identity or feelings of joy or peace from their reading of sacred texts; and others will find that reading such texts gives them an experience of spiritual communion – a sense of being in the presence of the Divine.

The research shows that therapists are actively drawing on sacred texts in therapy in a variety of different ways and that interventions drawing on sacred texts may be more frequently used than any other kind of spiritual intervention (Richards and Bergin 2005; West 2000). Therapists have quoted verses of sacred texts, offered their interpretation of sacred texts to clients or made indirect references to sacred texts while taking about or teaching religious concepts. Sometimes therapists will also encourage clients to read or study particular parts of sacred texts outside therapy sessions or to memorise or reflect on specific verses or passages. Furthermore, sacred texts may also be used to challenge client's dysfunctional thinking. Therapists view the purpose of such interventions in various lights. For example, they may use them to help clients reframe their experience from a spiritual perspective, to challenge and modify clients' irrational beliefs, to strengthen clients' sense of their own spiritual identity and purpose or to help clients find appropriate guidance, insight or consolation. Pargament (2007) also argues that sacred texts can offer stories (such as the story of Job in the Bible) which provide clients with valuable models of strength, resilience, hope, compassion and self–care in times of suffering.

Practical guidelines

Drawing this all together, it seems clear that there may, at least potentially, be considerable benefits to be derived from the use of some forms of spiritual interventions in the context of therapy. There are also, however, significant risks and dangers. Richards and Bergin (2005) contend that it should be possible to minimise the risk by being fully aware of the potential dangers, following basic guidelines for competent and ethical practice and undertaking further research into the effectiveness of such spiritual interventions. In order to minimise such risks, there are, I think, a number of basic practical and ethical guidelines that therapists need to follow, irrespective of their therapeutic orientation, when drawing on spiritual resources in the context of therapy.

Before using spiritual interventions

The first of these guidelines is that in drawing on spiritual resources, we should work hard to avoid making any assumptions. We should not, for example, assume that because clients describe themselves as religious or spiritual, they will want to talk about their spirituality or to draw on spiritual resources as part of the therapeutic process. We should also not assume that when clients share our own spiritual tradition, they will believe what we do, relate to the transcendent as we do, find the same spiritual resources helpful or even speak the same spiritual language. Some of the most unhelpful spiritual interventions arise out of making such assumptions, often on the basis of little or no evidence. For example, while it is possible that the use of prayer in therapy might be very welcome to some clients, others might see it as an unwelcome intrusion or as a source of pressure to meet the therapist's expectations. If prayer has been imposed, they may even experience it as threatening, frightening or abusive. Moreover, if the client is in the midst of a crisis of faith which is often accompanied by an unwillingness or inability to pray, then the therapist's introduction of prayer may give rise to feelings of guilt or inadequacy or a perception of the therapist as having a 'special relationship' with the Divine in a way that the client does not. It is also important to recognise that religious clients may find it very difficult to say 'no' to prayer even if the suggestion is made very tentatively and sensitively and with explicit permission not to take it up.

While it did not take place in the context of therapy, my own experience of being prayed for when I was not comfortable with it was that it was very unhelpful. At the time, I was in a very difficult place in my spiritual journey and the last thing I wanted was to pray or be prayed for. Prayer was, furthermore, offered at a point in the session when I was in considerable emotional distress and in a way that made it very difficult for me to say 'no' ('I think it might be helpful if we prayed together now.') There was no attempt to ascertain that I felt at ease with it and if I did, how I would like to pray. The person working with me knew relatively little about my spirituality, used language which she assumed would be meaningful to me (and was not) and did not explore the impact of her intervention with me afterwards. I felt awkward, incongruent, angry, confused, guilty and spiritually inadequate, but too vulnerable and distressed to voice what I was feeling. The prayer brought me no sense of comfort and furthermore, the content of it effectively shut down the cathartic release of my distress. I left feeling that I had not been heard or held in the place I was in and with a sense of failure in relation to my faith. It also left me wondering if perhaps the level of my distress was too much for others to bear.

A second related guideline is that before drawing on spiritual resources in any way in the context of therapy, it is crucial to have developed both a secure enough relationship with the client and a sound enough understanding of the nature of the client's spirituality and of where they are on their spiritual journey. The timing of such interventions is therefore of considerable importance. It is also important here to hold in mind the uniqueness and complexity of each individual's spirituality and to recognise as Pargament (2007: 243) puts it that 'one size does not fit all'. He gives the example of suggesting to clients that they might find it helpful to engage in a form of meditation such as mindfulness or transcendental meditation and points out that clients from conservative religious traditions would be likely to find such practices unfamiliar and, I would add, possibly even threatening. He emphasises the importance of tailoring the use of spiritual resources to the client's specific needs and preferences rather than applying them in a rigid or formulaic way. I agree with Pargament and would argue that it is not possible for us to do so until we have a good enough understanding of the client's spiritual frame of reference and of the way in which they are living out their spirituality.

The third point I want to make is that before drawing on spiritual resources or interventions in therapy, it is also crucial to have identified and considered the potential ethical issues and concerns that arise in relation to their use. For example, while some therapists use prayer relatively freely in their work and see it as a facilitative, nurturing resource, others have significant anxieties and concerns about the role of prayer in therapy and experience some conflict in integrating this aspect of their faith with their therapeutic practice. Rose (1996; 2002) and Gubi (2008) identify a number of key areas of concern expressed by therapists. For some, the process of praying for clients may be seen as exerting some form of potentially damaging unconscious influence on them, or introducing a subtle, covert form of direction into the process. Some therapists even have concerns about the ethics of praying privately for a client without their knowledge and consent. Rose (2002) voices their concern that such covert prayer could still exert a form of influence on the client. She also recognises that some forms of covert prayer could be seen as 'acting on behalf of the client' in a way that might be seen as contravening ethical guidelines.

It is possible, for example, that in the course of praying for clients during a session, therapists might inadvertently reveal hopes and dreams for them which may differ from their clients' own desires and aspirations, thereby subtly introducing their own agenda into the process. They may also intentionally or unintentionally reveal to clients an image or concept of the Divine which is different to theirs and thereby risk imposing their own beliefs on them. Rose (2002) argues, furthermore, that prayer can be wrongly used to give the client certain messages in a powerful way. Because of the power differential in the relationship and because these messages are often given 'in God's name', they may carry greater power and authority and be harder for the client to reject when they do not 'fit'. Particularly where the prayer involves a request for a specific outcome, prayer can become a means of asking God to bring about what the therapist believes should happen. This clearly does not sit easily with a process which is believed to be essentially non–directive. Bridger and Atkinson (1994: 222) also draw attention to such possible misuse of prayer in the context of the counselling relationship, seeing it as 'unhelpfully manipulative'.

Sadly, I have also come across flagrant abuses of power and authority where therapists have used prayer in a way that has effectively pressurised, coerced or manipulated clients in a variety of ways. In my practice as a therapist and as a tutor, I have come across many people who have been damaged by the inappropriate, insensitive and unethical use of prayer in the context of therapy. One of my clients described how a Christian counsellor she had worked with had imposed a prayer time both at the beginning and the end of each session without any discussion or consultation with her. While the client had felt very uncomfortable with this, she had not felt able to say so and complied with it because she felt it was expected of her 'as a good Christian'. Given that she was experiencing a serious faith crisis at the time, this was a profoundly unhelpful intervention. Another client had been given 'a word from the Lord' (what is sometimes referred to by Christians as a 'word of knowledge') after an in–session prayer time which had again been initiated by her Christian therapist. The therapist disclosed that God had revealed to her in prayer that the client had been sexually abused as a child by her father. The client herself had no memory of any abuse. Nor had she disclosed any concern or fear that she might have been abused. Given the power differential in the relationship and the fact that the therapist claimed that this revelation came directly from God, it was extremely difficult for the client to dismiss it and to trust her own 'gut sense' that the therapist was wrong. Such an intervention is, I believe, profoundly unethical and the emotional and spiritual damage it caused took a long time to resolve.

Such ethical concerns also exist in relation to drawing on sacred texts in the context of therapy. For example, Hurding (1992) highlights the danger of handling scriptures in a heavy–handed or insensitive way that risks 'bludgeoning needy people with the word of God' (p. 155). He is specifically talking here about the prescriptive use of scripture and argues that much Christian or biblical counselling is 'blighted by a hard–edged emphasis on the written word that tends towards aridity and judgmentalism' (p. 158). As a person–centred therapist, I see particular dangers in offering clients my own interpretations of passages from sacred texts or in encouraging clients to memorise or reflect on particular passages that I might see as being beneficial to them. There is a real danger here of slipping into the role of 'religious expert' and therefore crossing the boundary between therapist and religious leader unhelpfully. This has the potential, furthermore, to lead to transference and projection issues which might impact adversely on the therapeutic relationship. For example, unresolved feelings of disappointment with or anger towards God or religious authorities may be transferred or projected onto the therapist, thereby potentially damaging the relationship. Furthermore, because of the power imbalance in the therapeutic relationship and because of what Rennie (1994) calls 'client deference' – the tendency of clients to defer to their therapists even when they do not find their interventions helpful – it may also be difficult for clients to challenge their therapist's suggestions or interpretations even though internally, they may disagree or find them unhelpful. This has the potential to be very damaging, particularly for those whose locus of evaluation is very externalised.

The fourth guideline I would offer is that before drawing on spiritual resources in therapy, it is essential to assess the risk of doing so with the particular client we are working with and to identify any possible contraindications. Richards and Bergin (2005) outline a number of such contraindications. It goes without saying that the use of such interventions is clearly inadvisable where clients are averse to or have no interest in spirituality or have indicated (however subtly) that they are not comfortable with or do not wish to participate in spiritual interventions. Richards and Bergin argue that they are also contraindicated where the client's spirituality is not directly relevant to the presenting problems (or where the client does not acknowledge its relevance) or where the client is seriously psychologically disturbed – particularly where psychotic or delusional behaviour is being displayed. In addition, they hypothesise that spiritual interventions are less likely to be effective where the client is young (in childhood or adolescence) or in the relatively early stages of their spiritual journey, where the client's images of a personal God are negative ones or where the client has what Pargament et al (1988) call a passive or deferring religious coping or problem–solving style – that is, where people 'defer the responsibility' of problem solving to God rather than taking the responsibility of actively working to resolve the problem themselves[3]. While I accept that working with clients who have predominantly negative images of God can be very difficult, I do not, however, see this as a contraindication to the use of any spiritual interventions in my work with them. Indeed, my experience tells me that drawing on clients' sacred texts can at times be helpful in enabling them to explore and revise their negative images of God.

The fifth guideline is that we should ensure as far as is possible that we are clear about our aims in introducing spiritual interventions and are not using them to meet our own needs as therapists rather than our clients'. Therapists sometimes offer such interventions when they are feeling out of their depth, when they are feeling overwhelmed or powerless, when they are struggling to stay with the client's emotional pain or when they have lost hope or trust in the therapeutic process. There is a danger here that the use of such interventions can become a substitute for relationship, for simply being there in the midst of the darkness and confusion, for staying alongside clients as they face and work through their pain and distress. It is important therefore to consider carefully how a particular intervention might be therapeutically beneficial to the client and to reflect on the specific therapeutic outcomes we are hoping for.

For example, one of my supervisees reported that at the end of a counselling session, she had offered to pray for her client. She had never done this before. When I asked her what had prompted her to pray for the client at this point in the process, it emerged that the session had been an extremely difficult and painful one for the client and had left her feeling visibly shaken and distressed. As she talked it through, my supervisee came to the realisation that she had felt the need to end the session on a positive note and to leave the client with a sense of hope for her eventual healing. She had also been deeply distressed herself by aspects of the client's story and as she recognised, felt the need to 'hand the session and the client over' to God. The client had accepted her offer and my supervisee had then voiced a prayer that the client would feel a sense of God's presence in the midst of her distress and that God would give her the strength to work through the difficulties she was facing. On reflecting on this in supervision, she could see that her decision to pray for the client in this way arose out of her own needs rather than the client's and that it could potentially have been unhelpful in a number of ways. On checking this out with the client the following week, it became apparent that the client's reaction to it was a mixed one. While the therapist's offer to pray had enabled her to feel cared for, she was at a difficult point in her spiritual journey and was struggling with feelings of being abandoned by God. She had wanted to say no to the therapist's offer but had felt unable to do so in case it upset her. The client was also left with a concern that her level of emotional distress might be too much for the therapist.

A related guideline is that it is important to consider the possible impact of the use of spiritual interventions on the dynamics of the therapist–client relationship. For example, a concern that therapists often voice is that praying overtly for or with the client in therapy, teaching the client about spiritual or religious concepts or offering one's own understanding or interpretation of sacred texts or doctrines might subtly alter the balance of power within the relationship and thereby heighten the inevitable power imbalance within it. This is particularly likely to be the case where the therapist comes to be seen as a spiritual expert or authority figure whose understanding or interpretations cannot be questioned. Alternatively, the therapist may be regarded as in some way having 'a hot line to God'. In such circumstances, the client's self–disclosure may then become inhibited through fear of judgement. Clients may, for example, shy away from disclosing aspects of their experience or behaviour which they see as unacceptable or sinful or as evidence of what they may see as their weakness or inadequacy as a person of faith. There is also a danger here of therapists imposing their own beliefs on the client or of undermining the client's own locus of evaluation.

The last of these guidelines is primarily related to the use of prayer in therapy. It is important to recognise that some uses of prayer in therapy may be defensive. Rose (1996: 9) points out that where prayer is used as a mixture of escapism or flight from responsibility or where it involves a search for magical solutions or a 'quick fix', '... prayer can be used as a very powerful defence.' For example, Christians often talk of 'lifting to God' or 'giving to God' a particular problem or situation in a way that some would argue might involve an abdication of personal responsibility. Prayer can also be used either by therapist or client to avoid, deny or suppress emotional pain or particular feelings or reactions such as anger which the client may see as unacceptable or even sinful (Gubi 2002). In such situations, the therapist may be concerned about the possibility of colluding with a form of prayer that is considered to be psychologically unhealthy or 'inauthentic' or that may in some way be seen as 'working against' what the therapeutic process is seeking to achieve. For example, Gubi (2008) argues that prayer might be considered to be unhealthy or inauthentic where it acts as a form of wish–fulfilment (that is, where it arises out of the expectation that God will answer prayer in the way one wishes); where it is characterised by supernatural assumptions, superstition or a desire for magical interventions; where it is unhealthily egotistical or self–centred; where it involves a form of infantile regression (retreating into a child–like state); or where it seeks to overturn the laws of nature or to attempt to influence God's will according to our own wishes or desires (Gubi 2008: 36).

For example, one client that I worked with briefly wanted prayer to play a substantial role in our work together. She requested in our first session together that we introduce a time of prayer whenever and for as long as she felt she needed it during sessions. She wanted me to pray specifically that God would change the difficult circumstances she found herself in and would bring her emotional healing. A deeper exploration of the reasons for her request made it very clear that she believed that only prayer and God's direct intervention could resolve her problems. It became clear, moreover, that she had sought such prayer on many occasions in the past in a number of different contexts without experiencing any significant benefit. It was evident that her religious coping style was a deferring one (Pargament 2007). Another concern for me was that for this client, prayer would essentially be a defensive strategy, that she would see it as providing a magical 'quick fix' which would obviate the necessity for her to face her considerable emotional pain. Consequently, on this occasion, I chose not to agree to her request and in so doing, to hold the boundary between therapy and the prayer ministry[4] she appeared to be seeking.

Guidelines for using in–session spiritual interventions

The first of these practical guidelines is that when drawing on spiritual resources in therapy, it is even more important than it is normally for the therapist to be very clear about what is being suggested or proposed and how it might be helpful to clients; to obtain consent, ensuring that clients are given explicit permission to say 'no' at any point; and even if permission is given, to be alert for any signs of discomfort or unease throughout the process. This is of course good practice in relation to any form of intervention. Because it can be so difficult for religious clients to decline the use of spiritual interventions, however, the therapist may have to work harder to ensure that the client does not feel any pressure to give consent. Spiritual interventions thus have to be offered with tentativity, sensitivity and the utmost respect in order to ensure that the therapist's values, beliefs and goals are not imposed on the client, however unintentionally. Particularly with clients whose locus of evaluation is externalised or who evidence a tendency to see the therapist as a spiritual authority or to defer to the therapist, it may be helpful to go as far as exploring what it would be like for the client to say 'no'.

This leads me to the next important guideline. Whatever the nature of the spiritual intervention, it is also of vital importance to debrief it fully in order to explore its impact on the client and on the therapeutic relationship. As well as enabling the therapist to assess how helpful the intervention has been, debriefing it may also enable clients to identify barriers or blocks that are preventing them from benefiting fully from it. It also helps to ensure that any rupture that may have occurred in the relationship as a direct result of the intervention can be brought to the surface and worked through.

Finally, it is, I believe, very important for therapists to work authentically and within their own personal and professional role boundaries and competence when they work with spiritual resources. The role boundary between therapist and minister or pastor must be firmly held. Furthermore, it is important for therapists not to draw on spiritual resources in a way that is inconsistent with their normal spiritual practice or that may result in them working outside the limits of their experience and competence. Pargament (2007) adds that it is vitally important to recognise that spiritual resources and practices are designed primarily to facilitate spiritual growth and to deepen the client's relationship with the transcendent. As such, they are, as Pargament (2007) puts it, 'sacred resources' which should not be regarded merely as therapeutic tools or techniques. When drawn on in therapy, he argues, their 'sacred character' should always be recognised and respected.

In conclusion

What has struck me in researching this area is that even those who advocate drawing on spiritual resources in therapy are both cautious about their use and keen to emphasise the potential pitfalls and contraindications involved. This is, I think, particularly true of the use of prayer. For example, Gubi (2002) describes the explicit use of prayer in therapy as a 'contentious intervention' and recognises that at worst it can be used abusively. He also acknowledges that he has never explicitly used prayer in his counselling work in over two decades of practice (Gubi 2008). Richards and Bergin (2005) also speak of their 'serious reservations' about therapists praying overtly with clients during sessions and with some exceptions, hold the position that they should not.

My own position with regard to the use of spiritual interventions in therapy is a similarly cautious one. In relation to drawing on prayer in therapy, I do sometimes pray for clients outside the context of the therapy sessions, drawing on a practice of holding the client silently in mind which is very similar to that described by Thorne (2002). Thorne speaks of the longing that therapists may experience for the well–being of their clients whilst at the same time maintaining neutrality in relation to the goals and outcomes of the process. He describes this as 'a silent and passionate accompaniment without expectation but with absolute commitment to the client's evolution towards the fullness of being' (p.42). This captures beautifully the way I see and experience this form of prayerful holding of the client. It is for me a way of drawing on prayer which I believe is neither unethical, nor inconsistent with my person–centred philosophy and practice. Like Clinebell (1984) and Thorne (2003a), I also draw regularly on a number of spiritual practices as a way of facilitating my own personal and spiritual growth and preparing myself for my work as a therapist. Clinebell (1984: 130) sees prayer as an important resource for the counsellor's own preparation for the work of facilitating spiritual growth. He describes the process of '... seeking to maintain a continuous awareness, in the background of one's consciousness, of the here–and–now presence of the Spirit of love and liberation. It means keeping oneself open to the flow of the inner Light of the divine presence.' Similarly, Thorne (2003a) talks of the importance of 'putting himself in the presence of God', something he sees as 'an exercise in total surrender'. He outlines his own five point programme of spiritual practice – a form of spiritual discipline, the sole purpose of which, as he sees it, is to help him to develop and maintain 'a loving disposition towards himself.' He argues that this form of discipline can enable therapists to develop a deeper self–acceptance and self–love which then enhances their unconditional acceptance of and love for the client. He also believes that it increases the possibility of a 'transcendental encounter' between therapist and client.

Generally, I would consider it to be inappropriate to pray overtly with or for a client during sessions. In my initial interview with clients, I always offer them the opportunity to indicate whether they have any particular expectations or wishes in relation to the therapeutic process. I do not, however, mention prayer specifically. Nor would I ever initiate a discussion about prayer or offer to pray with or for a client during sessions even where it is clear that the client has a religious faith. Occasionally, clients may request that prayer form a part of the therapeutic process. In my experience, this has been relatively rare, even where I have been working in a pastoral setting. Where it does happen, I would consider it imperative to explore the request for prayer very fully with the client before deciding how to respond to it and to hold the boundary between therapy and prayer ministry very firmly. For example, when I was working in a pastoral context, one of my clients raised the issue of prayer as part of an early review of our work together. She had been disappointed that I had not asked her whether she wanted prayer to be part of the process as it played a very significant role in her life. She believed that it was important for her 'to invite God into the room' as we were working together. We spent some time exploring what prayer meant to her, how she experienced and benefited from it and how she thought it would help her to engage with the therapy. She talked of her commitment to enter into the therapeutic process as fully as she was able and her belief that praying at the start of each session would remind her of God's presence with her and enable her to feel held by God as she faced the pain she knew that she had to work through.

It was clearly very important to the client that prayer should be part of the process in this way and I was concerned about how refusing to allow her to pray might impact both on her and on our developing relationship. Furthermore, given the depth of her engagement with the therapeutic process even at this early stage and the kind of prayer she wanted to be able to draw on, I felt reasonably confident that in these circumstances, it was unlikely to impact negatively on the therapeutic process or relationship in any way. I did not offer to pray for the client but gave her the option of praying briefly herself at the start of a session, whether verbally or silently, should she wish to do so. At such times, I would hold her silently in mind. Rather than committing ourselves to do this routinely, we agreed that she would make the decision as to whether to pray at the start of each session. In the early stages of our work together, the client reported finding this helpful and there was certainly no evidence of her failing to engage fully in the therapeutic process.

Interestingly, however, she decided a little later in our work together that she no longer needed to begin the session in this way.

I have also drawn on the client's sacred texts in therapy in a variety of ways. In so doing, I generally prefer to work with what the client brings into the room and to focus more on their own way of interpreting, making sense of and finding meaning in sacred writings and how this might relate to the problems with which they are struggling. Occasionally, when clients' interpretations of particular passages are clearly having an adverse effect on their psychological or spiritual well–being, I might consider either drawing their attention to other passages from the text that might offer them another perspective or giving them the information that there are other possible interpretations and understandings of the passage that they might find helpful to explore for themselves. For example, one of my clients who had a deeply committed Christian faith was experiencing the symptoms of severe burnout. As a result of her church's teaching, she had interpreted a passage in the book of Romans (Rom.12: 1 – 2) as a command to deny her own needs and wants and to concentrate wholly on serving God through meeting the needs of others. In trying to be 'a living sacrifice', she had exhausted herself physically, emotionally and spiritually. Furthermore, in failing to continue to meet others' needs in this way, she had come to see herself as failing God. The client had herself made reference to the passage from Romans during the session. Having explored what it had come to mean to her, I chose to draw her attention to other passages in the Bible which describe the ways in which Jesus looked after himself and took care of his own needs during his ministry. I asked her how these other biblical passages might fit with her understanding of the passage from Romans.

Intuitively, this feels like a riskier intervention. It certainly needs to be handled tentatively and sensitively and as with all challenges, care needs to be taken in exploring its impact on the client. However, providing the therapist does not impose his or her own interpretation of the passages and engages the client in doing the work, I believe this can be an effective and ethical intervention. In this case, it opened up an exploration of the issue of self–love (often a difficult concept for Christians) and of the client's images of God as a 'slave driver' and 'killjoy' God who demands nothing less than perfection. In time, this enabled her to reach a healthier and more balanced perspective in relation to being 'a living sacrifice'. This allowed her to begin the process of recovery from burnout.

Finally, at times I also draw on more contemporary spiritual interventions in the course of therapy such as working creatively with the client's spiritual imagery where it seems relevant to the work they are doing in therapy or inviting clients to engage in a dialogue either with their emerging core self or with the Divine. These interventions are tentatively offered as a potential resource to draw on and I always work hard to ensure that clients do not feel any sense of pressure to engage in something that they are not comfortable with or that has no meaning for them. I have also found that such interventions are more likely to be effective if they emerge naturally out of the work we are doing together at the time. I shall explore this kind of work further in the next chapter.

Effective spiritually–oriented therapy rests, I believe, on an attitude of profound respect for the client's spirituality. It requires us to honour the client's emerging spiritual self and to tread with sensitivity and respect on their sacred ground. It asks of us that we are as attentive to the spiritual dimension of our clients' being and experience as we are to any other aspect of their lives. It engages us in a process of inquiring into the sacred as the client experiences it and of receiving the client's spiritual story with acceptance and empathy, however, different it may be from our own. It also requires that we are willing to work with the client's spirituality, where appropriate, whenever they choose to bring it into the room. In the next chapter, I shall explore some of the challenges and difficulties that face the spiritually–oriented therapist in working with the kinds of spiritual issues that may surface in the context of therapy.

Chapter 7 notes

1. Active imagination is a therapeutic technique developed by Jung (1973). It draws on the imagination in a way that enables clients to engage with, dialogue with and interpret the contents of their unconscious as they are revealed in dreams or fantasies or in creative works of art. In the context of Jungian therapy, it is seen as a way of accessing material from the unconscious in the form of images, thereby bringing it into conscious awareness. Guided imagery or fantasy is an intervention used in the context of transpersonal therapy in which clients are asked to imagine a particular symbolic image or scene. To a greater or lesser degree, the therapist then guides the process of enabling the imagery to evolve further (Rowan 1993).

2. Christian or biblical counselling approaches such as those of Crabb (1977) and Hughes (1981) are more explicitly biblical in orientation in the sense of actively incorporating biblical principles and concepts within the counselling process. They tend to draw heavily on techniques adapted from cognitive–behavioural approaches but also involve the explicit use of Christian resources such as the Bible and prayer.

3. Pargament el al (1988) identify two other styles of 'religious coping': the 'self-directing' style in which people do not rely on any intervention from God and see themselves as taking sole responsibility for resolving their problems; and the

'collaborative' coping style in which people see themselves as working together with God in dealing with the difficulties they face.

4. In the context of the Christian faith, prayer ministry relies on the presumed supernatural power of prayer to bring about physical and emotional healing. The direct source of the healing is believed to be God and therefore the quality of the relationship between the person praying and the person being prayed for is generally seen as of less importance.

8: Working with the spiritual

It is my experience that clients rarely present with obvious or explicit spiritual or existential issues in the early stages of therapy. There are, however, a number of common spiritual problems or concerns which may come to the surface later in the process, either implicitly or explicitly, when the therapeutic space has become safe enough. Whether religious or not, clients generally bring spiritual concerns into therapy because they are struggling with some aspect of their spirituality and need a safe place in which to explore it outside the context of their faith communities. At this point, they may or may not recognise how their spirituality may be impacting on the psychological problems they are experiencing. Alternatively, the therapist may offer clients an invitation to explore aspects of their spirituality because it has become clear in the course of the work that it is in some way inhibiting the resolution of the difficulties they are facing.

Over the years, I have, for example, found myself working with clients who were experiencing what might be thought of as an existential depression. These clients have no motivating sense of purpose. They see life as essentially meaningless or pointless and experience it as grey and empty. They seem to value nothing sufficiently to make life worthwhile. They are, as I see it, living in a 'spiritual vacuum', profoundly disconnected from their core self, existing rather than living. Sometimes their depression is so deep that they have all but lost the will to live. I have also encountered clients whose anxiety is existential in nature, who are intensely preoccupied with their own mortality or what Tillich (1952) called 'the threat of non–being'. Such clients cannot face death. Their fear of it is intense and, in religious clients, is often accompanied by a fear of hell and of God's judgement or condemnation.

Wrestling with chronic feelings of guilt and shame is also common, particularly in religious clients. For many clients, the guilt is inappropriate or false guilt – what Bradshaw (1988) calls 'toxic guilt'. For others, it may originally have been appropriate but has remained unresolved, sometimes over many years. Such clients often find it impossible to forgive themselves or to accept the forgiveness of others. Often, this is accompanied by an intense, unhealthy preoccupation with sinfulness. Much harder to work with is what Bradshaw (1988) calls chronic 'toxic shame' or a perception of oneself as being essentially flawed, defective, inferior or bad as a human being. Such feelings of shame are generally very deep–seated and difficult to uproot. In clients whose religious faith is theistic – that is, who have a belief in a personal god or gods – they are often accompanied by a conviction of being utterly unacceptable to God or of being undeserving of God's forgiveness.

Such clients may also wrestle with distorted perceptions, images or understanding of God. They may, for example, see God as a punitive 'judge and executioner'; as a 'slave–driver' God who is harsh, demanding and expects perfection; as a controlling or manipulative God; or as an unapproachable or distant God who has little concern for them and little interest in their lives. Such negative images of God often give rise, furthermore, to difficulties in relating to God. These may include an inability to trust or be intimate with God; fear of God (as distinct from awe); the inability to feel accepted or loved by God; feeling rejected or abandoned by God; feeling distant from God; or feeling disappointment or anger with God.

In thinking about the spiritual problems people often wrestle with, Pargament (2007) distinguishes between what he calls 'problems of spiritual destinations' and 'problems of spiritual pathways'. Problems relating to spiritual destinations are concerned with the way in which we perceive or image the Sacred in our lives. Such images – what he calls 'small gods' – are often too restrictive. Effectively, they put god in a box that is too small, that cannot encompass the full range of our experience of the Divine and that does not fully reflect the nature of the Divine. There are also 'false gods', gods which are not gods such as alcohol, drugs, sex, fame or power but which can attain a god–like status in our lives. Problems can also occur when a person holds conflicting images of a personal god simultaneously. As Pargament points out, it is possible for one person to see such a god as both loving and punitive, as both close and distant. Finally, people can 'demonise' both themselves and others (seeing themselves or others as evil) or attribute their problems to the demonic (for example, seeing themselves as under 'spiritual attack') in an attempt to externalise responsibility for the problems they face.

Problems relating to spiritual pathways relate to the breadth and depth of our spirituality and how well it is integrated into our lives. Pargament (2007: 152) points to research evidence which indicates that where spirituality is no more than 'a loose set of beliefs, practices, relationships, and experiences' rather than 'a way of being that is broad and deep, touching on virtually every dimension of life', it is less likely to support good psychological functioning and may actually cause psychological problems. This echoes Allport's distinction between intrinsic and extrinsic religiousness (Allport and Ross 1967). People with an extrinsic religious orientation rely on their religion to meet their own needs for security, comfort, status, self–esteem or social support. Their religion is effectively instrumental and compartmentalised rather than fully integrated into the rest of their lives. For people with an intrinsic orientation, on the other hand, their religion is their 'master motive' and a fundamental aspect of their concept of self. It is fully incorporated into their lives to the extent that, as Allport and Ross (1967) put it, they 'live' their religion. Swinton (2001) highlights a review of the relevant research relating to Allport's two religious orientations which suggests a positive correlation between an intrinsic orientation and mental health and a negative correlation between an extrinsic orientation and mental health (Mickley et al 1995).

I have also worked with many people who were experiencing some kind of faith crisis. Sometimes, clients may find it difficult to make sense of or come to terms with profound spiritual experiences they have had such as conversion experiences, mystical experiences or spiritual desert experiences. Often this is because what has happened to them is outside their normal range of experience and they have no conceptual framework that enables them to make sense of it. In rare circumstances, such experiences can be so powerful that they create what has been referred to as 'a spiritual emergency' (Grof and Grof 1989). A spiritual emergency occurs when, as the result of a particularly powerful spiritual experience or a period of rapid spiritual development, the conscious self is overwhelmed by the experience and cannot assimilate or integrate it. Normal psychological functioning can then become disrupted for a period of time and the person may need help and support in processing the experience and integrating it into his or her spiritual framework and life. Cortright (1997: 173 – 178) offers a useful discussion of how such spiritual emergencies are best handled from a transpersonal psychotherapy perspective.

Alternatively, clients may be experiencing a loss of faith (or an intense fear of losing faith), often following a significant life crisis or trauma and frequently accompanied by a profound sense of loss. Others may be caught up in a difficult and disturbing transition from one faith stage to another, more often than not, between Fowler's stages 3 and 4 (Fowler 1995, 1996). Such transitions are often profoundly disorientating and distressing and it can be very difficult for people to find their way through them without support. One might argue that faith communities themselves are in the best position to support people through such spiritual crises and in an ideal world, this would indeed be the case. Sadly, however, it is often very difficult for people to find the kind of support they need in the context of their faith communities and so their spiritual distress finds its way into the therapeutic encounter. The process they are going through is often significantly misunderstood and consequently, they are not given the information they need in order to enable them to see it as part of the normal, healthy process of spiritual development.

Finally, some of the most difficult work I have done has involved working with people who are recovering from an experience of being in some way spiritually abused or whose lives are being adversely affected by what

Clinebell (1984) calls 'pathogenic religion' – that is, a form of religion that is in some way damaging of our physical, mental or spiritual health and well–being. This is an issue I will return to later.

Working with spiritual issues in practice: a person-centred perspective

In order to illustrate the process of working with spiritual issues in therapy more clearly, I intend to draw on some of my client work. Over the years, much of my work as a therapist has been in pastoral settings where clients are made aware that the spiritual dimension of their lives is taken seriously and is viewed as one of many areas of concern that they might choose to bring to therapy. Because of the socio–cultural context within which I work, most of my work with religious clients has been with Christians whose religious faith is theistic – that it, it is based on a belief in and relationship with a personal god. I suspect, however, that the general principles that are important in working with spiritual issues in this context will also apply in other religious contexts.[1] I have also worked with a number of clients who would perhaps have described themselves as 'spiritual but not religious' or who would not have seen themselves as in any way religious or spiritual. They were nevertheless wrestling with spiritual concerns.

How then might a person–centred therapist work with such spiritual issues in practice when they come into the room? My experience tells me that at a practical level, working with such issues is in many respects no different than working with psychological issues. It does not require a significant shift in approach. It does not require the development of a new set of therapeutic skills or techniques. It does not necessarily require the use of specific spiritual interventions, although, as we have seen, these may in some circumstances be helpful. Furthermore, the fundamental importance of the quality of the therapeutic relationship remains the same whether we are working with the psychological or the spiritual dimension of experience.

One of the keys to working effectively with spiritual issues, I believe, is the willingness 'to go there' with the client. As a tutor and supervisor, I am aware of how difficult many trainee and qualified therapists find it to work in this area. Often they will back away from engaging at a meaningful level in dialogues about aspects of clients' spirituality, even when they are open to working in this area and have been trained to do so. Invitations from the client to attend to the spiritual are not recognised or are not taken up. Explorations of spiritual issues that the client raises are cut short, kept at a superficial level or not followed through in a focused way. Much–needed challenges in relation to aspects of the client's spirituality are not offered. There are many reasons for this, most of them rooted in fears of one kind or another. Overcoming this reticence is perhaps the first task facing the spiritually–oriented therapist and is essential if we are to work effectively with the spiritual dimension of life.

Another important key is that of learning to work comfortably within the client's spiritual framework. Griffith and Griffith (2002: 49) call this working within a person's 'familiar discourses' and see it as analogous to the position adopted by an anthropologist who seeks to learn about and understand an as yet unknown culture but ' not to disturb or harm it by intruding'. We need to be able to move around freely in the client's spiritual world, seeing it as they see it, treading softly and reverently on their sacred ground as we seek to understand the role that their spirituality plays in their life. We need to be able to receive and honour their spiritual story, however alien it might seem to us. We need to learn to understand and use the language of their spirituality, remembering that the particular words, metaphors and symbols they use may not mean the same thing as they do to other people, even when they share the same spiritual tradition.

And if we believe there are good grounds for challenging a particular aspect of the client's spirituality, we need to do so in a way that works from within their spiritual framework rather than from outside of it. This is not always easy. It requires that we are always open to learning from the client; that we are willing to be congruent when we do not understand; that we are prepared to acknowledge it when our assumptions have led to misunderstanding or miscommunication; and that we are willing to face our own prejudices when they threaten to disrupt our empathic connection with the client. This is, however, no different than it would be in relation to any other aspect of the client's experience or frame of reference.

Working with the issue of forgiveness

One of the spiritual issues that often surfaces in therapy, both in religious and non-religious clients, is that of forgiveness. I have chosen to focus on this issue in particular because it remains a controversial one. Research suggests that facilitating the process of forgiveness may be one of the spiritual interventions most commonly used by spiritually–oriented therapists (Richards and Bergin 2005). This is because there is a growing body of research that suggests, as Benner (1990) argues, that the ability to forgive often plays an important part not only in the process of recovering from a significant relational breakdown, but also in the process of healing from emotional wounds. Drawing on their own and others' research, Richards and Bergin (2005) maintain that forgiveness can increase our sense of emotional well–being, impact positively on both our physical and mental health, restore our sense of personal power, facilitate our psychological growth and in some circumstances, bring about reconciliation with those who have hurt us. In secular therapy, however, there is little recognition of this despite the fact that in recent years, there has been an increasing focus on the process of forgiveness from a non–religious perspective (Thoresen et al 1998).

In my work with a client whom I shall call Dee, the theme of forgiveness was a prominent one. Dee was a practising Christian who had come to therapy in her mid–forties in order to work through the emotional and spiritual impact on her of having had an abortion as a teenager. She had fallen pregnant accidentally in her mid–teens. Her parents who were both practising Christians themselves had reacted very badly to this. Dee wanted to go ahead with the pregnancy and to keep the baby but her parents refused to support her in this decision and insisted that Dee have an abortion. They told her that she had shamed herself and her family and that they would not stand by and allow this shame to become public knowledge. Dee felt that she had no choice but to submit to her parents' wishes. She was also told that if she ever told anyone about the pregnancy, they would disown her. Consequently, she had carried the secret of her abortion for over thirty years without any emotional support. She saw herself as wholly responsible for the abortion. Furthermore, she had never allowed herself to acknowledge or express the anger she felt towards her parents (both now dead) for pressurising her into taking a course of action that went against the values and beliefs that were so important to her. She struggled with a deep sense of shame and guilt, low self–esteem and an inability to forgive herself for what she saw herself as having done. She had also not fully grieved the child she lost.

From a core self model perspective, Dee's problems were compounded by elements of her belief system as a Christian which were preventing her from reaching a resolution of her difficulties. Her image of God was one of a righteous, stern and unforgiving God (an image that had been strongly portrayed to her by her parents) and she believed that she had committed an unforgivable sin in taking her child's life. She was intensely preoccupied by her own innate sinfulness as she saw it, and believed that however hard she tried, she would never be able to 'wipe the slate clean' and earn God's forgiveness and love. She talked of having confessed her sin to God on numerous occasions and of having been reassured by her pastor that God had forgiven her. She had also received prayer ministry from her church a number of times. She had not, however, felt forgiven and nothing had shifted her persistent sense of guilt and shame. Moreover, as her anger towards her parents began to surface in therapy, she was eventually able to acknowledge that she had never really forgiven them. That failure then became another stick to beat herself with.

Working with Dee's issues relating to forgiveness was a complex and difficult process that needed very careful handling. Forgiveness is a core value and central element of the Christian faith and the Bible is interpreted as commanding Christians to seek God's forgiveness and to forgive others as they themselves have been forgiven by God (Col. 3: 13; Luke 6: 37; Matt. 18: 21 – 22). Receiving God's forgiveness is, furthermore, seen as being dependent on one's willingness and ability to forgive others (Matt. 6: 14 –16). Dee was fully aware of this and part of her difficulty in accepting God's forgiveness was her awareness that she had not yet found it possible to let go of her anger towards her parents.

Forgiveness is, however, a very difficult task to achieve whether we look at it from a psychological or spiritual perspective (Worthington 1998). It is also a process which is often misunderstood as it was by Dee. Forgiveness is a process not a one–off event as West (2004) and others have emphasised. It is also a process that may take a very long time, that may never be fully completed and that for some people, may never begin. Timing is, I believe, all important. Indeed encouraging what is often referred to as 'premature forgiveness' is therapeutically unproductive and potentially damaging to the client.

Benner (1990) sees the work of emotional healing as involving three major tasks. The first task is that of re–experiencing the pain, an emotional task which involves 're–connecting with the pain of the emotional injury'. The second is that of re–interpreting the hurt. This is an intellectual task which involves changing distorted perceptions of the hurtful experience, the people who hurt us and of ourselves and learning to identify and empathise with the offender. The third and final task is that of releasing the anger, a volitional task which involves letting go of anger and moving into forgiveness. This is similar to Enright's twenty step process model of forgiveness (Enright and Coyle 1998) which outlines four key phases, each of which has a number of 'forgiveness guideposts'. The phases are those of uncovering anger (acknowledging the pain and exploring the injustice); deciding to forgive (exploring forgiveness and making a commitment to working towards it); working on forgiveness (reframing, developing empathy and compassion for the offender and bearing the pain); and the deepening of forgiveness which eventually leads to the experience of healing.

Benner (1990) argues that premature attempts at forgiveness can actually interfere with the healing process. This fits well with my own experience of working with the process of forgiveness. Genuine forgiveness is only possible once we have acknowledged, faced and expressed our feelings of anger, resentment and hurt. This was something that Dee had not yet done, in part because she saw anger itself as sinful and in part because she was afraid of becoming an angry person like her father. The depth of her father's anger had often frightened her as a child and she was determined to root out all traces of anger in herself.

Forgiveness is also not the same as forgetting, excusing, ignoring, condoning or overlooking the hurt. Benner (1990) argues that to forget the hurt is effectively to repress it. He also points out that forgiveness does not erase the memory of the hurt though it may lessen preoccupation with it and enable it to be recalled with less emotional pain. He sees excusing the offense, making allowances for it, overlooking it, ignoring it or minimising it as ways of defending against the pain. There may be reasons why people act as they do and seeking to understand those reasons is part of the process of reinterpreting the hurt. He points out, however, that reasons are not the same as excuses. In most instances of serious hurt, the behaviour of the other person is genuinely inexcusable and attempts to excuse may actually block the process of forgiveness.

Dee had engaged in all of these defensive processes. She had tried as far as possible to distance herself from the memory of her abortion and of her parents' behaviour at that time. She had made excuses for their reactions and minimised the part they had played in causing the intense emotional pain she had experienced. Encouraged by her church, she had engaged in a premature act of forgiveness as a young adult which resulted in further repression of her hurt and anger. She had not yet fully faced the pain her parents had caused her and so inevitably, had not been able to move towards forgiveness in the way she desired. Her expectations of the outcome of forgiveness were also unrealistic. She believed that once she had forgiven her parents, she would no longer experience any pain. As Benner (1990: 124) points out, however, the act of forgiveness '…is not a magic formula to eliminate pain.' Feelings of hurt and anger often persist for some time afterwards but this does not mean that the act of forgiveness is not genuine. She also saw it as a 'one–off' act rather than as a process. Benner (1990) argues, however, that we may need to forgive the hurt many times to complete the process.

Enabling Dee to work through her inability to forgive herself, her fear that she had not been forgiven by God and her inability to forgive her parents required working with her issues in relation to forgiveness on a number of different levels. In relation to her inability to forgive herself, the process of 're-interpreting the hurt', as Benner (1990) calls it, eventually enabled her to move towards a more realistic attribution of responsibility in relation to the abortion and a more compassionate understanding and acceptance both of herself and of her parents. In relation to her inability to forgive her parents, initially this involved affirming her strong desire, intention and commitment to forgive, normalising her struggle to do so and pointing her to a specific resource which gave her information about the process of forgiveness. This enabled Dee to reframe her experience and struggle to forgive and to see herself as in the process of forgiving rather than as failing to forgive.

Then followed the emotional work of 're–experiencing the pain', as Benner (1990) describes it. Telling the story of the abortion for the first time ever was an important part of that process and enabled her to begin to allow herself to feel the pain that she had been suppressing for so long. In relation to her feelings of anger, this process required not only addressing her fear of her own anger, but also gently challenging the mis–interpretation of scripture which was fuelling her belief that anger is sinful. This was a difficult challenge to offer, in part because her beliefs about anger had been shaped to a degree by her church's teaching (or at least by her interpretation of it) and in part because Dee's locus of evaluation was largely externalised.

Griffith and Griffith (2002) argue that it is often riskier to focus on a person's religious beliefs rather than on their spiritual stories, experiences and metaphors. This may be particularly true for those who have a Christian or Muslim faith. Christianity and Islam attach a great deal of importance to beliefs not only about God, but also about the authority of their sacred texts. Holding 'the right beliefs' can, therefore, be very important for many Christians and Muslims. In Judaism, Hinduism and Buddhism, however, such beliefs serve a lesser role. Griffith and Griffith (2002: 143) also distinguish between convictions and assumptions. Convictions – that is, 'commitments to what is regarded to be of ultimate reality or ultimate in its importance' – are generally strongly held, often to the point of being unshakeable, even in the face of clear evidence or compelling arguments to the contrary. Assumptions are more loosely and less rigidly held and are therefore more readily reality–tested. They also point out, furthermore, that the same religious belief can be held as an assumption by one person, but as a conviction by another. Convictions are passionately and strongly defended, often to the point that anybody holding different beliefs or challenging the convictions will come under attack.

Griffith and Griffith (2002) argue that it is often counterproductive for a therapist to treat such convictions as if they were testable hypotheses. Richards and Bergin (2005) also emphasise the importance of avoiding getting into a scriptural or theological debate or argument with the client, arguing that this could lead to the unethical imposition of the therapist's beliefs and values on the client. In my work with Dee, I was very conscious of the danger of doing so or of appearing to set myself up as a religious authority who was directly challenging the teaching and authority of her church leaders. Moreover, in relation to Dee's spiritual development, there were many elements of her spirituality which appeared to fit with Fowler's description of Stage 3 – the synthetic-conventional stage of faith which is characterised by a strong dependence on and loyalty to one's faith community and to external religious authority, an absence of doubt and questioning and a lack of critical reflection on beliefs and values (Fowler 1995). I was also aware of the tensions involved in continuing to respect and work from within Dee's own spiritual framework, while at the same time challenging an aspect of that framework which was impeding her psychological growth and healing.

Instead of challenging the rationality of such damaging beliefs, Griffith and Griffith (2002) advocate helping the client, wherever possible, to explore the real–life consequences of holding the belief. Similarly, Pargament (2007) talks about what he calls 'pragmatic challenges' – challenges which invite clients to explore the negative consequences for them of holding the particular beliefs they do. For Dee, the real–life consequence of holding the belief that anger is sinful was that she was suppressing her anger, a strategy that we know is likely to have negative consequences for her, both emotionally and physically. In so doing, she was blocking her own emotional healing. Giving her information about the process of forgiveness and about the importance of expressing the hurt and anger before moving into forgiveness went some way towards encouraging a loosening of her belief. In Dee's case, however, it was not enough to enable her to let go of it altogether.

Pargament (2007) also identifies two other kinds of interventions that can be used to challenge rigidly held spiritual beliefs which are in some way detrimental to the client. He suggests that it can often be helpful to identify what he calls 'spiritual inconsistencies' between clients' beliefs and sacred teachings and, where appropriate, to offer alternative passages from scripture (or from other forms of spiritual writings) which enable the client to see that there may be other possible interpretations of those teachings. Another intervention which I have found useful is that of helping clients to explore how they came to adopt a particular belief. Identifying the influences that have shaped a particular belief can enable clients to step back from it and encourage them to be more reflective about it. Questions such as 'How does it fit with the way you think?' or 'How does it fit with your experience?' can also encourage clients to consider the belief from their own internal frame of reference in a way that they may not have done, or had 'permission' to do, before.

This is an intervention that proved very helpful in Dee's case. Challenging her interpretation of scripture also involved my pointing her towards stories in the

Bible in which Jesus clearly felt and displayed anger and inviting her to consider how this fitted with her belief that all anger is sinful. It then involved giving her information that there might be other ways of understanding the passages she was concerned about and pointing her to a particular resource that offers a balanced exploration of the issue of anger. This book was written from within a Christian framework that was close enough to her own and therefore was unlikely to be too threatening to her.

Moving into the final stage of releasing her anger and of moving towards forgiveness proved easier for Dee once she had faced the pain she had been suppressing. Benner (1990) sees this as a process which has three steps – preparation, execution and repetition. The task of preparation is partly concerned with developing the client's understanding of the process of forgiveness and helping them to adjust their expectations of what will result from the act of forgiveness (both largely a matter of information–giving). With some clients who are experiencing difficulty in letting go of their anger despite their willingness to do so, it may also involve exploring their resistance in an accepting and nonjudgmental way. Benner highlights a number of possible reasons why clients may resist the movement towards forgiveness. These include not being ready to give up the feelings of moral superiority and power that they might have in relation to the person who hurt them; wanting to punish the person who hurt them and seeing withholding forgiveness as a way of doing so; not wanting to feel vulnerable or to take the risk of being hurt again; and believing that forgiveness should only be offered if the person who hurt them has requested it and therefore deserves it.

The task of execution is the act of forgiveness itself. Benner (1990: 126) argues that forgiveness should always be related to specific acts or behaviour and that attempts at what he calls 'global forgiveness' are rarely effective. He also suggests that forgiveness is often most meaningful when it involves verbally expressing forgiveness for each offense (not necessarily directly to the person concerned). It may also involve taking some form of action such as writing a letter expressing forgiveness (which may not be sent) or changing one's behaviour towards the offender.

Dee decided that it would be helpful for her to write down all the specific things her parents did and said that had hurt her and, when she felt ready to do so, to destroy the piece of paper that she had written them on. This took the form of a simple ritual that she chose to carry out during a therapy session. It proved very meaningful and cathartic for her and it did seem that it somehow 'sealed' or brought to completion the process of forgiveness in the way that Benner suggests. Dee's own words were that it had 'finally given her closure'.

The third task is that of repetition which strictly speaking is not a separate task in itself, but simply a recognition that the execution of the act of forgiveness may need to be repeated a number of times. In his five step REACH model of the process of forgiveness, one that overlaps considerably with that of Benner (1990), Worthington (1998) refers to this as the task of 'holding on' to the forgiveness. Again, it can be helpful here to indicate to clients that there may be a need to repeat an act of forgiveness, even if it feels complete at the time. Dee left therapy feeling that she had finally found closure, but also aware of the possibility that the need to forgive might surface again.

Finally, in relation to Dee's inability to feel forgiven by God, this also required work on a number of different levels. It included focusing on Dee's images of God and the way in which they had been formed. It also involved a gentle process of challenging her negative images in order to enlarge her understanding of God. People often have more than one image of God and these may be in conflict with each other. This was certainly true for Dee. One of her images of God was that of a very strict and unforgiving God who would not tolerate imperfection. Another, however, was the God portrayed by the biblical story of the prodigal son, which interestingly was her favourite passage from the Bible. As we explored these conflicting images in therapy, she began to realise the extent to which her negative image of God had been shaped by her parents and particularly by her father's disciplining of her as a child. In effect, she slowly came to recognise that she had transferred many of her perceptions of and feelings about her father on to her relationship with God.

Another intervention which I have found helpful is that of encouraging clients, where appropriate, to draw on their own spiritual experience in reflecting on the images of God they hold. Dee had recounted to me a very positive spiritual experience she had had during a time of prayer which she described as being 'totally flooded by God's presence'. I asked her to reflect on this experience and to think about what she had learnt from it about the nature of God. She had no hesitation in describing the God she experienced in those moments as accepting, forgiving and deeply loving. Her difficulty in the past had been in trusting her own experience, an issue that we then explored in its own right.

Exline and Rose (2005) suggest a number of possible interventions that may be helpful in enabling people to enlarge their understanding of God. These include encouraging the client to engage in a two–way conversation with God in which the client speaks to God and then imagines God's response. This can be done verbally in therapy or through writing letters or journaling. Dee embarked on this process spontaneously during the course of her therapy. She kept a spiritual journal and found herself on one occasion writing a letter to God. She brought the letter with her to the next session and having read it through, I asked her how she imagined God would respond to it. At that moment, she started to cry because, as she disclosed when the tears finally subsided, she suddenly 'knew' exactly what God would say to her. We were nearing the end of the session so I asked her if she thought it might be helpful to try and write down what she thought God would say at some point during the week. She seemed eager to do so. The following week she returned with a letter she had written to herself, voicing God's response to her as she imagined it. She was deeply moved by this process and I believe that it did play an important role in enabling her to reshape her images of God.

As she moved towards a more positive imaging of God, a more realistic attribution of responsibility in relation to the abortion and a deeper acceptance of her own struggle to forgive her parents, she was finally able to feel that God had forgiven her for getting pregnant – the only aspect of her behaviour that she now saw as needing forgiveness. This process then led her, again unprompted, into a profoundly touching two way dialogue with the child she had lost. This proved to be the final aspect of our work together. It was instrumental in enabling Dee not only to come to terms with the abortion she had had, but also to move forwards in the grieving process, both in relation to her lost child and in relation to her parents.

It goes without saying that clients should never be pressurised to forgive when they are not willing or able to do so. In fact, I believe that it is generally inappropriate to bring the issue of working towards forgiveness into the room unless the client has already indicated that he or she has concerns about it or wishes to address it. Clients who cannot forgive because the hurt is too severe and runs too deep within them need not our judgment, but our acceptance and empathy. Having said that, my experience of working with this issue in therapy tells me that, when well–timed, sensitively and carefully handled and successfully negotiated, the process of forgiving can have significant benefits for the client as it undoubtedly did in Dee's case.

The impact of pathogenic religion

My work with another client whom I shall call Tim touches on an issue that is of serious concern in relation to what Clinebell (1984) called 'pathogenic religion' – that is, religion that is unhealthy or growth–inhibiting. It is also the story of someone in the stormy waters of transition (Fowler 1996) who, as is so often the case, was not receiving the acceptance, understanding and support he needed in order to enable him to keep his head above water.

Tim was in his late thirties. He came to therapy struggling with feelings of deep depression, anxiety, low self–esteem, shame and guilt. Very early on in our work together, he also expressed his fear that he was losing his Christian faith, a prospect that was deeply disturbing to him. He spoke of feeling that spiritually he was 'standing on shifting ground', that in relation to his faith, nothing made any sense to him anymore and that he no longer knew what he thought or whom or what he believed in. As Tim told his story, it became apparent that on a spiritual level, what he was experiencing was a transition between Fowler's Stage 3 (the synthetic–conventional stage of faith) and Stage 4 (the individuative–reflective stage) – the most difficult of the faith transitions to negotiate (Fowler 1995). This process had started about a year before he entered therapy, but it had been intensified by his recent experience of being spiritually abused by members of the faith community to which he belonged.

I would define spiritual abuse in the following way. Spiritual abuse occurs when someone with real or perceived spiritual authority uses that authority to coerce, control, exploit or otherwise mistreat others with the result of harming their psychological or spiritual well–being and undermining their spirituality. This results in what Johnson and Van Vonderan (1991) call 'toxic faith' – a damaging and destructive relationship not with the Divine, but with a religion or religious system that seeks to manipulate people and to control their lives in ways that are damaging of their psychological or spiritual well–being and that inhibit their growth.

This concept of 'toxic faith' is closely related to Clinebell's concept of 'pathogenic religion' (Clinebell 1984). The word 'pathogenic' comes from two Greek roots: 'pathos' (disease) and 'genesis' (bringing into being). Literally, therefore, it means bringing dis–ease into being. A pathogenic religion is a religion which is at some level damaging of our well–being and which blocks, impedes or limits our overall growth and development. A religion can be pathogenic at one of more of the following levels: at the level of its system of beliefs giving rise to pathogenic theology; at the level of its moral codes and practices giving rise to pathogenic laws, rules and practices (such as rites, ceremonies and forms of prayer or worship); and at the level of the systems within which it is practised giving rise to pathogenic faith communities.

Clinebell (1984: 118 – 119) identified a number of criteria which he believed can be useful in assessing the extent to which a particular religion is pathogenic or salugenic (health–promoting). Drawing on Clinebell's criteria and on what I have learnt both from my own personal and practical experience, I have attempted to identify a set of characteristics which, taken together, depict the nature of pathogenic religion as I see it. Pathogenic religion stresses the sinfulness, evilness and worthlessness of humanity rather than its inherent worth. It fosters distorted images of the Divine and emphasises divine judgment and punishment rather than divine love and grace. It inhibits rather than fosters psychological and spiritual growth and well–being. It is autocratic and authoritarian rather than democratic; it is controlling and oppressive rather than valuing of individual autonomy and freedom. There is an over–emphasis on obedience and submission. It is dogmatic, narrow–minded and unquestioning rather than open–minded, questioning and critically reflective. It treats beliefs as facts and is not open to differing perceptions, viewpoints and interpretations. It discourages rather than promotes independent thinking. It suppresses challenge and stifles genuine dialogue and debate rather than encouraging it. It requires conformity rather than valuing diversity and allowing people to find their own answers and their own way.

It is excluding of those who do not 'fit the mould' rather than inclusive and tolerant. It is socially oppressive (for example, of women or of gay people) rather than liberating. It is preoccupied with religious performance and values doing more than being. It is legalistic and rule–bound to the point that there is an excessive adherence to laws and a strong emphasis on 'thou shalt not' teachings which must be rigidly adhered to rather than applied with flexibility, tolerance and compassion. It is demanding and perfectionist rather than gracious and it places heavy burdens on people. As such, it gives rise to unhealthy life strategies such as people pleasing and perfectionism in an attempt to ensure acceptability to the Divine. It punishes those who 'fall short' or do not comply rather than accepting people's woundedness and vulnerabilities. It is guilt– and shame–inducing rather than compassionate and forgiving. It is disempowering rather than empowering.

Such abuse of power may not always be obvious or extreme such as when individual leaders use their position of spiritual power and authority to meet their own needs for power, influence or emotional or sexual gratification. It may also be very subtle and therefore harder to identify. It occurs whenever an individual uses his or her spiritual position to control, manipulate or dominate another person; when an individual fails to respect the feelings and opinions of another, or attacks or belittles another's feelings or opinions without any concern for that person's spiritual or emotional well–being; when people are pressurised to conform or live up to a 'spiritual standard' in a way that promotes external 'spiritual performance'; when an individual uses his or her spiritual authority to pressurise people to take part in activities with which they are not comfortable; or when people are shamed into conforming, supporting a particular belief or position or not asking legitimate questions.

The impact of significant spiritual abuse can be devastating. Furthermore, it can impact people at all levels of their being. At a spiritual level, it can lead to spiritual disempowerment and a sense of being inadequate, unacceptable or inferior as a spiritual person. It can result in the development of distorted images of and inability to trust the Divine or an excessive fear of the Divine. It can give rise to a preoccupation with divine punishment and with spiritual performance, often accompanied by extreme perfectionism and intense feelings of guilt and shame. It can bring about a range of difficulties in relating to the Divine and accepting the forgiveness of the Divine. It can also lead to a faith crisis, a faith transition, loss of faith or conversion to another faith.

Depending on the nature and severity of the abuse, it can also lead at an emotional level to a wide range of negative emotions such as depression, anxiety, feelings of inadequacy or failure, loss of self–worth, self–blame or self–hatred, feelings of guilt and shame, feelings of powerlessness and intense confusion, feelings of hurt and anger and feelings of having been traumatised. At a psychological level, it can result in a range of psychological problems such as an externalised locus of evaluation; a distorted self-image and shame–based identity; a fear of failure or making mistakes; a strong pattern of people pleasing; an inability to hold appropriate boundaries or to say 'no'; an inability to look after self; difficulties in taking appropriate personal responsibility; and an over–dependence on others at the same time as a difficulty in trusting them.

Tim was evidencing a significant number of the difficulties outlined above. Moreover, at the start of therapy, he was very confused about the problems he was experiencing in his relationship with his church community. These difficulties began when Tim took the risk of disclosing to the leadership team at his church that he is gay. This was a very significant risk for him to take as he knew that the particular church he was attending regarded the practising of homosexuality as a sin and that there were some members of the church community who were markedly homophobic.[2] Furthermore, Tim had struggled with his sexual orientation for many years to the extent that he had kept it secret from virtually everyone in his life. On a number of occasions in the past, he had sought prayer ministry and what is known as conversion therapy[3] outside the context of his church in the hope that this might bring about a change in his sexual orientation. He had only recently begun to come to terms with the fact that he is gay and as part of that process had reached the decision to start being open with others about it. He also talked with the leadership about the faith crisis he was experiencing and his fear that he might lose his faith altogether.

The leaders of the church community to which Tim belonged reacted very badly to his disclosures. They urged him very strongly to continue seeking help through prayer ministry and told him that he could undoubtedly change his sexual orientation if he really wanted to and if his faith and trust in God's healing power was strong enough. They also told him that he would have to withdraw from his voluntary position as a youth worker in the church with immediate effect. When he refused further prayer ministry, this was seen as evidence of his sinfulness and unwillingness to repent and of a 'spirit of disobedience' from which he needed to be delivered. Tim also felt he had been subtly threatened with expulsion from the community if he did not defer to the leadership. At the point at which Tim entered therapy, he had written to his church leaders to say that he needed time out from church to reflect and that he did not wish any further contact with the community until he was ready to return. Despite this request, he received what he described as 'a barrage' of highly distressing letters, telephone calls and emails urging him to reconsider and telling him that he was putting himself 'outside of God's love' and risking his salvation. One of these went as far as making reference to a passage from the book of Leviticus in the Bible which refers to homosexual acts as 'an abomination'. Furthermore, it became clear from some of the messages he received that the leadership had publicly informed the rest of the community about the reasons for his withdrawal, despite his request that his disclosure should be kept confidential.

As a result of these experiences, Tim's world was, as he put it, 'falling apart'. It felt to him as if the community which he had hoped would support him had abandoned and betrayed him when he did not comply with their demands. He felt isolated and desolate, emotionally and spiritually. He no longer knew who God was or if God cared about him. He felt guilty about abandoning his search for 'a cure' for his homosexuality, guilty that his faith was not strong enough to bring about the sexual healing he strongly desired and guilty about withdrawing from church. He saw himself as a failure on almost every level.

Working with Tim was a long and difficult process. In relation to the spiritual abuse he had experienced, this involved addressing a number of key tasks which I believe are central to the process of recovery. The first of these is that of facilitating the recognition that spiritual abuse has occurred. This involves encouraging the telling of the survivor's story by offering a safe space in which the story can be told and received with acceptance and empathy. It also requires that the survivor's feelings of having been abused are validated and that any denial or minimisation of the abuse is challenged. In Tim's case, he was able relatively early in the process to verbalise his awareness that he had found some of the behaviour of his church leaders very unhelpful and at times, harassing and threatening. He did not use the term 'abuse' at this stage and neither did I as I suspected it was not a term with which he would have been comfortable. Validating the strength of his feelings was, however, very important. It enabled him to work through his confusion over what had happened and to reach a place of recognition that his reactions were justifiable and not out of proportion.

The second task is that of facilitating awareness of the impact of the abuse. This involves helping the abuse survivor to identify and explore the impact of the abuse on their emotional, psychological and spiritual well–being and to make and understand the connections between the abuse and their current difficulties. This is closely allied to the third task – that of expressing and working through the emotional pain caused by the abuse. This requires giving survivors the space, freedom and permission to express their emotional pain fully without fear of judgement (particularly feelings that they might believe to be unacceptable or sinful such as anger). It also involves gently challenging any resistance to this process.

In Tim's case, being given a book on spiritual abuse by a close friend who was supporting him proved to be a turning point. It gave him the information he needed both to understand his experience and to become more aware of the complexity of its impact on him. Indeed, had he not been offered this resource outside the context of therapy, it is an intervention I would have considered. One of the difficulties Tim experienced in relation to working through his emotional pain was a sense of being disloyal not only to his church (which in many respects had been very supportive of him in the past), but also to God. This is not an uncommon difficulty. Where it does occur, helping clients to separate out their relationship with the abusive spiritual community from their relationship with God may be necessary.

The fourth task is that of re–empowering the survivor. This involves developing survivors' trust in their own experience and internal locus of evaluation and enabling them to begin to consider alternative more empowering perceptions and interpretations of that experience and of their behaviour. It also requires a process of deconditioning. This may include challenging distorted beliefs about self, others or God which have developed as a result of the abuse and addressing interpretations of sacred texts which have been used to manipulate and control the survivor. Finally, the therapist may also need to challenge the survivor's inappropriate self–blame and to encourage an appropriate reattribution of responsibility.

For Tim, this process of re–empowering was made easier by the fact that he was already caught up in a faith transition before the abuse occurred and so was beginning to question and reflect critically on elements of his faith tradition (including its beliefs about and attitudes to homosexuality). Re–empowering him involved enabling him to re–interpret the abuse (a process that is very similar to that described by Benner 1990) and to develop an understanding of why it had occurred. Eventually, he reached the conclusion that his church had acted primarily out of concern for him and that the abuse he felt he had experienced was not in any way intentional. He came to see it as arising out of a particular theological framework which had been rigidly applied to a very complex and difficult situation. He also concluded, however, that their approach had been very unhelpful and inadvertently damaging of him on many levels. At times, this process of re–interpretation required the use of challenging interventions such as the ones Pargament (2007) describes to help him reach his own decisions about how to interpret particular passages of the Bible and how to apply them to his own particular situation. Mostly, however, it involved working to re–establish his trust in his own experiencing and locus of evaluation, a trust that had been undermined by his faith community's emphasis on an unquestioning acceptance of their version of biblical truth. It also involved normalising the process of de–constructing faith that he was engaged in.

Finally, the sixth task is that of supporting the survivor in making desired life changes and addressing resolution issues such as finding meaning in the experience, addressing identity issues and issues relating to the process of forgiveness. For Tim, this revolved primarily around making what was for him a very difficult decision about whether to leave his church community; considering whether to seek spiritual accompaniment in order to find the support he needed in coping with the faith transition he was experiencing; and dealing with issues relating to his negative shame–based image of himself, his preoccupation with what he saw as his own sinfulness and his chronic feelings of guilt (largely inappropriate or false guilt).

In relation to the process of faith transition, I believe that spiritually–oriented therapists can potentially play a very important part in supporting people through this stage of the spiritual journey. As we have seen, because of their general lack of awareness and understanding of this stage of the journey, many church communities are unable to support or resource people as they begin to deconstruct their faith and often, as Tim's church did, see the process as one that needs at all costs to be suppressed. This leaves people in transition with nowhere to go at a time when they feel profoundly disoriented and disconnected with all that they were once deeply committed to. Supporting Tim through this healthy process of transitioning involved normalising and validating his experience and his growing need to reflect more critically on his spiritual beliefs and values (mainly an information–giving process which may involve the use of bibliotherapy or other similar interventions); offering a safe, accepting and non–judgmental space in which his fears, confusion and feelings of loss could be heard and held; working with him to identify and resolve the childhood–related issues that were inhibiting his trust in his own organismic experiencing and locus of evaluation; and supporting him in locating resources for himself which could inform and sustain him throughout the process.

Soul work

Finally, my work with a client whom I shall call Julia illustrates a dimension of therapy that I call soul work. I would define soul work as that aspect of therapeutic work that is primarily focused on the making of the soul journey – that is, the process of deepening our connection with the innermost part of our being, of letting go of the false self and embracing the true self, of 'giving birth' to and nurturing the emerging core self or soul. Julia entered therapy in her early fifties. Ostensibly, she had come to explore the impact on her of her recent divorce and indeed this was the primary focus in the early stages of our work together. Gradually, however, it became apparent that there was a deeper underlying issue that the breakdown of her marriage had brought to the surface. She began to talk of feeling that she had 'lost her way' in life, something that she believed had begun to happen long before her divorce. She saw her marriage as having 'sapped all of her energy', as having 'cut her off' from something deep inside herself that she intuitively felt to be of vital importance. She could not as yet put into words what this 'something' was but sensed that it was 'precious' and 'life–giving' and that she was 'in mourning' for it. Julia was clearly caught in the throes of an experience of 'alienation' as Slee (2004) calls it. She was profoundly disconnected from her core self to the point that she could speak of no longer knowing who she was or what she wanted. She recognised in herself a deep sense of longing but did not know what it was she was aching for. She was beginning to awaken.

At the start of one of our sessions, she told me of a dream she had had during the week. She spoke of feeling powerfully drawn to enter a dark cave that she had stumbled across whilst walking through a wood. In her dream, she knew that was searching for a treasure that she had mislaid. She did not know where to find it but knew instinctively that it was there, hidden deep in the recesses of the cave. As she descended deeper into the cave, she became aware that she was not alone, that someone was there walking with her in the semi–darkness. When I asked her who it was, she described a wise old woman who she knew intuitively had come to guide her – not to tell her what to do or where to go but to accompany her as she found her own way to the treasure she was seeking. In my experience, such dreams are not uncommon in this stage of awakening and the image of the wise old woman (or man) is an archetypal image that often plays an important role in the process.

Working with this dream in therapy proved to be a significant aspect of Julia's soul work. This was not so much a matter of helping her to understand and find meaning in the dream though it was important to her to try and make sense of what she was experiencing. As a person–centred therapist, my role in this process was not one of offering my insights and interpretations, but of sitting with her as she found her way to her own. Asking clients what a particular image means to them, how it is speaking to them, what associations they have to it or how they make sense of it themselves enables them to trust and draw on their own inner resources and wisdom. It avoids the danger of imposing an interpretation which may not fit, which may undermine their own internal spiritual authority and which may also divert or even shut down the imaginal process. The meaning a particular form of imagery holds for the therapist or has held for others may bear little or no relation to what it may mean for the client. Moreover, even if the therapist's interpretation were to be accurate, the client may not be ready to embrace it and may therefore be threatened by it. Where clients are struggling to make sense of their experience, I believe it is generally better to encourage them to sit with the 'not knowing' and wait patiently for the meaning to emerge, rather than to offer them another's analysis and understanding.

The most important part of this work with Julia, however, involved her continuing to work with the imagery of the dream both on her own and in therapy. Essentially, this was a process of allowing the imagery to continue to emerge and evolve as she attended to it. Sometimes this would happen in the course of what Watkins (1976 cited in Rowan 1993) calls 'waking dreams'. Waking dreams are hard to define. A waking dream is not a form of daydreaming. It is a dreamlike experience which occurs while the person is awake. Watkins (1976: 31) describes it as 'an experience of the imagination undertaken with a certain quality or attitude of awareness'. My experience of such waking dreams is that it seems as if the imagery is unfolding spontaneously as I immerse myself in it. In other words, it does not feel as if I am consciously directing or controlling the imagery as it surfaces. It seems, as I experience it, to have 'a life of its own'. Julia's waking dreams would often happen outside the context of therapy. Sometimes, however, they occurred as we were working together during the session. Julia would begin by reading a passage from her journal in which she had described the continuing unfolding of her imagery. What seemed significant is that she had chosen to write in the present rather than the past tense. The process of recounting her waking dream in this way then seemed to take her back into it and the story continued to emerge. This fits with my own experience of recounting a significant dream I had had to my therapist who encouraged me to tell the story of the dream in the present tense. As I came to the end of the dream story, I entered spontaneously into a waking dream in which the imagery of the dream continued to unfold.

As I see it, my role as a therapist in this work is simply to trust the emerging process and through being fully present, to be with and hold the client as he or she engages with it. I have learnt from experience that over–directing it is unhelpful and so I make very few interventions. I do not at any point introduce my own symbols or images or offer my own understanding or interpretation of what is emerging. A few reflections and simple questions (such as 'what is happening now?' or 'what else can you see?') are generally all that is needed to facilitate the imaginal process.

As Julia's imagery continued to unfold, she began to explore a number of different passageways in her cave. She had a strong sense that at the end of each passage there was something or someone she needed to find before she could eventually reclaim the treasure she had lost. The first of these passages led her to an encounter with what she called her 'child self'. At a psychological level, this was a part of herself that she had repressed as a result of a number of difficult childhood experiences which had left her feeling deeply shamed. Her encounter with and reclaiming of this part of herself was a very important part of her therapeutic journey. At a spiritual level, I believe that this process of reconnecting with her child self was in itself an aspect of Julia's soul journey. The child archetype is another important archetypal image in Jungian psychology. Jung (1973) saw the inner child as a symbol of wholeness. Abrams (1990: 1 – 6) sees it as 'a primordial image of the Self, the very centre of our individual being' and so identifies it directly with the soul. He sees the inner child as 'a uniting symbol' which plays an important part in the process of personality integration and believes that it surfaces within us when we become open to inner change and transformation. As such, it is 'a bearer of renewal through rebirth'. In Julia's case, her encounter with her child self resulted in the child joining forces with the wise old woman in accompanying and guiding her on her journey through the cave. When the two characters first met in her waking dream, she had the strong sense that they already knew each other, that they were already intimately connected and her child self continued to play an important role in her spiritual journey for some time to come.

Julia's soul journey is still unfolding. In her imaginal cave, she has since encountered and begun to reclaim other unlived parts of her core self – for example, her creative self, her sensual, sexual self, her 'strong woman' and her spiritual self – all of which she had at least partially repressed in the process of creating a false self that would enable her to survive in an environment where her needs were rarely met. In my experience, it is not uncommon for the imagination (the capacity for image–making) to play such a prominent role in soul work, both in men and in women. Elkins (1998: 47) believes that the soul 'works in the medium of imagination', that it discloses itself primarily through images, fantasies, dreams and symbols. Similarly, Hillman (1975) sees the imagination as 'the royal road to soul–making'. In the process of working with clients who are caught up in this process of becoming, I have encountered the image of the cave several times. Other similar imaginal journeys have centred on exploring the rooms in a house or other similar building, following the course of a stream or river, journeying to the heart of a forest, walking to the centre of a labyrinth or entering into a deep pool or lake of water. At one level, what is happening here is that particular archetypal growth processes are being symbolised. The process of letting go of the false self may, for example, be symbolised as a snake shedding its old skin (Rupp 1996). Similarly, the process of the emerging of the core self may be symbolised in a variety of ways such as a butterfly emerging from a chrysalis or as giving birth to a child (Monk Kidd 1990). The emerging soul may also appear in symbolic images which can take a number of forms. For Julia, the image of a multi–faceted diamond became very important to her and came to represent the treasure for which she was searching. For others such symbols have taken the form of a person (such as a particular character from mythology, literature or film) or an animal (such as a butterfly, a bear or a lion).

I have found that working at this soul level in therapy is profoundly growthful for the client at both a psychological and spiritual level. In my experience, it happens more commonly in clients who are in mid–life and in the context of a therapeutic encounter in which a degree of relational depth is developed. What I have learnt in facilitating this kind of therapeutic work is that it is important to trust both the client and the process and to encourage the client to do the same; to go 'with the flow' of what is emerging and to offer minimal direction, especially when the client's imaginal process is unfolding; to expect the unexpected, the surprising and the mysterious; to have a strong sense at times of standing on sacred ground; and to be open to change and growth in myself as well as in my clients.

Holding the boundaries

There are some writers such as May (1992) and Leech (2001) who might argue that therapy is not an appropriate context in which to address spiritual issues and that referring the client on – for example, to a religious leader or spiritual director – is the right course of action. I do not believe this to be the case. There may well be particular spiritual issues which might be more appropriately dealt with outside the context of therapy (such as, for example, a client's desire to explore alternative forms of prayer or to discuss alternative interpretations of sacred texts) and it goes without saying that therapists should not work outside the limits of their professional competence. However, as we have seen, spiritual problems are often inextricably interwoven with psychological problems. Each may be caused by the other and each may be exacerbated by the other. Moreover, the process of spiritual growth is closely intertwined with the process of psychological growth to the point that, at times, they seem virtually inseparable.

Spiritual direction or accompaniment is the process of accompanying another on his or her spiritual journey. I would argue that to hold the boundary between therapy and spiritual accompaniment too tightly is likely to weaken the effectiveness of both. Writing as a spiritual director, May (1992: 14) argues that 'to look to the spirit without addressing the mind is as absurd as caring for the mind without attending to physical health.' The reverse, I believe is also true. To look to the psychological without, where relevant, addressing the spiritual is equally absurd. Veness (1990) maintains that while therapists' primary focus is on psychological healing and growth, they also need to be comfortable working with the spiritual dimension. Similarly, spiritual directors or accompaniers, whose principal task is that of accompanying others on their spiritual journey, should also have some knowledge of and capacity to work with the psychological problems that may surface along the way. Separating out the two roles of therapist and spiritual director, she argues, can potentially lead to 'an artificial break in what should be a continuum of experience' (p. 259). Gubi (2012: 20) argues that within both disciplines of therapy and spiritual accompaniment, there can be 'a process of oscillation... between the work being psychologically–orientated or soul–orientated.' I refer to this process of oscillation as working 'in the overlap' between the two disciplines and I believe that to be maximally effective, both therapist and spiritual accompanier need to be willing and able to work in this overlap. Harborne (2012:129) would, I think, agree and goes as far as posing 'the heretical question' as to whether spiritual direction or accompaniment could usefully be seen as 'a particular and specific modality of psychotherapy'.

I have received both therapy and spiritual accompaniment. I have trained in both and offered both. My experiences of doing so have taught me that at the level of the relationship and encounter between client and therapist or client and spiritual accompanier, it is generally very hard to distinguish between the two processes. Gubi (2012: 19) echoes this when he asserts that in his experience, both disciplines have felt 'qualitatively "the same" in the nature of the encounter'.

What I have also learnt from these experiences is that both processes are more effective when there is a willingness on the part of the therapist or spiritual accompanier to move between the psychological and spiritual dimensions of being and experience in response to the client's own needs and agenda. This does not mean that there is no boundary to be held or that there is no difference at all between the two processes. There are undoubtedly key differences in structure, intention and primary focus and to a lesser degree, in the dynamics of the relationship. There are also times when spiritual accompaniment may be a more appropriate space within which the client can continue to explore his or her spiritual journey. For example, having worked with one of my clients for a number of months, it became apparent to both of us that our work together was becomingly increasingly focused on her developing spirituality and that she no longer needed the regular weekly sessions that she had had up to that point. The problems that she had presented in therapy had been largely resolved but as she put it, she had learnt so much about herself and grown to such an extent both psychologically and spiritually, that she wanted to continue the journey and to be accompanied in so doing. Moving into spiritual accompaniment with its gentler pace and stronger focus on the spiritual journey seemed a logical choice given the stage she had reached in her particular journey of becoming.

When working as a spiritual accompanier, there are also times when it may be appropriate to refer the client to a therapist in order to address the psychological issues that have emerged. Some months after I had begun working with another client as a spiritual accompanier, she disclosed an experience of childhood sexual abuse. She had never told anyone of this experience before and it was clear from her level of emotional distress that she needed to explore its impact on her in some depth. I would not consider spiritual accompaniment to be an appropriate context within which to do this work and so referred her to a therapist. At the same time, we continued to meet regularly, focusing on her experience of abuse only as it was impacting on her developing spirituality.

In general, however, it has been my experience that working in the overlap between spiritually–oriented therapy and spiritual accompaniment has been profoundly growth enhancing at both a psychological and spiritual level.

Implications for training and supervision

Richards and Bergin (2005) argue that in the USA, there is at present a gap between professional beliefs about the importance of including a focus on religion and spirituality in therapy training and what actually happens in practice. They point out that, despite a growing recognition in the profession that training courses should pay some attention to the spiritual dimension of experience, very few courses do so and when they do, their coverage of the topic tends to be somewhat superficial. I believe this to be true also of the majority of therapist training courses in the UK.

As far back as the late 1990s, Shafranske and Maloney (1996) identified a number of measures that they believe need to be taken in order to address the current deficiency in therapist training in relation to spirituality. They saw the ideal curriculum as having four key elements: a focus on values in therapy, a focus on the psychology of religion, a focus on working with spiritual issues in therapy and a focus on comparative religion. Drawing on Shafranske and Maloney's work, Richards and Bergin (2005) also make a number of recommendations in relation to standards of education and training for therapists. They argue that all therapists should receive training in multicultural attitudes and skills which should include a focus on religion and spirituality. They suggest that therapists should study a good range of the literature relating to spirituality and religion, the psychology and sociology of religion, the relationship between religion and mental health, the use of spiritual interventions and working with spiritual issues in therapy. They recommend that therapists should read one or two good books on world religions and develop a more specialised knowledge of those religious and spiritual traditions which they may encounter in the course of their work – for example, by reading relevant literature and where possible, by immersing themselves in the culture of that religion. This might even involve talking to people who practise it or perhaps attending a worship service.

Similarly, West (2000) makes a number of suggestions as to what preparation therapists might need in enabling them to work effectively with spiritual issues in the context of therapy. His recommendations overlap to some degree with those of Richards and Bergin (2005) but he also believes that therapists should have some awareness and understanding of the main maps and models of spiritual development; that they should study spiritually–oriented counselling approaches; that they should be familiar with the literature relating to spiritual experience; and that they should develop an awareness and understanding of the assessment issues relating to spirituality, including when and to whom to refer clients when they have reached the limits of their professional competence. He also suggests that they should have a good understanding of the similarities and differences between pastoral care and counselling, spiritual accompaniment and therapy.

In addition, he argues that it is important for spiritually–oriented therapists to be engaged in some form of spiritual development themselves and to have explored their own their own biases and prejudices in relation to spirituality and religion. Finally, he points out the importance of working with a supervisor who has the appropriate knowledge and understanding to support them in working with the spiritual dimension of their clients' lives.

For the past sixteen years, I have been involved in the development and delivery of a Higher Education training programme for professional counsellors in the UK. While the programme covers the same ground that would be covered in any good training programme of this nature, a substantial element of it is focused on equipping therapists to work with the spiritual dimension of experience. More recently, I have also been involved with a colleague of mine in the development of a modular nine month Continuing Professional Development course for qualified therapists. This course is specifically designed to deepen their understanding of human spirituality, both religious and non–religious, and to equip them to work effectively with the spiritual dimension of their clients' experience and problems in living, however that spirituality may be expressed.

The curriculum of both courses incorporates those areas that Richards and Bergin (2005) and West (2000) highlight but goes beyond them in a number of respects. The core self model that I have outlined in this book explicitly incorporates the spiritual dimension of human experiencing in a more systematic, in–depth way than is generally the case, other than in transpersonal and pastoral approaches. At a theoretical level, there is a primary focus on deepening students' understanding of spirituality and spiritual experience, both religious and non–religious; on developing their knowledge and understanding of a range of models of spiritual development including psychological, transpersonal and religious models; on exploring the complex relationship between spirituality and mental and physical health and well–being; and on looking at the concepts of pathogenic and salugenic religion.

At a practical level, the curriculum focuses on developing students' ability to work effectively with the spiritual dimension of experience; to understand the difficulties and ethical issues relating to the use of spiritual interventions in the context of therapy; and to work effectively with the kind of spiritual issues commonly encountered in therapeutic work. Students are introduced to a number of different spiritually–oriented therapeutic approaches and there is also an emphasis on the challenges of working cross–culturally, including a focus on how this relates specifically to religion and spirituality. Finally, at a personal development level, students are challenged to explore their own attitudes, beliefs and values; to articulate and reflect critically on their own philosophical and spiritual framework; to explore their own spiritual journeys; and to identify and work with their prejudices and biases in relation to religion and spirituality. Furthermore, throughout the course, students are encouraged to engage in a process of spiritual reflection on the theoretical concepts and ideas they are encountering and on their practice as part of the process of learning to integrate spirituality and practice.

I believe that such a curriculum gives students a very solid grounding at both a theoretical and practical level. It gives them the confidence to work with the client's spirituality when it comes into the room and the knowledge and skills to do so effectively. It also resources them in working with their own process issues in relation to working with clients whose spirituality may differ radically from their own. My challenge both to the developers and directors of counselling and therapy training programmes and to national organisations such as the BACP who set the standards for such programmes is to take the spiritual dimension of human experience much more seriously and to incorporate a reasonably in–depth focus on human spirituality in all professional training programmes, irrespective of their therapeutic orientation. I have also been deeply concerned at ex–students' anecdotal accounts of encountering ignorance, misunderstanding, lack of respect and prejudice in their tutors in relation to spirituality and religion. Given that BACP 'considers it important to respect the convictions of clients who have an allegiance to a faith community'; that BACP 'encourages high standards of training and awareness in spirituality and especially in its relationship to counselling and psychotherapy; and that BACP 'encourages counsellors and psychotherapists to engage with the aspects of faith and culture if their clients bring these to counselling/psychotherapy' (Thresholds summer 2010: 22), this is a serious failing that cannot be ignored.

A related challenge for the profession is to ensure that supervisors are adequately equipped to support and resource their supervisees in working with the spiritual dimension of their clients' problems in living. This is, as West (2000) points out, a very significant challenge given the failure of the majority of therapy (and supervision) training courses to address the issue of spirituality in any depth. His research has indicated that it is not uncommon for spiritually–oriented therapists to experience difficulties and tensions in their supervisory relationships when they are seeking supervision of their work in this area. At best, supervisors often feel ill–equipped to supervise work of this nature. At worst, they may actively discourage or oppose it.

In conclusion

As I have already discussed, it appears that the Zeitgeist is changing. There is an upsurge of interest in spirituality. Many people are spiritually hungry. Many are searching for a deeper meaning and purpose in life, for an inner peace that eludes them and for ways of nurturing their soul. But at the same time, more and more people are struggling with organised religion. Many do not feel at home within its walls and are following alternative spiritual paths, often in relative isolation. All too often, this leaves them with nowhere to go for help and support when they experience difficulties or face challenges in their spiritual lives or when aspects of their spirituality are impacting adversely on their well–being and growth. Some have been so damaged by organised religion that they are fearful of crossing its threshold again.

I believe that spirituality is going to come into the room more and more often in therapy as people seek a safe space to talk about their spiritual stories and to explore those aspects of their spiritual journey that are troubling them. Most would not think of seeking spiritual accompaniment or even know that such a possibility exists. Moreover, spiritual accompaniers are generally only trained to work with people who share their own religious tradition and often have little awareness or understanding of non–religious spirituality or of the close inter–relationship between spiritual and psychological development.

Properly trained and resourced spiritually–oriented therapists are, I think, well placed to meet this need. My hope is that the profession will rise to rather than avoid the challenge and in so doing, will 'put the soul back' in psychotherapy where it belongs.

Chapter 8 notes

1. Richards and Bergin (2000) present a series of articles on therapeutic work with clients from a range of religious and spiritual backgrounds including Christianity, Judaism, Islam, Hinduism, Buddhism and ethnic–centred spirituality (such as Native American spirituality).

2. Religious attitudes to homosexual orientation and practice vary widely. They range from outright condemnation of what is seen as unnatural and sinful to total acceptance, even within the same religious tradition. In general, the more liberal and progressive religious people are in their worldview and beliefs, the more accepting they are likely to be of homosexuality.

3. Conversion therapy (also known as reparative or reorientation therapy) is a highly controversial approach that seeks to change the client's sexual orientation from homosexual to heterosexual. There is no reliable evidence that conversion therapy is ever effective and strong evidence that it is psychologically harmful, often leading to significant emotional distress, self–harm and suicidal thoughts and behaviour (American Psychiatric Society Taskforce 2009). Leading national counselling bodies in the UK such as the British Association for Counselling and Psychotherapy (BACP), the National Counselling Society (NCS) and the Association of Christian Counsellors

(ACC) have all spoken out against the practice of conversion therapy which they consider to be unethical. All have issued statements instructing their members not to engage in its practice.

References

Abrams, J. (ed.) (1990) *Reclaiming the Inner Child*. London: Thorsons.

Ainsworth, M.D.S. (1985) 'Attachment across the Lifespan', *Bulletin of the New York Academy of Medicine*, 61: 792-812.

Alexander, C.N., Rainforth, M.V. and Gelderloos, P. (1991) 'Transcendental meditation, self-actualization, and psychological health: A conceptual overview and statistical meta-analysis', *Journal of Social Behavior and Responsibility*, 6: 189-247.

Allport, G.W. (1969) *The Individual and his Religion*. Ninth edition. New York: Macmillan.

Allport, G. W. and Ross, M. (1967) 'Personal Religious Orientation and Prejudice', *Journal of Personality and Social Psychology*, 5, 4: 432-443.

Armstrong, K. (1999) *The History of God*. London: Vintage.

Assagioli, R. (1975) *Psychosynthesis: A collection of basic writings*. New edition. Wellingborough: Turnstone Books.

Assagioli, R. (2000) *Psychosynthesis: A collection of basic writings*. Reprint. Amhurst, Mass: Synthesis Centre.

Astley, J. and Francis, L. (eds) (1992) *Christian Perspectives on Faith Development*. Leominster: Gracewing/Eerdmans.

Augsburger, D.W. (1986) *Pastoral Counseling Across Cultures*. Philadelphia: Westminster Press.

Baer, R.A. (2003) 'Mindfulness Training as a Clinical Intervention: A conceptual and empirical review', *Clinical Psychology: Science and Practice*, 10: 125-143.

Baldwin, M (ed.) (2000) *The Use of Self in Therapy*. Second edition. New York: Haworth.

Bartholomew, K. (1990) 'Avoidance of intimacy: An attachment perspective', *Journal of Social and Personal Relationships*, 7: 147-178.

Batson, C.D., Schoenrade, P. and Ventis, W.L. (1993) *Religion and the Individual: A social-psychological perspective*. New York: Oxford University Press.

Baumeister, R.F. and Leary, M.R. (1995) 'The Need to Belong: Desire for interpersonal attachments as a fundamental human motivation', *Psychological Bulletin*, Vol. 117, No. 3: 497-529.

Beauregard, M. and Paquette, V. (2006) 'Neural correlates of a mystical experience in Carmelite nuns', *Neuroscience Letters*, 405: 186-90.

Beck, A.T. (1976) *Cognitive Therapy and the Emotional Disorders*. New York: International Universities Press.

Benner, D.G. (1989) *Psychotherapy and the Spiritual Quest*. London: Hodder & Stoughton.

Benner, D.G. (1990) *Healing Emotional Wounds*. Grand Rapids, MI: Baker Book House.

Benner, D.G. (2002) *Sacred Companions: The gift of spiritual friendship and direction*. Downers' Grove, Ill: IVP.

Bly, R. (1988) *A Little Book on the Human Shadow*. New York: Harper Collins.

Bowlby, J. (1979) *The Making and Breaking of Affectional Bonds*. Oxford: Psychology Press.

Bozarth, J.D. (1998) *Person-Centred Therapy: A Revolutionary Paradigm*. Ross-on-Wye: PCCS Books.

REFERENCES

Bozarth, J.D. and Wilkins, P. (eds) (2001) *Rogers' Therapeutic Conditions: Evolution, theory and practice. Volume 3: Unconditional Positive Regard.* Ross-on-Wye: PCCS Books.

Bradshaw, J. (1988) *Healing the Shame That Binds You.* Deerfield Beach, Florida: Health Communications Inc.

Brazier, D. (1993) 'Congruence', cited in G. Wyatt, (ed.) (2001) *Rogers' Therapeutic Conditions: Evolution, theory and practice. Volume 1: Congruence.* Ross-on-Wye: PCCS Books.

Brenner, R.R. (1980) *The faith and doubt of Holocaust survivors.* New York: Free Press.

Bridger, F. and Atkinson, D. (1994) *Counselling in Context: Developing a theological framework.* London: Darton, Longman and Todd.

Bridges, W. (1980) *Transitions: Making sense of life's changes.* Reading, Massachusetts: Addison-Wesley.

Brierley, P. (2006) 'Pulling Out of the Nosedive. A contemporary picture of churchgoing: What the 2005 English church census reveals', *Christian Research.*

Buber, M. (1951) 'Distance and relation', *Hibbert Journal: Quarterly Review of Religion, Theology and Philosophy*, Vol. XL1X (2): 105-114.

Buber, M. (1958) *I and Thou.* London: T&T Clark. Translated by R.G. Smith.

Bugental, J.F.T. (1976) *The Search for Existential Identity: Patient-therapist dialogues in humanistic psychotherapy.* San Francisco: Jossey-Bass.

Cahn, B.R. and Polich, J. (2006) 'Meditation States and Traits: EEG, ERP, and Neuroimaging Studies', *Psychological Bulletin*, Vol. 132, No. 2: 180-211.

Cameron, R. (2003) 'Emotional and Subtle Contact', in J. Tolan, *Skills in Person-Centred Counselling and Psychotherapy.* London: Sage. pp. 100-109.

Cassidy, S. (1988) *Sharing the Darkness.* London: Darton, Longman and Todd.

Christ, C.P. (1986) *Diving Deep and Surfacing: Women writers on spiritual quest.* Boston: Beacon Press.

Clark, F.V. (1977) 'Transpersonal perspectives in psychotherapy', *Journal of Humanistic Psychology*, 17 (2): 69-81.

Clinebell, H.J. (1979) *Growth Counseling: Hope-centred methods of actualizing human wholeness.* Nashville: Abingdon.

Clinebell, H.J. (1984) *Basic Types of Pastoral Care and Counselling.* London: SCM Press.

Cooper, M (1999) 'If you can't be Jekyll be Hyde: An existential-phenomenological exploration of lived-plurality', in J. Rowan and M. Cooper (eds), *The Plural Self.* London Sage. pp. 51-70.

Cooper, M. (2005) 'Therapists' experiences of relational depth: a qualitative interview study', *Counselling and Psychotherapy Research*, 5 (2): 87-95.

Cooper, M. (2008) *Essential Research Findings in Counselling and Psychotherapy: The facts are friendly.* London: Sage.

Corbett, L. and Stein, M. (2005) 'Contemporary Jungian Approaches to Spiritually Oriented Psychotherapy', in L. Sperry and E.P. Shafranske, *Spiritually Oriented Psychotherapy.* Washington, DC: American Psychological Association. pp. 51-73.

Cortright, B. (1997) *Psychotherapy and Spirit.* Albany NY: State University of New York Press.

Crabb, L. J. (1977) *Effective Biblical Counseling: A model for helping caring Christians become capable counselors.* Grand Rapids: Zondervan.

Dalai Lama (2005) *Essence of the Heart Sutra: The Dalai Lama's Heart of Wisdom Teachings.* Somerville, MA: Wisdom Publications. Translated & edited by Geshe Thupten Jinpa.

REFERENCES

Daniels, M. (2002) 'The Transpersonal Self: 2. Comparing Seven Psychological Theories', *Transpersonal Psychology Review*, Vol. 6, No. 2: 4-21.

Davis, J., Lockwood, L. and Wright, C. (1991) 'Reasons for not reporting peak experiences', *Journal of Humanistic Psychology*, 31 (1): 86-94.

De Chardin, T. (2008) *The Phenomenon of Man*. New York: Harper Perennial.

Dickinson, E. (1891) cited in T.W. Higginson, 'Emily Dickinson's Letters', *The Atlantic Monthly*, Volume 68, No. 4: 444-456.

Dystra, C. and Parks, S. (eds) (1986) *Faith Development and Fowler*. Birmingham, A: Religious Education Press.

Eliade, M. (1961) *The Sacred and the Profane*. New York: Harper and Row.

Elkins, D.N. (1998) *Beyond Religion: A personal program for building a spiritual life outside the walls of traditional religion*. Wheaton, IL: Quest Books.

Elkins, D.N. (2005) 'A Humanistic Approach to Spiritually Oriented Psychotherapy', in L. Sperry and E.P. Shafranske (eds), *Spiritually Oriented Psychotherapy*. Washington, DC: American Psychological Association. pp. 131-152.

Elkins, D.N. (2009) *Humanistic Psychology: A clinical manifesto. A critique of clinical psychology and the need for progressive alternatives*. Colorado Springs, CO: Colorado School of Professional Psychology Press.

Elkins, D.N., Hedstrom, J.L., Hughes, L.L., Leaf, J.A. and Saunders, C. (1988) 'Towards a Humanistic-Phenomenological Spirituality: Definition, description and measurement', *Journal of Humanistic Psychology*, 28, 4: 5-18.

Elkins, D.N., Lipari, J. and Kozora, C.J. (1999) 'Attitudes and values of humanistic psychologists: Division 32 survey results', *The Humanistic Psychologist*, 27: 329-342.

Ellis, A. (1980) *The Case Against Religion: A psychotherapist's view and the case against religiosity*. New Jersey: American Atheist Press.

Ellison, C.W. (1983) 'Spiritual Well-Being: Conceptualization and measurement', *Journal of Psychology and Theology*, 11: 330- 340.

Enright, R.D. and Coyle, C.D. (1998) 'Researching the process model of forgiveness with psychological interventions', in E.L. Worthington, Jr. (ed.), *Dimensions of forgiveness: Psychological research and theological perspectives*. London: Templeton Foundation.

Erikson, E. (1958) *Young Man Luther: A study in psychoanalysis and history*. New York: W.W. Norton.

Erikson, E. (1968) *Identity, Youth and Crisis*. New York: W.W. Norton.

Erikson, E. (1980) *Identity and the Life Cycle*. New York: W.W. Norton.

Exline, J.J. and Rose, E. (2005) 'Religious and spiritual struggles', in R.F. Paloutzian and C.L. Park (eds), *Handbook of the Psychology of Religion and Spirituality*. New York: Guilford Press. pp. 315-330.

Ferenczi, S. (1956) cited in P. Halmos (1965) *The Faith of the Counsellors*. London: Constable.

Fisher, M.P. (2000) *Religions Today: An introduction*. Abingdon: Routledge.

Fisher, M.P. (2011) *Living Religions*. Eighth edition. London: Lawrence King.

Fowler, J.W. (1987) *Faith Development and Pastoral Care*. Philadelphia: Fortress Press.

Fowler, J. W. (1995) *Stages of Faith: The psychology of human development and the quest for meaning*. San Francisco: Harper Collins.

Fowler, J.W. (1996) *Faithful Change: The Personal and Public Challenges of Postmodern Life*. Nashville TN: Abingdon Press.

REFERENCES

Fowler, J.W., Streib, H. and Keller, B. (2004) *Manual for Faith Development Research*. Third edition. Atlanta: Center for Research in Faith and Moral Development, Emory University.

Frankl, V.E. (1997) *Man's Search for Meaning: An Introduction to logotherapy*. New York: Simon & Schuster.

Frankl, V.E. (2000) *Man's Search for Ultimate Meaning*. New York: Perseus Books.

Freud, S. (1920) 'Beyond the Pleasure Principle', in J. Strachey (1955), *The Standard Edition of the Complete Psychological Works of Sigmund Freud, Volume XVIII (1920-1922): Beyond the Pleasure Principle, Group Psychology and Other Works*. London: Hogarth Press and the Institute of Psychoanalysis. pp. 1-64.

Freud, S. (1961) *The Future of an Illusion*. New York: Norton. Edited and translated by J. Strachey.

Friedman, H., Krippner, S., Riebel, L. and Johnson, C. (2009) 'Transpersonal and Other Models of Spiritual Development', *International Journal of Transpersonal Studies*, 28: 112-118.

Fromm, E. (1956) *The Art of Loving*. New York: Bantam Books.

Goldsmith, M. and Wharton, M. (2004) *Knowing Me, Knowing You: Exploring personality type and temperament*. New edition. London: SPCK.

Goldstein, K. (1939) *The Organism: A holistic approach to biology derived from pathological data in man*. New York: Zone Books.

Grant, B. (1995) 'Perfecting the therapeutic attitudes: Client-centered therapy as a spiritual discipline', *The Person-Centered Journal*, 2(1): 72-77.

Griffith, J.L. and Griffith, M.E. (2002) *Encountering the Sacred in Psychotherapy: How to talk with people about their spiritual lives*. New York: Guilford Press.

Grof, S. (1975) *Realms of the Human Unconscious*. New York: Viking.

Grof, S. and Grof, C. (1989) *Spiritual emergency*. Los Angeles: Tasker.

Gubi, P.M. (2002) 'Practice behind closed doors – challenging the taboo of prayer in mainstream counselling culture', *Journal of Critical Psychology, Counselling and Psychotherapy*, 2, 2: 97-104.

Gubi, P.M. (2004) 'Surveying the extent of, and attitudes towards, the use of prayer as a spiritual intervention among British mainstream counsellors', *British Journal of Guidance and Counselling*, 32, 4: 461-476.

Gubi, P.M. (2008) *Prayer in Counselling and Psychotherapy*. London: Jessica Kingsley Publishers.

Gubi, P.M. (2012) 'Counselling and spiritual direction: the same, but distinct', *Thresholds: Counselling with spirit*, Summer. BACP publication. pp. 18-21.

Halmos, P. (1965) *The Faith of the Counsellors*. London: Constable.

Harborne, L. (2008) 'Working with Issues of Faith, Spirituality or Religion', *BACP Information Sheet G13*, Lutterworth: BACP publication.

Harborne, L. (2012) *Psychotherapy and Spiritual Direction: Two languages, one voice?* London: Karnac Books.

Harris, M (1988) *Women and Teaching*. New York: Paulist Press

Harris, M. (1989) *Dance of the Spirit: The seven steps of women's spirituality*. New York: Bantam Books.

Harris, T. (1973) *I'm Ok, You're Ok*. London: Arrow Books.

Haugh, S. and Merry, T. (eds) (2001) *Rogers' Therapeutic Conditions: Evolution, theory and practice Volume 3: Empathy*. Ross-on-Wye: PCCS Books.

REFERENCES

Hay, D. (1982) *Exploring Inner Space: Scientists and Religious Experience*. Harmondsworth: Penguin.

Hay, D. (2002) 'The Spirituality of Adults in Britain', S*cottish Journal of Healthcare Chaplaincy*, Vol. 5: 1

Hay, D. (2006) *Something There: The Biology of the Human Spirit*. London: Darton, Longman and Todd.

Hay, D. and Heald G. (1987) 'Religion is Good for You', *New Society*, 17 April.

Hay, D. and Hunt K. (2000) 'Understanding the Spirituality of People who don't go to Church'. *Final report of the Adult Spirituality project*, Nottingham University.

Hawkins, J. (2010) 'Walking the Talk: Potent therapy is a risky business', in J. Leonardi (ed.), *The human being fully alive*. Ross-on-Wye: PCCS Books.

Helminiak, D. (1987) *Spiritual Development: An interdisciplinary study*. Chicago: Loyola University Press.

Hermsen, E. (1996) 'Person-centered psychology and Taoism: the reception of Lao-tzu by Carl R. Rogers', *International Journal for the Psychology of Religion*, 6 (2): 107-25.

Heron, J. (1998) *Sacred Science: Person-centred inquiry into the spiritual and the subtle*. Ross-on-Wye: PCCS books.

Hillman, J. (1975) *Re-visioning Psychology*. New York: Harper & Row.

Hillman, J. (1996) *The Soul's Code*. New York: Random House.

Hoare, C.H. (2002) *Erikson on Development in Adulthood: New insights from the unpublished papers*. New York: Oxford University Press.

Holmes, U.T. (1982) *A History of Christian Spirituality: An analytical introduction*. New York: Harper One.

Hood, R.W., Jr. (2001) *Dimensions of Mystical Experience: Empirical studies and psychological links*. Amsterdam: Rodopi.

Horney, K. (1950) *Neurosis and Human Growth*. New York: W.W. Norton & Co.

Hughes, S. (1981) *A Friend in Need: How to help people through their problems*. Eastbourne: Kingsway Publications.

Hurding, R. (1992) *The Bible and Counselling*. London: Hodder and Stoughton.

Jackson, C. (2003) *The Gift to Listen: The Courage to Hear*. Minneapolis, MN: Augsburg Fortress.

James, W. (1985) *The Varieties of Religious Experience*. New York: Penguin Classics. Originally published in 1902.

Jamieson, A. (2002) *A Churchless Faith*. London: SPCK.

Jensen, J.P. and Bergin, A.E. (1988) 'Mental health values of professional therapists: A national interdisciplinary survey', *Professional Psychology: Research and Practice*, 19: 290-297.

Johns, H. (1996) *Personal Development in Counselling Training*. London: Cassell.

Johnson, D. and Van Vonderan, J. (1991) *The Subtle Power of Spiritual Abuse: Recognizing and escaping spiritual manipulation and false spiritual authority within the church*. Bloomington, M: Bethany House Publishers.

Jung, C.G. (1960) 'Stages of Life', in *The Structure and Dynamics of the Psyche, Volume 8 of Collected Works of C.G. Jung*. Princeton, NJ: Princeton University Press.

Jung, C.G. (1961) *Modern Man in Search of a Soul*. London: Routledge & Kegan Paul.

Jung, C.G. (1969) *The Archetypes and the Collective Unconscious*. Second edition. Princeton: Princeton University Press. Translated by R.F.C. Hull.

Jung, C.G. (1973) *Collected Works*. London: Routledge & Kegan Paul.

Kahle, P.A. (1997) 'The influence of the person of the therapist on the integration of spirituality and psychotherapy'. Unpublished doctoral dissertation. Denton: Texas Woman's University College of Arts and Sciences.

Kahn, M. (1997) *Between Therapist and Client: The new relationship*. New York: Holt Paperbacks.

Kegan, R. (1982) *The Evolving Self: Problems and process in human development*. Cambridge: Harvard University Press.

Kierkegaard, S. (1941) *The Sickness Unto Death*. Princeton University Press.

Kirkpatrick, B. (2005) *The Creativity of Listening: Being there, reaching out*. London: Darton, Longman and Todd.

Kirschenbaum, H. and Land Henderson, V. (1990a) *Carl Rogers in Dialogue*. London: Constable.

Kirschenbaum, H. and Land Henderson, V. (1990b) *The Carl Rogers Reader*. London: Constable.

Knox, R. (2008) 'Clients' experiences of relational depth in person-centred counselling', *Counselling and Psychotherapy Research*, 8(3): 182-188.

Knox, R., Murphy, D., Wiggins, S. and Cooper, M. (eds) (2012) *Relational depth: New perspectives and developments*. Basingstoke: Palgrave Macmillan.

Koenig, H.G., McCullough, M.E. and Larson, D.B. (2001) *Handbook of Religion and Health*. Oxford: Oxford University Press.

Kohlberg, L. (1984) *Essays on Moral Development, Vol. 2: The Psychology of Moral Development*. San Francisco: Harper & Row.

Korzybski, A. (1933) *Science and Sanity: An introduction to non-Aristotelian systems and general semantics*. New York: The International Non-Aristotelian Library Publishing Company.

Laing, R.D. (1965) *The Divided Self: An existential study in sanity and madness*. London: Pelican.

Laing, R.D. (1977) *Self and Others*. Second edition. Harmondsworth: Penguin.

Lartey, E.Y. (2003) *In Living Color: An intercultural approach to pastoral care and counselling*. Second edition. London: Jessica Kingsley.

Leech, K. (2001) *Soul Friend: Spiritual direction in the modern world*. Revised edition. New York: Morehouse Publishing.

Leonardi, J. (2006) 'Self-Giving and Self-Actualizing: Christianity and the person-centred approach', in J. Moore and C. Purton (eds), *Spirituality and Counselling: Experiential and theoretical perspectives*. Ross-on-Wye: PCCS Books. pp. 204-217.

Leonardi, J. (ed.) (2010) *The human being fully alive*. Ross-on-Wye: PCCS Books.

Levinson, D. (1978) *The Seasons of a Man's Life*. New York: Knopf.

Lewis, C.S. (1966) *A Grief Observed*. London: Faber and Faber.

Liebert, E. (2000) *Changing Life Patterns: Adult development in spiritual direction*. Atlanta, GA: Chalice Press.

Lietaer, G. (1984) 'Unconditional Positive Regard: a controversial basic attitude in client-centered therapy', in R.E. Levant and J.M. Shlien (eds), *Client-Centered Therapy and the Person-Centered Approach: New directions in theory, research and practice*. New York: Praeger.

Lietaer, G. (2001) 'Being Genuine as a Therapist: congruence and transparency', in G. Wyatt (ed.), *Rogers' Therapeutic Conditions: Evolution, theory and practice. Volume 1: Congruence*. Ross-on-Wye: PCCS Books.

Lines, D. (2006) *Spirituality in Counselling and Psychotherapy*. London: Sage

Loevinger, J. (1976) *Ego Development: Conceptions and theories*. San Francisco: Jossey-Bass.

Lynch, G. (2003) *Losing My Religion: Exploring the process of moving on from evangelical faith*. London: Darton, Longman and Todd.

Lynch, G. (2007) *The New Spirituality: An introduction to progressive belief in the twenty-first century*. New York: I.B. Taurus.

Mabry, J.R. (2006) *Faith Styles: Ways people believe*. New York: Morehouse Publishing.

MacMillan, M. (1999) 'In you there is a universe: person-centred counselling as a manifestation of the breath of the merciful', in I. Fairhurst (ed.), *Women Writing in the Person-Centred Approach*. Ross-on-Wye: PCCS Books. pp. 47-62.

Maslow, A.H. (1943) 'A Theory of Human Motivation', *Psychological Review*, 50: 370-396.

Maslow, A.H. (1962) 'Lessons from the peak experiences', *Journal of Humanistic Psychology*, 2(1): 9-18.

Maslow, A.H. (1968) *Towards a Psychology of Being*. Second edition. New York: Van Nostrand Reinhold Co.

Maslow, A.H. (1969) 'The farther reaches of human nature', *Journal of Transpersonal Psychology*, 1(1): 1-9.

Maslow, A.H. (1971) *The Farther Reaches of Human Nature*. New York: Viking Press.

Maslow, A.H. (1976) *Religions, values, and peak experiences*. New York: Penguin.

May, G.G. (1987) *Will and Spirit: A Contemplative Psychology*. New York: Harper Collins.

May, G.G. (1992) *Care of Mind, Care of Spirit*. New York: Harper Collins.

May, R. (1958) 'The Origins and Significance of the Existential Movement in Psychology', in R. May, E. Angel and H.F. Ellenberger (eds), *Existence: A new dimension in psychiatry and psychology*. New York: Basic Books.

May, R. (1982) 'The problem of evil: An open letter to Carl Rogers', *Journal of Humanistic Psychology*, 22 (3): 10-21.

McAdams, D.P. (1977) *The Stories We Live By: Personal myths and the making of the self*. Second edition. New York: Guilford Press.

McDowell, J. (1985) *His Image, My Image*. London: SP Trust.

McLeod, J. (1993) *An Introduction to Counselling*. Maidenhead: Open University Press.

McLeod, J (2009) *An Introduction to Counselling*. Fourth edition. Maidenhead: Open University Press.

McMillan, M. (2004) *The Person-Centred Approach to Therapeutic Change*. London: Sage.

Mearns, D. (1996) 'Working at relational depth with clients in person-centred therapy', *Counselling*, 7 (4): 306-11.

Mearns, D. (2003) *Developing Person-Centred Counselling*. Second edition. London: Sage.

Mearns, D. and Cooper, M. (2005) *Working at Relational Depth in Counselling and Psychotherapy*. London: Sage.

Mearns, D. and Thorne, B.J. (1999) *Person-Centred Counselling in Action*. Second edition. London: Sage.

Mearns, D. and Thorne, B.J. (2013) *Person-Centred Counselling in Action*. Fourth edition. London: Sage.

Mearns, D. and Thorne, B.J. (2000) *Person-Centred Therapy Today: New frontiers in theory and practice*. London: Sage.

REFERENCES

Merry, T. (1999) *Learning and Being in Person-Centred Counselling.* Ross-on-Wye: PCCS Books.

Mickley, J.R., Carson, V. and Soecken, K.L. (1995) 'Religion and Adult Mental Health: The state of the science in nursing', *Issues in Mental Health Nursing,* 16: 345-360.

Miller, A. (1987) *For Your Own Good: The roots of violence in child-rearing.* London: Virago Press.

Mohandas, E. (2008) 'Neurobiology of Spirituality', *Mens Sana Monographs,* Vol. 6, Issue 1: 63-80.

Momen, M. (2009) *Understanding Religion: A thematic approach.* Oxford: One World.

Monk Kidd, S. (1990) *When the Heart Waits: Spiritual direction for life's sacred questions.* New York: Harper One.

Moody, H.R. and Carroll, D. (1997) *The Five Stages of the Soul: Charting the spiritual passages that shape our lives.* New York: Anchor Books.

Moore, J. (2001) 'Acceptance of the truth of the present moment as a trustworthy foundation for unconditional positive regard', in J.D. Bozarth and P. Wlkins (eds), *Rogers' Therapeutic Conditions: Evolution, Theory and Practice. Volume 3: Unconditional Positive Regard.* Ross-on-Wye: PCCS Books.

Moore, J. and Purton, C. (eds) (2006) *Spirituality and Counselling: Experiential and theoretical perspectives.* Ross-on-Wye: PCCS Books.

Moore, T. (1992) *Care of the Soul.* London: Piatkus.

Moore, T. (2002) *The Soul's Religion.* London: Bantam Books.

Nelson, J.M. (2009) *Psychology, Religion, and Spirituality.* New York: Springer.

Nelson-Jones, R. (1988) *The Theory and Practice of Counselling Psychology.* London: Continuum International Publishing.

Newberg, A.B., Alavi, A., Baime, M., Pourdehnad, M., Santanna, J. and D'Aquili, E.G. (2001) 'The measurement of regional cerebral blood flow during the complex cognitive task of meditation: a preliminary SPECT study', *Psychiatry Research: Neuroimaging,* 106: 113-22.

Newberg, A.B., Pourdehnad, M., Alavi, A. and D'Aquili, E.G. (2003) 'Cerebral blood flow during meditative prayer: Preliminary findings and methodological issues', *Perceptual and Motor Skills,* 97: 625-630.

Nouwen, H.J.M. (1996) *Reaching Out: The three movements of the spiritual life.* Second edition. London: Fount Paperbacks.

Nouwen, HJM, McNeill, DP and Morrison, DA (1982) *Compassion: A reflection on the Christian life.* London: Darton, Longman and Todd.

O'Donohue, J. (1997) *Anam Cara: Spiritual wisdom from the Celtic world.* London: Bantam Books.

O'Donohue, J. (2000) *Eternal Echoes: Exploring our hunger to belong.* London: Bantam Books.

O'Donohue, J. (2004) *Divine Beauty: The invisible embrace.* London: Bantam Books.

O'Donohue, J (2007) *Benedictus: A book of blessings.* London: Bantam Press.

Oord, T.J. (ed.) (2007) *The Altruism Reader: Selections from writings on love, religion and science.* Pennsylvania: Templeton Foundation Press.

Osmer, R. and Fowler, J.W. (1993) 'Childhood and Adolescence - A faith development perspective', in R.J. Wicks, R.D. Parsons and D. Capps (eds), *Clinical Handbook of Pastoral Counseling.* Vol. 1: 171-212.

REFERENCES

Otto, R. (1926) *The Idea of the Holy: An inquiry into the non rational factor in the idea of the Divine*. Whitefish MT: Kessinger Publishing. Translated by John W. Harvey.

Page, S. (1999) *The Shadow and the Counsellor: Working with the darker aspects of the person, the role and the profession*. London: Routledge.

Paloutzian, R.F. and Park, C.L. (eds) (2005) *Handbook of the Psychology of Religion and Spirituality*. New York: Guilford Press.

Pargament, K.I. (1997) *The Psychology of Religion and Coping: Theory, research and practice*. New York: Guilford Press.

Pargament, K.I. (1999) 'The psychology of religion and spirituality? Yes and no', *International Journal for the Psychology of Religion*, 9: 3-16.

Pargament, K.I. (2007) *Spiritually Integrated Psychotherapy: Understanding and addressing the sacred*. New York: Guilford Press.

Pargament, K.I., Falgout, K., Olsen, H., Reilly, B., Van Heitsma, K. et al (1988) 'Religion and the problem-solving process: Three styles of coping', *Journal for the Scientific Study of Religion*, 27: 90-104.

Parks, S. (1990) 'Faith Development in a Changing World', *The Drew Gateway*, 60, 1: 4-21.

Patterson, C.H. (1974) *Relationship Counseling and Psychotherapy*. New York: Harper & Row.

Peck, R.C. (1968) 'Psychological developments in the second half of life', in B. Neugarten (ed.), *Middle age and aging*. Chicago: University of Chicago Press. pp. 88-92.

Peck, M.S. (1990a) *The Different Drum: Community-making and peace*. New edition. London: Arrow.

Peck, M.S. (1990b) *The Road Less Travelled: A new psychology of love, traditional values and spiritual growth*. London: Arrow Books.

Peck, M.S. (1993) *Further Along the Road Less Travelled: The unending journey towards spiritual growth*. London: Simon & Schuster.

Perrin, D.B. (2007) *Studying Christian Spirituality*. New edition. London: Routledge.

Piaget, J. (1929) *The Child's Conception of the World*. London: Routledge & Kegan Paul.

Purton, C. (1996) 'The deep structure of the core conditions: A Buddhist perspective', in R. Hutterer, G. Pawlowsky, P.F. Schmid and R. Stipsits (eds), *Client-Centered and Experiential Psychotherapy: A paradigm in motion*. Frankfurt-am-Main: Peter Lang.

Purton, C. (1998) 'Unconditional positive regard and its spiritual implications', in B.J. Thorne and E. Lambers (eds), *Person-Centred Therapy: A European perspective*. London: Sage.

Raphel, M.M. (2001) 'The status of the use of spiritual interventions in three professional mental health groups'. Doctoral dissertation. Dissertation Abstracts International, 62(2), 779A.

Rennie, D. (1994) 'Client's Deference in Psychotherapy', *Journal of Counseling Psychology*, 41, No. 4: 427-437.

Richards, P.S. and Bergin, A.E. (eds) (2000) *Handbook of Psychotherapy and Religious Diversity*. Washington, DC: American Psychological Association.

Richards, P.S. and Bergin, A.E. (2005) *A Spiritual Strategy for Counseling and Psychotherapy*. Second edition. Washington, DC: American Psychological Association.

Rogers, C.R. (1942) *Counseling and Psychotherapy: New concepts in practice*. Boston: Houghton Mifflin.

REFERENCES

Rogers, C.R. (1951) *Client-Centered Therapy*. London: Constable.

Rogers, C.R. (1956) cited in H. Kirschenbaum and V. Land Henderson (1990a) *Carl Rogers in Dialogue*. London: Constable.

Rogers, C.R. (1957a) 'A Note on "The Nature of Man"', *Journal of Consulting Psychology*, Vol. 4, No. 3: 199-203.

Rogers, C.R. (1957b) 'The necessary and sufficient conditions of therapeutic personality change', *Journal of Consulting Psychology*, 21, (2): 95-103.

Rogers, C.R. (1959) 'A theory of therapy, personality and interpersonal relationships as developed in the client-centred framework' in S. Koch (ed.), *Psychology: a Study of Science, Vol. 111. Formulations of the Person and the Social Context*. New York: McGraw Hill. pp. 184-256. An abridged version of this paper is also published in H. Kirschenbaum and V. Land Henderson (1990b) *The Carl Rogers Reader*. London: Constable.

Rogers, C.R. (1966) 'Client-Centred Therapy', in S. Arieti (ed.), *American Handbook of Psychiatry Vol. 3*. New York: Basic Books. pp. 183-200.

Rogers, C.R. (1967) *On Becoming a Person*. London: Constable.

Rogers, C.R. (1973) 'The interpersonal relationship: the core of guidance', in C.R. Rogers and B. Stevens, *Person to Person: The problem of being human*. London: Souvenir Press.

Rogers, C.R. (1974) 'Remarks on the future of client-centred therapy', in D. Wexler and L. Rice (eds), *Innovations in Client-Centred Therapy*. New York: John Wiley. pp. 7-13.

Rogers, C.R. (1980) *A Way of Being*. New York: Houghton Mifflin.

Rogers, C.R. (1982) 'Reply to Rollo May's letter', *Journal of Humanistic Psychology*, 22(4): 85-89.

Rogers, C.R. (1986) 'A client–centered/person–centered approach to therapy', in I.L.Kutash and A. Wolf (eds), *Psychotherapist's casebook: Theory and technique in the practice of modern times*. San Francisco: Jossey-Bass. pp. 197-208.

Rogers, C.R. (1989) 'A newer psychotherapy 1942', in H. Kirschenbaum and V. Land Henderson (eds) (1990a) *Carl Rogers in Dialogue*. Boston: Houghton Mifflin.

Rogers, C.R. and Sanford, R.C. (1984) 'Client-Centred Psychotherapy', in H.I. Kaplan and B.J. Sadock (eds), *Comprehensive Textbook of Psychiatry, IV*. Baltimore: Williams and Wilkins Co. pp. 1374-88.

Rogers, C.R. and Stevens, B. (1973) *Person to Person: The problem of being human*. London: Souvenir Press.

Rohr, R. and Ebert, A. (1990) *Discovering the Enneagram: An ancient tool for a new spiritual journey*. North Blackburn, Victoria: CollinsDove.

Rose, J. (1996) A Needle-Quivering Poise: Between prayer and practice in the counselling relationship. *Contact Pastoral Monographs No. 6*. Edinburgh: Contact Pastoral Trust.

Rose, J. (2002) *Sharing Spaces?: Prayer and the counselling relationship*. London: Darton, Longman and Todd.

Rossano, M.J. (2006) 'The Religious Mind and the Evolution of Religion', *Review of General Psychology*, Vol. 10, No. 4: 346-364.

Rowan, J. (1993) *The Transpersonal: Psychotherapy and Counselling*. London: Routledge.

Rupp, J. (1996) *Dear Heart, Come Home: The path of midlife spirituality*. New York: Crossroad Publishing.

Satir, V. (1972) *Peoplemaking*. Palo Alto CA: Science and Behaviour Books.

Schmid, P.F. (2001a) 'Acknowledgement: The art of responding. Dialogical and ethical perspectives on the challenge of unconditional relationships in therapy and beyond', in J.D. Bozarth and P. Wilkins (eds), *Rogers' Therapeutic Conditions: Evolution, Theory and Practice Volume 3: Unconditional Positive Regard*. Ross-on-Wye: PCCS Books.

Schmid, P.F. (2001b) 'Comprehension: The art of not knowing. Dialogical and Ethical Perspectives on Empathy as Dialogue in Personal and Person-centred Relationships', in S. Haugh, and T. Merry (eds), *Rogers' Therapeutic Conditions: Evolution, Theory and Practice Volume 3: Empathy*. Ross-on-Wye: PCCS Books.

Schulkin, J. (2007) 'An Instinct for Spiritual Quests: Quiet religion', *Journal of Speculative Philosophy*, 21.4: 307-320.

Seeman, J. (1983) *Personality Integration: Studies and reflections*. New York: Human Sciences Press.

Shafranske, E.P. (2000) 'Religious involvement and professional practices of psychiatrists and other mental health professionals', *Psychiatric Annals*, 30: 525-532.

Shafranske, E.P. and Maloney, H.N. (1996) 'Religion and the clinical practice of psychology: A case for inclusion', in E.P. Shafranske (ed.), *Religion and the Clinical Practice of Psychology*. Washington DC: American Psychological Association. pp. 561-586.

Sheldrake, P. (1994) *Befriending Our Desires*. London: Darton, Longman and Todd.

Slee, N.M. (1996) 'Further on from Fowler: Post-Fowler Faith Development Research', in L. J. Francis, W.K. Kay and W.S. Campbell (eds), *Research in Religious Education*. Leominster: Gracewing.

Slee, N.M. (2004) *Women's Faith Development: Patterns and processes*. Aldershot: Ashgate Publishing.

Smith, H. (2009) *The World's Religions*. 50th anniversary edition. San Francisco: HarperSanFrancisco.

Sperry, L. and Shafranske, E.P. (2005) *Spiritually Oriented Psychotherapy*. Washington, DC: American Psychological Association.

St. Augustine (1950) 'De quantitate animae', in *Ancient Christian Writers: The Works of the Fathers in Translation*. Westminster, Maryland: Newman Press. Originally written circa 388. Translated by J.M. Colleran.

St. Augustine (1999) *The Fathers of the Church: St Augustine: Retractions*. Washington: Catholic University of America Press. First published in 428.

St. John of the Cross (2003) *Dark Night of the Soul*. New York: Dover Publications.

Stairs, J. (2000) *Listening for the Soul: Pastoral care and spiritual direction*. Minneapolis: Fortress Press.

Standal, S. (1954) 'The need for positive regard: a contribution to client-centred theory.' Doctoral dissertation, University of Chicago.

Steere, D. (1985) cited in B. Kirkpatrick (2005) *The Creativity of Listening: Being there, reaching out*. London: Darton, Longman and Todd.

Steger, M.F., Frazier, P., Oishi, S. and Kaler, M. (2006) 'The Meaning in Life Questionnaire: Assessing the presence of and search for meaning in life', *Journal of Counseling Psychology*, Vol. 53, No. 1: 80-93.

Stern, D.N. (1985) *The Interpersonal World of the Infant: A view from psychoanalysis and developmental psychology*. New York: Basic Books.

Stern, D.N. (2004) *The Present Moment in Psychotherapy and Everyday Life*. New York: WW Norton.

Streib, H. (2001) 'Faith Development Theory Revisited: The religious styles perspective', *International Journal for the Psychology of Religion*, 11: 143-158.

Streib, H. (2003) 'Faith development research at twenty years', in R. Osmer and F. Schweitzer (eds), *Faith Development and Public Life*. St Louis, MO: Chalice Press.

Swinton, J. (2001) *Spirituality and Mental Health Care*. London: Jessica Kingsley.

Taylor, S. (2010) *Waking from Sleep*. London: Hay House.

Teasdale, W. (1999) *The Mystic Heart*. Novato, CA: New World Library.

Tepper, L., Rogers, S.A., Coleman, E.M. and Maloney, H.N. (2001) 'The Prevalence of Religious Coping With Persistent Mental Illness', *Psychiatric Services*, 52: 660-665.

Thoreau, H.D. (1995) *Walden: Or, Life in the woods*. New edition. New York: Dover Publications Incorporated. Originally published in 1854.

Thoresen C.E., Luskin, F. and Harris, A.H.S. (1998) 'Science and forgiveness interventions: reflections and recommendations, in E.L. Worthington, Jr (ed.), *Dimensions of Forgiveness, Psychological Research and Theological Perspectives*. London: Templeton Foundation.

Thorne, B.J. (1991) *Person-Centred Counselling: Therapeutic and spiritual dimensions*. London: Whurr Publishers.

Thorne, B.J. (1992) *Carl Rogers*. London: Sage.

Thorne, B.J. (1998) *Person-Centred Counselling and Christian Spirituality*. London: Whurr Publishers.

Thorne, B.J. (2002) *The Mystical Power of Person-Centred Therapy: Hope beyond despair*. London: Whurr Publishers.

Thorne, B.J. (2003a) 'Developing a spiritual discipline', in D. Mearns, *Developing Person-Centred Counselling*. Second edition. London: Sage. pp. 45-50.

Thorne, B.J. (2003b) *Infinitely Beloved: The challenge of divine intimacy*. London: Darton, Longman and Todd.

Tillich, P. (1952) *The Courage to Be*. London: Yale University Press.

Tillich, P. (1957) *Dynamics of Faith*. New York: Harper & Row.

Tillich, P. (1964) *The Shaking of the Foundations*. London: Penguin Books.

Tolan, J. (2003) *Skills in Person-Centred Counselling and Psychotherapy*: London: Sage.

Tournier, P. (1957) *The Meaning of Persons*. London: SCM Press.

Tournier, P. (1965) *The Adventure of Living*. New York: Harper.

Travis, F. (2001) 'Autonomic and EEG patterns distinguish transcending from other experiences during Transcendental Meditation practice', *International Journal of Psychophysiology*, Vol. 42, Issue 1: 1-9.

Underhill, E. (1995) *Mysticism: The development of humankind's spiritual consciousness*. London: Greener Books. Originally published in 1911.

Van Belle, H. (1980) *Basic Intent and Therapeutic Approach of Carl Rogers*. Toronto: Wedge Publishing Foundation.

Van Kaam, A. (1976) *Dynamics of Spiritual Self Direction*. Denville, NJ: Dimension Books.

Vaughan, F.E. (1995) *The Inward Arc: Healing in psychotherapy and spirituality*. Boston: New Science Library.

Vernon, G. M. (1968). 'The religious "nones": A neglected category', *Journal for the Scientific Study of Religion*, 7: 219-229.

Veness, D. (1990) 'Spirituality in counselling: A view from the other side', *British Journal of Guidance and Counselling*, 18 (3): 250-260.

Wachholtz, A.B. and Pargament, K.I. (2005) 'Is spirituality a critical ingredient of meditation?: Comparing the effects of spiritual meditation, secular meditation, and relaxation on spiritual, psychological, cardiac and pain outcomes', *Journal of Behavioural Medicine*, 28, 369-384.

Walsh, R. and Vaughan, F.E. (eds) (1993) *Paths beyond ego: The transpersonal vision.* New York: Perigee Books.

Watkins, M. (1976) *Waking Dreams.* New York: Harper Colophon.

West, W.S. (1998) 'Therapy as a Spiritual Process', in C. Feltham (ed.), *Witness and Vision of the Therapists.* London: Sage.

West, W.S. (2000) *Psychotherapy and Spirituality: Crossing the line between therapy and religion.* London: Sage.

West, W.S. (2004) *Spiritual Issues in Therapy: Relating experience to practice.* Basingstoke: Palgrave Macmillan.

Whitmore, D. (2004) *Psychosynthesis Counselling in Action.* Third edition. London: Sage.

Wilber, K. (1977) *The Spectrum of Consciousness.* Wheaton IL: Quest Books.

Wilber, K (1980) *The Atman Project.* Wheaton, IL: Quest Books.

Wilber, K (2004) *Integral Spirituality: A startling new role for religion in the modern and postmodern world.* Boston, MA: Shambala.

Wilkins, P. (2000) 'Unconditional positive regard reconsidered', *British Journal of Guidance and Counselling*, 28, (1): 49-115.

Wilkins, P. (2003) *Person-Centred Therapy in Focus.* London: Sage.

Worthington, E.L., Jr (1986) 'Religious Counseling: A review of published empirical research', *Journal of Counseling and Development*, 64, 421-431.

Worthington, E.L., Jr (1989) 'Religious Faith Across the Life Span: Implications for counseling and research', *The Counseling Psychologist* ,Vol. 17, no. 4: 555-612.

Worthington, E.L., Jr (ed.) (1998) *Dimensions of Forgiveness: Psychological research and theological perspectives.* London: Templeton Foundation.

Wosket, V. (1999) *The Therapeutic Use of Self: Counselling practice, research and supervision.* London: Routledge

Wyatt, G. (ed.) (2001) *Rogers' Therapeutic Conditions: Evolution, theory and practice Volume 1: Congruence.* Ross-on-Wye: PCCS Books.

Yalom, I.D. (1991) *Love's Executioner and Other Tales of Psychotherapy.* London: Penguin Books.

6786695R00148

Printed in Great Britain
by Amazon.co.uk, Ltd.,
Marston Gate.